AF505946

Framing the troubles online

Manchester University Press

Framing the troubles online

Northern Irish groups and website strategy

PAUL REILLY

Manchester
University Press
Manchester and New York

distributed in the United States exclusively
by PALGRAVE MACMILLAN

Published by Manchester University Press
Oxford Road, Manchester M13 9NR, UK
and Room 400, 175 Fifth Avenue, New York, NY 10010, USA
www.manchesteruniversitypress.co.uk

Distributed in the United States exclusively by
Palgrave Macmillan, 175 Fifth Avenue, New York,
NY 10010, USA

Distributed in Canada exclusively by
UBC Press, University of British Columbia, 2029 West Mall,
Vancouver, BC, Canada V6T 1Z2

British Library Cataloguing-in-Publication Data
A catalogue record for this book is available from the British Library

Library of Congress Cataloging-in-Publication Data applied for

ISBN 978 0 7190 8233 7   *hardback*

First published 2010

The publisher has no responsibility for the persistence or accuracy of URLs for any external or third-party internet websites referred to in this book, and does not guarantee that any content on such websites is, or will remain, accurate or appropriate.

Typeset in ITC Charter
by Servis Filmsetting Ltd, Stockport, Cheshire
Printed in Great Britain
by CPI Antony Rowe, Chippenham, Wiltshire

Contents

List of tables

List of illustrations

Every attempt has been made to obtain permission to reproduce the figures illustrated in this book. If any proper acknowledgement has not been made, copyright-holders are invited to inform the publisher.

List of abbreviations

32CSM	32 County Sovereignty Movement
ANEM	Association of Independent Media
BGM	Birches Guerrilla Movement
CAIN	Conflict Archive on the Internet
DUP	Democratic Unionist Party
ETA	Euskadi Ta Askatasuna
EZLN	Ejercito Zapatista de Liberacion National
FBI	Federal Bureau of Investigation
ICTs	information and communication technologies
IDF	Israel Defence Force
IICD	Independent International Commission on Decommissioning
IMC	Independent Monitoring Commission
INLA	Irish National Liberation Army
IRA	Irish Republican Army
IRSP	Irish Republican Socialist Party
ISP	Internet service provider
LVF	Loyalist Volunteer Force
PFLP	Popular Front for the Liberation of Palestine
PSNI	Police Service of Northern Ireland
PUP	Progressive Unionist Party
RHC	Red Hand Commandos
RSF	Republican Sinn Fein
RUC	Royal Ulster Constabulary
SDLP	Social and Democratic Labour Party
UDA	Ulster Defence Association
UDP	Ulster Democratic Party
UFF	Ulster Freedom Fighters
UKUP	United Kingdom Unionist Party
UPRG	Ulster Political Research Group

URL	universal resource locator
UUP	Ulster Unionist Party
UVF	Ulster Volunteer Force
YCV	Young Citizen Volunteers

Acknowledgements

This book could not have been written without Sarah Oates, who not only served as my supervisor but also encouraged and challenged me throughout my postgraduate research. I would also like to thank both staff and students of the Department of Politics at the University of Glasgow for their support and inspiration over the past few years. Assistance given by the Belfast Interface Project, the Belfast Conflict Resolution Consortium, the East Belfast Mission, Interaction Belfast, and the Short Strand Community Forum was also very much appreciated. In addition, this undertaking could not have been realised without the support of my family and friends. My thanks, in particular, go to Mum, Dad, Mark, Emma, Colin, Jack and Lucia for your patience and understanding. The research presented in this book would also not have been possible without the support given by James Barker, Paul Beattie, Roger Gay, Martin McElroy, Richard McGuinness, Derek Milne, Martin Smith, Peter Smith and Scott Young. Thanks to Tony Mason, Reena Jugnarain, Judith Oppenheimer, and their colleagues at Manchester University Press for their support and assistance in the publication of this book.

Introduction

Synopsis

This book explores the ways in which civil and uncivil groups in Northern Ireland use the Internet during a period of conflict transformation, with a particular emphasis on their framing of their positions in respect of the acceptability of the use of violence in pursuance of larger political goals and thus also their attitudes to the peace process. The book considers whether there are any qualitative differences between the online framing of terrorist-linked groups and the constitutional parties in the region. The websites of solidarity actors are also analysed to determine whether these actors are more or less likely to justify political violence on their websites than are their respective terrorist organisations. The book addresses these research issues by analysing the websites of Loyalist and Republicans in 2004 and 2005, a period before the advent of Web 2.0, in which these websites were the only visible presence of these actors in cyberspace. While the primary focus of this research will be on the frames adopted by both civil and uncivil actors in the region, the book also considers the implications of these website strategies for community relations in Northern Ireland today. The websites of rival residents' groups are examined to determine whether the Internet is a safe environment in which these groups can foster better cross-community relations, and perhaps even bridge social capital, across sectarian interfaces. The frames adopted by residents of interface areas are compared to assess whether these websites strengthen in-group identities or facilitate a form of mediated dialogue between these communities. The online audience for Northern Irish terrorists is explored through examination of Internet usage patterns and the ranking systems used by Internet search engines. Internet usage patterns are examined to define the potential audience available to Northern Irish terrorists via their websites.

The research suggests that there is little to differentiate between the websites of terrorist-linked groups and the websites of constitutional parties. While Loyalist and Republican 'fans' often use paramilitary insignias on their websites to demonstrate their opposition to the peace process, these websites do not appear to constitute a new dimension of terrorist threat to the peace process. Moreover, the book suggests that the online audience for these actors is likely to consist of Internet users who use the web for political research and Loyalist and Republican supporters in the 'offline' world. The prospects for better community relations did not appear to be enhanced by the websites of residents' groups in Northern Ireland. Both sides use their web presence to claim that they were constantly under threat of attack from the community situated at the other side of the 'peaceline'. Yet, the relatively underdeveloped and infrequently updated websites of Northern Irish community groups do not provide an accurate picture of community relations in these interface areas. The research presented in this book suggests that these groups are meeting on a regular basis in the real world and are wary of using the Internet for fear of their message being misinterpreted by members of rival interface groups.

Outline

The book is organised into five chapters. In Chapter 1, the relationship between the Internet and politics is explored, with a particular focus on how information and communication technologies (ICTs) are used to support political violence and frame conflict in contemporary nation-states. This chapter presents an overview of the debate about the transformative potential of the Internet, often characterised as a battle between cyberoptimists and cyberpessimists, in order to contextualise the research presented in the book. The relationship between terrorism and the Internet is also explored, with a particular focus on how the ability to communicate with potential global audiences might reduce the rationale for the use of publicity-oriented terrorism during a period of conflict transformation. The chapter concludes by introducing the methodologies used throughout the rest of the book, including framing theory and a coding scheme used to analyse website functionality.

The next chapter considers the extent to which the online frames adopted by terrorist-linked parties differ from those of constitutional parties in Northern Ireland. Some commentators have suggested that the Northern Irish media helped build cross-community support for the Good Friday Agreement (1998) through their adoption of a 'peace frame'. This peace frame created a bond between pro-peace groups from both camps, making a clear distinction between the political fronts that were engaged in the process and the violence associated with their terrorist sponsors (Wolfsfeld, 2001: 36). In this chapter, the frames used by Northern Irish political parties will be examined to assess the extent to which they have been influenced by the peace frame employed by the Northern Irish media in the late 1990s. The websites of political fronts and constitutional political parties are analysed to determine whether these groups have realised the potential of the web as a tool for mobilisation and organisational linkage. The study suggests that the websites of organisations closely linked to Northern Irish terrorist groups not only do not differ markedly from those of 'civil' groups, but also do not seem to offer any new dimension of terrorist threat.

In Chapter 3, the book will focus upon the websites of so-called terrorist 'fans'. Authors such as Hoffman (1998) and Weimann (2004) suggest that the Internet has made political violence more accessible to people who are not formally linked to terrorist organisations. The study will examine to what extent the peace frame, which differentiates parties such as Sinn Fein from their terrorist organisations, influences the content of Loyalist and Republican solidarity websites. Websites dedicated to dissident Loyalists and Republicans will also be analysed to determine whether their webmasters are posting material online that contravenes anti-terrorist legislation. This will also allow a direct comparison between the online frames adopted by official terrorist organisations and actors that purport to be part of their support network. The chapter suggests that these websites do not constitute a new dimension of terrorist threat in Northern Ireland. Although many of these webmasters use paramiliary insignias and pictures of hooded gunmen on their websites, there was no evidence to suggest that they are engaged in terrorism themselves. Indeed, many of these websites appeared to have no links to the terrorist organisations from which they took their names, suggesting that these actors should be considered fans of terrorist organisations rather than active participants in their campaigns.

In Chapter 4, the online audience for Northern Irish terrorists will be discussed with reference to data already available in the public domain, such as Internet usage patterns and the ranking systems used by Internet search engines. Factors such as the number of Internet users who use the web for political research will be included to determine the potential audience available to Northern Irish terrorists. This chapter will also inform the debate over whether bridging the digital divide might be a precondition for resolving terrorism. The cyberoptimist model is underpinned by an assumption that the Internet will facilitate the 'one to many' communication that undermines unequal power relations in democratic nation-states. In theory, terrorists might choose to abandon their armed struggle in favour of an online communication strategy if it enables them to mobilise a global audience of Internet users. The research presented in this chapter will investigate whether dissident Loyalists and Republicans are likely to attract a large audience via their websites. The study will consider the extent to which the online communication strategies of these groups are capable of replicating the oxygen of publicity generated by their respective military campaigns.

In Chapter 5, the focus will shift from analysis of the websites of terrorist fans and parties to a consideration of how the Internet is being utilised to foster better community relations across sectarian interfaces. Cyber enthusiasts such as Wellman (2001) and Dahlgren (2005) argue that ICTs have the potential to facilitate public debate in communicative spaces that are not present in the real world, opening up the possibility that in situations of community conflict, where neutral space may be difficult to access, online spaces may provide a viable alternative for improving community relations. Interface areas have suffered disproportionate levels of political violence since the outbreak of the Troubles in the late 1960s. Website functionality and online framing will be examined in order to test Chadwick's hypothesis that the Internet may generate bridging social capital between rival communities in interface areas. The online communications of Loyalist and Republican residents' groups will be analysed to assess the extent to which Northern Ireland's two main communities still perceive politics as a zero-sum game. In doing so, the analysis will provide further insight into the potential of the Internet as a tool to integrate marginal groups within ethnically divided societies. The chapter will conclude by considering whether community activists themselves believe that the Internet can help manage relationships between rival interface communities.

1

The Internet, politics and framing conflict

This book explores the ways in which civil and uncivil groups in Northern Ireland used the Internet in 2004 and 2005, with a particular focus on how they framed their positions in respect of the acceptability of political violence and their attitudes towards the peace process. This chapter contextualises the research presented in the book by looking at three issues, namely the nexus between the Internet and politics, the role of the Internet in war and peace, and theoretical perspectives on how framing can affect public opinion. A number of theories on the role of the Internet in nation-states will be discussed, from the three cyber paradigms (see below) to more recent research into the relationship between the Internet and social capital. Internet penetration and usage patterns in Northern Ireland will also be provided in order to determine the potential audience available to the actors under investigation. The chapter then explores how ICTs have been used to both shape and define conflict, with a particular focus on the Second Gulf War, which has been labelled by some authors as the first 'YouTube War' (see Carruthers, 2008). The analysis also explores how the Internet has been used to support conflict transformation in divided societies. The chapter concludes by introducing the methodologies used in this book, including framing theory and a coding scheme designed to measure website functionality.

The Internet and politics

Thus far, there has been no consensus amongst academics as to how ICTs will transform politics. One of the first attempts to categorise the competing perspectives regarding the transformative potential of the Internet can be found in *Digital Divide*, Pippa Norris's exploration of the relationship between the Internet and politics. According to Norris (2001), there are three cyber paradigms that describe the impact of ICTs on contemporary nation-states. These are:

1. The cyberoptimist model suggests that the Internet will undermine unequal power relations, creating a multiplier effect for marginal groups.
2. The cyberpessimist model proposes that the Internet will 'unleash new inequalities of power and wealth', reinforcing the gap between activists and the disengaged.
3. The cybersceptic model suggests that it is too early to tell whether ICTs will have a lasting effect upon patterns of political organisation and behaviour.

While authors such as Oates (2008) have questioned how useful it is to use these models to frame the debate over the transformative potential of the Internet, they do provide a framework for an exploration of the relationship between the Internet and political activism in contemporary nation-states. The research presented in this book will discuss which of these cyber paradigms, if any, are suitable conceptual tools for characterising the web activism of civil and uncivil groups in Northern Ireland.

The cyberoptimist view
Studies of online mobilisation have tended to be used as evidence to support either the cyberoptimist or cyberpessimist models identified by Norris in *Digital Divide*. The cyberoptimist model is often referred to as the Equalisation Model, which emphasises the potential of the Internet as a force multiplier for sub-state minorities (see Norris, 2001). Early research in the field tended to stress the role of the Internet in the reinvigoration of liberal democratic polities, with a particular focus on how ICTs would make it easier for people to participate in elections. Authors such as Corrado and Firestone (1996) and Budge (1996) suggested that low electoral turnouts might be partially remedied by the utility of electronic voting systems similar to the QUBE 'teledemocracy' piloted in California in the 1980s. Cyber enthusiasts have also argued that the Internet facilitates forms of communication and interaction that undermine unequal power relations both within and between nation-states (Dyson, 1998; Rheingold, 1993; Spears and Lea, 1994). Empirical evidence to support this hypothesis was provided by the Lusoli and Ward study of the Countryside Alliance online communication strategy (2006). Despite its conservative and predominantly rural membership, the Countryside Alliance was found to have used ICTs to both widen and deepen participation amongst its supporters, culminating in a number of high-profile demonstrations held in London in 2002. The Equalisation Model also suggests that nation-states in the developing

world would be likely to benefit from the reduction of social context in communication transactions afforded by the Internet. Governments could use ICTs to aid the more equitable distribution of resources in economically deprived regions and they afford these developing nation-states a degree of organisational coherence that allow them to 'punch above their weight' in the international community (Reilly, 2008).

Research has also suggested that the Internet might help to narrow the gap between established political institutions and minorities who perceive that they lack representation in their respective polities (see Bennett, 2003; Chadwick, 2006). The Internet appears to be the most influential medium for the three individual-level indicators of social capital – civic participation, interpersonal trust and personal content-ment – amongst young people. While social capital itself may be some-thing of a contested subject, studies have continued to suggest that the use of the Internet for information exchange has generally posi-tive effects for all generations in terms of civic activism and political engagement.[1] People who use the Internet for information exchange are considered likely to encounter more information and have greater opportunity to become involved in some form of civic engagement than those who do not use the Internet for such purposes (see Johnson and Kaye, 2003; Romer et al, 2009; Shah et al, 2001). For example, Owen (2006) suggests that the Internet has facilitated a new form of political activism amongst young people in the United States. Recent studies suggest that young people (aged between 18 and 29 years) use Internet information in their political decision-making, and are increasingly likely to produce political content online (Owen, 2006: 35). Romer et al (2009) went as far as to suggest that 'greater informational use of the Internet in the schools civics curricula would help to increase both political and civic engagement amongst young people' (p. 79).

Cyberoptimists also argue that the Internet has the potential to enrich the democratic process through the creation of a public sphere of 'rational-critical citizen discourse' (Dahlberg, 2001). They argue that the Internet provides communicative spaces that not only permit the circulation of 'information and ideas, but also the formation of political will amongst subcultures' (Dahlgren, 2005: 148). In this Habermasian public sphere, people would be encouraged to listen to other views and critically reflect upon their own opinions on a variety of issues (see Froomkin, 2003). Recent ICT developments, collectively dubbed Web 2.0, have aroused renewed interest in the cyberoptimist conception of the Internet as a public sphere in light of their emphasis on user-generated content. Sites such as Bebo and Facebook are perhaps the most visible elements of Web 2.0, the section of the World Wide Web that provides a platform for user-generated content. According to a recent Nielsen report (2009), Facebook is now the ninth most popular online brand in the world, with membership social networking websites now the fourth most popular online sector after search, portals and PC software applications. Cyberoptimists have gone so far as to suggest that these technological developments could help to foster a global civil society in which transnational advocacy networks operate across the globe to strengthen the voice of the developing world. They point to the Chiapas uprising in Mexico (1994) and Moveon.org[2] as examples of how ICTs can provide a critical multiplier effect for transnational advocacy networks (see Norris, 2001; Kaldor, 2003). Bennett (2003) suggests that the Chiapas mobilisation is an example of how the Internet is facilitating a new form of 'global protest politics'.[3]

The cyberpessimist view
Cyberpessimists argue that the Internet will reinforce the gap between rich and poor, as well as between activists and the disengaged (Norris, 2001: 12). They suggest that the Internet will reinforce existing patterns of political participation within liberal democracies. The digital divide, the gap between those able to benefit from ICTs and those who are not, is often cited as evidence that the Equalisation Model is unrealistic. Statistics from the Organisation for Economic Cooperation and Development (OECD) reflected the dominance of the First World in terms of Internet usage at the start of the 2000s decade. For example, an estimated 54.3 percent of Americans were said to have used the Internet on a regular basis in 2002, compared to a mere 0.4 percent of the population of countries situated in sub-Saharan Africa (Manrique, 2002: 7). The First World hegemony was also said to have been reflected in the predominance of English as the vernacular language of cyberspace. However, there has been a shift in research into the digital divide over the past decade, from an examination of who has access to information technology towards a study of who is actually benefiting from it. This has been prompted by the rapid growth of telecommunications in developing countries, as demonstrated by an 874.6 percent growth in Internet consumption in Africa between 2000 and 2007.[4] It is perhaps more useful to look at Internet usage patterns rather than access as a factor in how the Internet might affect power relations both within and between nation-states today.

There is already some empirical evidence to support the reinforcement model. Political bulletin boards appear to promote 'homophily' rather than to stimulate genuine political debate between societal groups. People choose to post to groups that contain people with similar political ideologies to their own. For example, a survey of political Usenet groups found that only 9.3 percent of leaders posted messages to ideologically dissonant groups (Hill and Hughes, 1997: 13). Moreover, Margolis and Resnick (2000) suggested that ICT usage by political parties has perpetuated 'politics as usual', insofar that the better-resourced parties are more likely to develop more professional and sophisticated websites than smaller, less well-resourced political parties. Studies suggest that political parties tend to use their websites for top-down communication rather than to encourage dialogue with their grass roots membership, with relatively low numbers of voters visiting candidate campaign websites (see Nixon et al, 2003; Gibson et al, 2008). Furthermore, peripheral political parties do not appear to have experienced the critical multiplier effect postulated in the cyberoptimist model. As Nixon et al assert, ICTs may 'allow these parties to survive, but they hardly allow them to strive' (p. 35). There is also evidence to suggest that parties and candidates may maintain websites to demonstrate the professionalism of their respective campaigns and compete with other party websites, what Selnow (1998) refers to as a 'me too effect'. Moreover, data collated from the Minnesota E-Democracy project suggests that a high level of 'cultural capital' is a fundamental prerequisite for political participation online.[5] The volunteers who subscribed to the project in 1994 tended to have university level education, incomes well above the national average, and an interest in politics in the offline world, while the project did not tend to attract volunteers who had little or no prior interest in politics (Jensen, 2006: 44). In this particular case study the widening potential of ICTs did not appear to be fulfilled.

While cyberoptimists suggest that technological developments such as social networking websites may extend the public sphere in democratic nation-states, authors such as Sunstein (2007) suggest that they may accelerate existing trends of 'cyberbalkanisation'. They argue that people do not tend to listen respectfully to the opinions of others on social networking websites and do not engage in the rational discourse associated with the Habermasian public sphere. Moreover, cyberpessimists refer to empirical evidence that suggests the relative anonymity of cyberspace may not necessarily liberate individuals from their offline identities, nor lower the threshold for political engagement. The Social Identity Model of Deindividuation Effect suggests that the relatively anonymity of computer mediated communication may in fact make some Internet users more highly sensitised to the social cues that appear in virtual communities. Cho and Lee (2008) studied how students from three different cultural groups used the Internet in both

Singapore and the United States. They found that individuals tended to select information sources from within their own social networks rather than from other cultural groups online. However, their study also suggested that individuals whose Internet use was motivated by a desire to obtain information immediately were more likely to look beyond the websites of members of their own social networks.

What is clear from the cyberoptimist vs cyberpessimist debate is that although the Internet retains the potential to both deepen and widen political participation, this potential may not necessarily translate into forms of collective action that alter power relations within democratic nation-states. The cybersceptic model discussed by Norris in *Digital Divide* suggested that it was perhaps too early to tell what effect ICTs will have upon politics. This 'wait and see' approach towards the Internet and politics has been evident in more recent research into new media technologies, with scholars such as Chadwick (2006) suggesting that the Web is both 'increasing and decreasing social capital and opportunities for political participation' (p. 112). The early indications are that the emphasis on user-generated content synonymous with Web 2.0 might not necessariy stimulate participation in democratic nation-states. Authors such as Gaines and Mondak (2008) suggest that social networking websites 'publicise socialising' and allow for the exploration of different facets of an individual's identity, many of which may not be overtly political in nature. This book will add to the debate over the transformative potential of the Internet by analysing what function websites fulfil for a variety of civil and uncivil actors in Northern Ireland and the implications of these website strategies for conflict transformation in the Province.

Internet usage patterns in Northern Ireland

The infrastructure for wired community relations in Northern Ireland was under construction during the period of data collection. According to the 2005 Ofcom Media Literacy Audit, Northern Ireland had the lowest rate of Internet penetration of the four regions in the United Kingdom, with only 48 percent of Northern Irish respondents claiming to have Internet access at home. Broadband Internet services had only reached 28 percent of all Northern Irish households during the period of data collection, much lower than in the rest of the United Kingdom.[6] The average time spent online by Internet users was also lower than in the rest of the United Kingdom. Email and looking for information about a private interest were the two most popular activities reported in Northern Ireland and the other regions of the United Kingdom.

However, the Northern Irish respondents were more likely than their English, Scottish and Welsh counterparts to use the Internet to look up information relating to their work or studies. For example, the study found that 57 percent of Northern Irish users used the Internet for research, in comparison to just 47 percent of the respondents from Wales.

There has been a significant growth in both the availability and take-up of Internet services in Northern Ireland since 2005. According to the latest Ofcom report (2009), Internet penetration has reached 68 percent in the Province, comparable with the UK average of 70 percent and higher than both Scotland and Wales. Residential broadband take-up was second only to England in the first quarter of 2009 at 64 percent, with DSL broadband now available in all households in Northern Ireland. However, the average time spent online by Internet users remains lower than in the rest of the United Kingdom, with the most recent study showing that Northern Irish users spend on average 9.6 hours per week online compared to users in England, who use the Internet for 12.4 hours per week.[7] In terms of the purpose of Internet use, email and general surfing were once again the two most commonly reported Internet activities. However, the number of respondents who use the Internet to aid their work or studies declined from 57 percent in 2005 to 40 percent in 2009. Social networking has become an increasingly popular online activity amongst both communities in Northern Ireland, with one in four households in Northern Ireland claiming to use one of the four most popular social networking websites, namely Bebo, Facebook, Myspace and YouTube. Ofcom also found that 36 percent of adult respondents from Belfast, where the majority of peace walls in the Province are located, used these websites on a regular basis. In sum, there have been significant improvements made to the digital infrastructure of Northern Ireland since 2005. This book will consider what impact, if any, the increased availability of Internet services in the Province will have upon the website strategies of political actors in the region.

The role of the Internet in conflict

Cyber dissent and authoritarian regimes
This book presents an analysis of how civil and uncivil actors in Northern Ireland used the Internet to frame their positions regarding the acceptability of political violence during a period of conflict transformation. Much of the literature in the field has tended to focus upon either the role of the Internet in shaping media coverage of

conflict or the threat of so-called cyberterrorism. In terms of media coverage of conflict, the Internet has continued to enable opposition voices to be heard in spite of authoritarian controls on press freedom during periods of unrest A few years after the Chiapas insurrection, the Internet enabled Radio B92 to continue broadcasting to international audiences after Yugoslav leader Slobodan Milosevic ordered the closure of the station. Although Milosevic managed to shut down the station premises in August 1999, radio transmissions were sent via satellite to other Association of Independent Media (ANEM) groups, who in turn transmitted the material on the Internet.[8] This enabled B92 to 'drip feed' information about the internal unrest within Yugoslavia to international audiences, with the radio station playing a critical role in organising the demonstrations that finally led to the overthrow of Milosevic's government in October 1999. This was just one of several authoritarian regimes that have faced increased international scrutiny due to the online activism of their citizens. For example, the use of the Internet by so-called Chinese cyber-dissidents in the late 1990s focused the attention of the international media upon alleged human rights abuses against members of the Falun Gong and pro-Tibetan protestors within China (Chase and Mulvenon, 2002). Although China has responded to this threat by erecting electronic firewalls, these controls can often be easily circumvented through the use of proxy servers that reconnect users to sites officially blocked by the state (Deibert, 2001). There have also been reported incidents of cyber dissent in countries such as Burma, Cuba and Libya.[9] While many of these authoritarian nation-states continue to develop strategies to minimise cyber dissent, it is fair to say that the Internet continues to provide a communicative space for their opponents to mobilise support for their cause.

Alternative perspectives on war
The Internet has also provided a communicative space for alternative perspectives on war. While embedded journalists faced certain restrictions in terms of both their freedom of movement and their ability to show civilian casualties, a number of blogs emerged providing details of everyday life for civilians living in Iraq during the Second Gulf War (Bell, 2008). Probably the most well-known of these bloggers was Salam Pax, otherwise known as the Baghdad Blogger. Pax posted information about his experiences living in Baghdad both during and after the 2003 Iraq invasion on a blog entitled Dear_Raed. The blog started to influence the British public's perception of the war in Iraq after it was picked up for syndication by the *Guardian* newspaper in the spring of 2003, in effect turning Pax himself into a celebrity (Pax, 2003).

The posting of videos on YouTube by insurgents and American troops has also informed public opinion vis-à-vis the conflict. The videos and pictures that emerged on the site showing American troops engaged in acts of abuse against Iraqi civilians in 2005 did little to build support for a war that was already deeply unpopular in parts of Europe and North America. Indeed, the US Department of Defense's decision to create its own official YouTube channel in 2007 to give a 'boots on the ground' perspective of events appears to have been designed to show a more positive image of US troops in the region. However, Christensen (2008) suggests that this creates a 'propagandistic dissonance' for the US Department of Defense YouTube channel insofar as positive images of US troops sit alongside videos that render such material impotent (p. 172).

The Iraq War appears to have set a precedent for how user-generated content may shape future media coverage of conflict. For example, social networking website Twitter was used to both organise and publicise demonstrations in the wake of alleged electoral fraud in the Iranian presidential election in June 2009. Despite efforts by the Iranian authorities to limit international news media coverage of the demonstrations, Twitter provided links to mobile phone footage of violent clashes between the media and protestors.[10] While commentators such as Gaurav Mishra have suggested that it is premature to talk of an 'Iranian Twitter Revolution', given the low number of users of the social networking site in Iran, the lessons for authoritarian regimes were clear.[11] It now appears that user-generated content may leave authoritarian regimes such as Iran impotent in their efforts to control the flow of information from within their borders. While access might appear to be the only method through which the state can clamp down on so-called cyber dissent, it may prove difficult for authoritarian regimes to stop all anti-regime content from reaching international audiences.

Cyberterrorism
The book will consider what function websites fulfilled for dissident Loyalist and Republican terrorists in 2004 and 2005, and the extent to which this differs from the terrorist uses of the Internet identified in previous studies. The Internet provides a new medium through which the terrorist can attack the nation-state. Both hackers and so-called 'cyberterrorists' manipulate content or block access to popular websites, although hackers do not tend to launch attacks that are intended to lead to violence or disrupt essential services (see Denning, 2000; Rogan, 2006). Cyberterrorism can be defined as the 'unlawful attacks and threats of attacks on computers, networks, and information stored

therein when done to intimidate or coerce a government or its people in furtherance of political objectives' (Denning, 2000: 1). So far, only a few terrorist organisations have engaged in cyberterrorism. In 1996, the Liberation Tigers of Tamil Eelam (LTTE) created a 'virtual blockade' around several Sri Lankan diplomatic missions, using a coordinated series of e-bombs to deny Internet users access to their websites (Zanini and Edwards, 2001). A group calling themselves the Internet Black Tigers was responsible for sending over 800 emails a day to these embassies during a two-week period (Denning, 2005: 8). The paralysis of the Sri Lankan missions represented a significant propaganda coup for LTTE insurgents. This highlights the similarities between the techniques used by hacktivists and cyberterrorists. Other examples of denial of services attacks include the Serbian Black Hand group, who were linked to attacks on an ethnic Albanian website during the Kosovo conflict in 1998, and the pro Hizbollah UNITY group, who launched attacks against Israeli financial and government websites in 2000.[12] Yet, cyberterrorism is differentiated from hacktivism by virtue of its destructive nature. It does not refer to terrorist use of the Internet for mobilisation or as a propaganda tool, or other functions of the Internet that are used by both civil and uncivil actors. For cyberterrorists, ICTs represent a weapon that may be used to intimidate or threaten a target audience. As Rogan (2006) suggests, the most important characteristic of cyberterrorism is its 'result in violence, or the threat of violence against persons and property' (p. 9). In the case of the LTTE and the Black Hand, these cyber attacks were used alongside attacks in the offline world to terrorise a target audience.

There is only limited evidence to support the hypothesis that terrorists are seeking to develop the ability to launch cyber attacks. Indeed, much of the literature on cyberterrorism acknowledges that to date there have been no recorded cyberterrorist attacks that have resulted in fatalities (see Weimann, 2004; Rogan, 2006; Gorge, 2007). Terrorism analyst Yonah Alexander claimed that Saddam Hussein had set up 100 websites, also known as Iraq Net, to enable denial-of-service attacks against the United States prior to the invasion of Iraq in 2001. However, Stohl (2008) states there is no evidence to support this assertion nearly 8 years later (p. 10). The Centre for the Study of Terrorism and Irregular Warfare identified radical Islamic groups as the most likely to develop hacking tools that cause mass disruption to critical infrastructures. Take, for example, the case of Al Qaida and its network of radical Islamic terrorist organisations. Synonymous with the most lethal terrorist attacks perpetrated around the globe over the past decade, there is some evidence to suggest that Al Qaida has used the Internet to support its offensive operations. Prior to 9/11, members of the Al Qaida network used the Internet to coordinate operations, recruit new members and solicit resources (see Goodman et al, 2006). In addition, evidence from the investigation into the terror attacks in Mumbai (November 2008) indicates that the perpetrators used anonymous email accounts to plan and coordinate their attacks.[13]

Nevertheless it would appear that the Al Qaida network has yet to reveal the full extent of its cyberterror capabilities. In 2002, Osama Bin Laden and Muslim cleric Omar Bakri Muhammad called for an electronic jihad, defined as 'small scale computer attacks motivated by the jihadist ideology' (Rogan, 2006: 27). This was followed in October 2004 by the declaration of an online fatwa on the Islamic Online website, a website affiliated with the Al Qaida network. However, there have been few other references to electronic jihad in subsequent communiqués issued by radical Islamic groups. Conversely, the evidence from intercepted Al Qaida communications and training manuals suggests that these organisations are building their own defences against potential cyber attacks from nation-states. Analysis of Al Qaida training materials that have been distributed online shows that these organisations are encouraging their members to hide passwords and protect passwords, in effect promoting defensive operations as opposed to the offensive operations envisaged by authors such as Arquilla and Ronfeldt in the mid-1990s (see Rogan, 2006; Hoffman, 2006). There have also been few examples of radical Islamist groups training their members how to hack websites, with the Forum al-Nusra being one of the few websites to provide links for its members to watch hacker training videos online (Rogan, 2006: 28). It would appear that the Al Qaida network has yet to realise the potential of ICTs as a weapon to be used against critical infrastructures. However, it is conceivable that the Al Qaida network may have developed the complex coordinated cyberterror capability already, but has not yet perpetrated a cyber attack. As demonstrated by the 9/11 atrocities, a sudden and unexpected terrorist attack in cyberspace might generate maximum publicity for the organisation. This might explain why there are so few references to hacking tools on radical Islamic websites such as Islamic Online. One might also speculate that if Al Qaida were planning a cyber attack, incriminating information would be omitted from websites that are likely to be monitored by intelligence agencies such as the Federal Bureau of Investigation (FBI).

Terrorist use of the Internet
Cyberterrorism is only likely to be pursued by terrorist organisations who can afford to invest in expensive hacking tools and recruit members

with the necessary technical knowledge to launch denial-of-service attacks. Attacks on computer networks may be counter-productive given the function that the Internet serves for most terrorist organisations. As Conway (2006a) suggests, there appears to be a consensus amongst authors who have studied how terrorists use ICTs. Authors such as Cohen (2002), Thomas (2003), and Furnell and Warren (1999) have identified broadly similar terrorist uses of the Internet, such as the dissemination of propaganda, fundraising and the planning of atrocities. Weimann (2004) identified other core terrorist uses of the Internet, such as data mining and information sharing, in an article entitled *WWW.terror.net: How Modern Terrorism Uses the Internet*. A synthesis of these studies suggests that there are five core terrorist uses of the Internet, namely publicity and propaganda, planning and coordination, data mining and information sharing, mobilisation and fundraising, and networking. Each of these functions demonstrates how the Internet may facilitate the perpetration of atrocities in the offline world.

Publicity and propaganda

Conway (2006b) suggests that the Internet allows terrorists to wage cybercortical warfare, a form of conflict conducted against minds to change the will of an enemy (Szafranski, 1997: 404). There is already some evidence to suggest that terrorists are using the Internet to 'claim that their enemy is the real terrorist' (Weimann, 2004: 3). Ethnonationalist terrorist organisations often use their websites to discredit their critics and define themselves as members of civil society. Thus, emotive words like 'freedom fighter' and 'state oppression' often permeate the solidarity websites of terrorist organisations such as the Basque separatists, Euskadi Ta Askatasuna (ETA).[14] In addition, terrorist organisations often seek publicity to further their psychological war against a target population. This may take the form of statements, released on the Internet, that are designed to intimidate a target audience. For example, terrorists have used the Internet to release images of their hostages to the conventional mass media. One such video, released on a number of Islamist websites in February 2002, showed the beheading of *Wall Street Journal* reporter Daniel Pearl.[15] In the video, Pearl states his captors' demands to the camera, calling for the immediate end of the US presence in Pakistan.[16] Subsequent to the Pearl video, jihadist groups have posted videos of other hostages being executed, including British contractor Ken Bigley and American entrepreneur Nick Berg (Conway, 2006a: 11).

Research into how terrorists use the Internet has tended to focus on the content of these online communications rather than their likely recipients. While terrorists do appear to be using the Internet to generate their own propaganda, they must attract an online audience if these messages are to intimidate a target population. In the case of Daniel Pearl, the extensive media coverage of his kidnapping may have led many people to search for the video of his execution on the Internet. This suggests that the online framing of terrorists may only influence public opinion if reported in the conventional mass media. As Conway points out, Hizbollah's 'cybercortical' campaign only came to prominence in 1999, when a news report about mangled remains of slain Israelis published on a Hizbollah website caused a political row between the Israel Defence Force (IDF) and the families of several murdered Israeli marines.[17] There is limited evidence to suggest that Hizbollah's efforts to attract an American audience to their website during this period proved successful, despite the provision of an English language facility on the three main Hizbollah websites (p. 11).

Planning and coordination

The Internet would appear to be an ideal arena for the planning of terrorist activity, as it offers both cheap and anonymous communication. Security sources believe that some terrorists use a single email account for intra-group communication, with the password and username of an email provided to each member of the group. Messages between group members are saved as draft, rather than sent to another email account. They are then deleted once read by the recipient (Hinnen, 2005: 39). This leaves no communication transaction that can be recorded by the Internet service provider (ISP). Terrorists already appear to be using ICTs to plan and perpetrate atrocities. Evidence gathered from a laptop belonging to Ramzi Yousef, the terrorist responsible for the failed 1993 World Trade Center attack, showed that there were itemised plans to destroy a number of US airliners on the same day (Eid, 2006: 8). There is also some evidence to suggest that Northern Irish terrorists may be using the Internet to plan and perpetrate atrocities. Loyalist terror groups such as the Ulster Freedom Fighters (UFF) have used the websites of their affiliates to identify potential targets. In March 2001 the *Belfast Telegraph* reported that a message on an 'Ulster Loyalist' website directed members of the Limavady UFF to attack a bar allegedly frequented by members of the Provisional Irish Republican Army (IRA).[18] Although this particular example came to the attention of the press, the scale of such covert utility of the Internet is difficult to assess.

Mobilisation and fundraising

Terrorists also use the Internet to mobilise supporters and solicit resources from sympathisers. Internet users may be asked to submit an email to the webmaster if they wish to join the organisation. For example, Fritz et al (2004) located an Iranian website that provided an application form for Internet users who wished to become martyrs (p. 9). Alternatively, terrorist recruiters may use online chat rooms to approach Internet users who are sympathetic to their cause (Weimann, 2004: 16). In addition, there appears to be significant evidence that terrorists are using the Internet to solicit resources from sympathisers. Fundraising may be facilitated through the website of an affiliate of a terrorist organisation, such as a political party or a charity, to avoid legal sanctions under anti-terrorist legislation such as the US Patriot Act (2001). Hinnen (2005) asserts that jihadists use sympathetic websites to post bank account details to which funds for various terrorist organisations can be transferred. One website, www.ummah.net, provided bank accounts for the Harkat ul Muhjadeen at the Allied Bank of Pakistan, urging Internet users to donate funds in support of the 'global jihad' (p. 38).

While most recent studies have focused on how jihadists use the Web for recruitment, there has been relatively little research conducted into whether ethno-nationalist terrorists are using ICTs to mobilise their supporters. Content analysis of the ULISNET website suggests that dissident Loyalist and Republican terrorists may be using the Web for mobilisation and resource solicitation. ULISNET claimed that its basic function was to provide the media with press releases from the dissident Loyalist group the Loyalist Volunteer Force (LVF). Yet the organisation appealed for information about rival Loyalist and Republican paramilitaries on its website. Internet users who had 'even the slightest information on active Republican terrorists' were invited to email the organisation through a secure email server.[19] Analysis of the 'Projects' section revealed that ULISNET was in fact part of the 'support network' for the LVF. For example, Internet users were asked to donate bulletproof vests to the organisation, for 'obvious uses'. Unsurprisingly, this website was shut down in late 2004.[20] Although this may be an isolated case, it raises issues around the extent to which 'pro-terrorist' webmasters are able to utilise the public spaces of the Web to attack liberal democracies. This research will add to the debate over how terrorists use the Internet, through an examination of the functionality of websites maintained by dissident terrorists in Northern Ireland.

Networking

Some terrorist groups have followed the lead of transnational corporations, using ICTs to organise themselves into decentralised networks. In theory, network-based terrorist organisations are immune to infiltration by the authorities, as they are 'based around the idea of "leaderless resistance"' (Tucker, 2001: 1). In the Middle East, network-based groups have gradually replaced old hierarchical groups such as the Popular Front for the Liberation of Palestine (PFLP). The Internet allows terrorist groups such as Hizbollah to communicate with like-minded groups based in diverse locations such as Chechnya, Palestine and Afghanistan (Weimann, 2004: 9). Still, it should be noted that network-based terrorist organisations are not a product of the 'Information Age'. The Palestinian Liberation Organisation, a network of smaller Palestinian groups, formed as early as 1964. Nevertheless, technological innovations like email have facilitated the restructuring of terrorist hierarchies into networks. Groups such as Hamas have developed a network structure of loosely connected autonomous actors which includes private individuals living outside the Middle East. The label 'amateur terrorist' can be applied to these individuals, who often 'have little or no formal connection to an existing terrorist group' (Hoffman, 1998: 185). While these individuals are not full members of the organisation, they nevertheless act to further the objectives of a terrorist group. For example, lone terrorists like Ramzi Yousef, the perpetrator of the 1993 World Trade Center bombing, have often retrospectively been linked to decentralised terrorist networks such as Al Qaida (Eid, 2006: 1).

Data mining and sharing information

Terrorists also use the Internet to obtain information on potential targets and share techniques with like-minded individuals. There is already some evidence to suggest that terrorists are using publicly available information to plan and coordinate atrocities. An Al Qaida training manual recovered in Afghanistan in 2002 stated that its operatives could gather 'at least 80 percent of information about the enemy through public sources'.[21] Terrorists may also share information with other terrorists online. For example, the Global Islamic Media Front offered a 'degree in jihad' to Internet users who visited its website in 2005. The webmaster offered specialisation in 'electronic media, spiritual and financial jihad' (Ariza, 2005: 1). The evidence presented at the trial of the men responsible for the Madrid train bombings in March 2004 suggests that other jihadist groups are using the Internet for research and information sharing. One of the attackers was shown to have downloaded a document entitled 'Jihadi Iraq: Hopes and Dangers' from a jihadist website (p. 2).

Each of the functions outlined above demonstrates the potential importance of the Internet to contemporary terrorist organisations.

While the Weimann thesis may not be applicable to all terrorist organisations in its entirety, it is important to recognise that terrorists do use the Internet for many of the same purposes as civil society organisations. While there still remains a high degree of uncertainty about the threat of cyberterrorism, there is more evidence to show that terrorists are using the Internet to plan and perpetrate atrocities in the offline world. Terrorist use of the Internet for these functions arguably poses a greater risk to nation-states than the cyber attacks envisaged in the mid-1990s.

The Internet and conflict transformation
While much of the literature in the field has focused upon the use of the Internet to perpetuate conflict, there has been relatively little research into how ICTs may aid the process of conflict transformation in divided societies. Cyber enthusiasts such as Wellman (2001) and Dahlgren (2005) argue that ICTs have the potential to facilitate public debate in communicative spaces that are not present in the real world, opening up the possibility that in situations of community conflict, where neutral space may be difficult to access, online spaces may provide a viable alternative for improving community relations. Amichai and McKenna (2006) argue that the Internet has the potential to facilitate effective intergroup contact by creating 'a secure environment, reducing anxiety, cutting geographical distances, significantly lowering costs, and by creating equal status, intimate contact, and cooperation' (p. 10). They suggest that a gradual model of interaction should be employed, starting with text-only interaction, moving on to videoconferencing and culminating in face-to-face interaction between members of the different social groups. These online interactions might conceivably lead to the development of bridging social capital in divided societies. There is already some empirical evidence to suggest that the Internet can be used by diasporas to help discourage people from engaging in intercommunal violence. Brinkerhoff (2006) found that members of the Somalinet virtual community tended to discourage acts of violence and encourage the development of a shared Somali identity amongst its members, who were drawn from a number of rival ethnic groups. Although there were still a large number of discussions that could be characterised as antagonistic, the analysis suggested that digital diasporas had the potential to alter the cost-benefit equation for those members who were considering violent engagement through an engendered sense of identity and shared understanding across different ethnic groups (p. 47).

Terrorism itself might be solvable should its perpetrators find a large audience on the Internet. Authors such as Castells (2001) and Elnur

(2003) argue that bridging the digital divide, the gap between those who are able to benefit from ICTs and those who are not, is a precondition for resolving terrorism. The cyberoptimist model implies that ICTs facilitate the 'one to many' communication that terrorists are invariably denied in the mass media (Chadwick, 2006). The Internet might enable these actors to reach large audiences without having to perpetrate violence in order to generate publicity for their cause. Authors as far back as Spears and Lea (1994) have suggested that the Internet facilitates 'forms of communication, interaction, and organisation that undermine unequal status and power relations' (p. 428). However, this hypothesis is based upon the assumption that terrorism is a rational communication strategy employed by sub state actors who lack both political power and regular access to the mass media. Wieviorka (1993) asserts that some terrorist actors may be less dependent upon the mass media for sustenance than others are, as they conceive their violence as an end in and of itself. Nevertheless, by definition, all terrorist actors use political violence as an instrument to achieve strategic political and 'military' objectives. The manipulation of the mass media via high-profile atrocities remains the most effective method of 'terrorising' a target audience. This book will consider whether the website strategies of dissident Loyalists and Republicans, who remain committed to the use of violence for political advantage, are able to reproduce the publicity they gain from the perpetration of high-profile atrocities. It will also provide further insight into the dialogic potential of the Internet and how this relates to the process of conflict transformation in divided societies such as Northern Ireland.

Methodologies

Frames
The book employs two research methodologies in order to examine the website strategies of Northern Irish political groups. In terms of a qualitative approach, the frames adopted by these actors in relation to the acceptability of political violence will be analysed throughout the book. The term 'frame' is used to describe two interrelated processes, namely how a speaker uses words and images to relay information about an issue or event to an audience, and an individual's cognitive understanding of a given situation (Goffman, 1974). The psychological origins of framing theory can be traced back to experimental work in the late 1970s that examined how people evaluated options that had been presented to them in different ways (Kahneman and Tversky, 1979). Subsequent research into how social organisations mobilised

their supporters found that frames fulfilled a number of critical group-maintenance functions. These included the development of group identity, problem definition, solution identification and engendering support amongst group members and allies for the proposed solution to the problem (Levin, 2005). Much of the recent literature in the field has tended to focus upon how the frames adopted by the media affect public opinion. Communication scholars such as Scheufele and Tewksbury (2008) suggest that the media can have potentially strong attitudinal effects, depending upon the 'predispositions, schema, and other characteristics of the audience that influence how they process media messages' (p. 11). A synthesis of the literature in the field suggests that frames are more likely to affect public opinion at an aggregate level if they are easily accessible in the media and resonate with the cultural values of the audience (Scheufele, 1999; Entman, 2003). However, the environment in which a frame emerges may also determine how it shapes an individual's cognitive understanding of an issue or an event, particularly if they have no prior knowledge of it. Whereas individuals with low levels of personal motivation may be motivated by competitive contexts to discriminate between strong and weak frames, they are likely to be affected by both in a non-competitive media environment (Chong and Druckman, 2007).

The 'Cascading Activation' model proposed by Entman (2003) is probably the most-cited recent study of media framing. This model is congruent with previous studies of political communication that suggested that elites use culturally resonant news frames to manufacture consent for their foreign policies (Hallin, 1986; Herman and Chomsky, 2002). Entman (2003) asserts that the framing of US foreign policy post 9/11 as a 'war on terrorism' helped the Bush administration to 'dampen elite dissent, dominate media texts and reduce the threat of negative public reaction' to US military engagement in these areas (p. 423). Examples of this 'high resonance' framing can be found in the emotionally charged language used by President Bush during his media appearances, with terms such as 'evil' and 'war' frequently used to frame the 9/11 attacks. The 'war on terrorism' frame convinced many Americans that military engagement in Afghanistan was the best solution for Islamic terrorism, despite a stronger case existing for military intervention against Saudi Arabia.[22] Initially the Democrats and the US news networks provided little or no resistance to this frame, for fear of seeming 'unpatriotic', with the exception of a few editorials that highlighted the link between Saudi officials and Osama bin Laden. However, a frame challenge did emerge as the elite consensus for the 'war on terrorism' started to fracture in the summer of 2002. The Bush administration's decision to invade Iraq as the next stage of its 'war on terrorism' divided Republicans both within and outside the government. Leading figures within the administration such as Secretary of State Colin Powell voiced their scepticism about the Iraq option, while former Secretaries of State such as James Baker were openly critical about the proposed military intervention. However, Entman (2003) attributes the emergence of a frame challenge to the professional norms of journalists rather than to the divisions within the ruling elite. The US news media were to play an important role in covering not only the divisions within the Bush administration but also the growth of the anti-war coalition during this period (p. 428).

Although scholars such as Zhou and May (2007) assert that framing fails to take account of how online public opinion may shape public discourse, it remains an important conceptual tool for analysing the nexus between terrorism and the media. In *Framing Terrorism: The News Media, the Government and the Public*, Norris et al (2003) used framing theory to analyse how both terrorists and governments manipulate the media to shape public perceptions of political violence. Congruent with the literature in the field, the authors in this volume found that news frames can alter how audiences evaluate terrorism if there is a consensus view held by both political elites and journalists within a community. Frames have also been deployed to compare and contrast media coverage of terrorism in the United Kingdom and the United States. Barnet et al (2007) found that CNN coverage of the 9/11 attacks tended to be more sensationalist than BBC coverage of the 7 July 2005 terrorist attacks in London. Furthermore, there were differences in how both news organisations framed the government response to terrorism, with CNN criticising the US government for its inability to prevent the 9/11 attacks while the BBC praised UK public officials for their quick response to the London attacks. Post 9/11, there has also been a renewed interest in the psychological impacts of how the media frame terrorism. Bucy (2003) studied how audiences reacted to statements made by President Bush when they were played after graphic images of the 9/11 atrocities. He found that presidential statements were unlikely to allay viewer anxiety if they were paired with high-intensity images of terrorism. A synthesis of these studies suggests that media framing of terrorist attacks has the potential to not only influence how audiences interpret political violence but also build support for government responses to terrorism.

Framing and soft power in Northern Ireland
This book will consider whether the ability of Northern Irish terrorists to frame their positions regarding the acceptability of political violence

in cyberspace is likely to translate into soft power for these actors. Soft power is defined here as the 'ability to get what you want by attracting and persuading others to adopt your goals' (Nye, 2004: 5). Recent empirical studies have tended to focus on how terrorists use militaristic language on their websites to generate soft power and mobilise supporters. Authors such as Weimann (2004) suggest that terrorists often depict themselves as freedom fighters on their websites in an effort to counter their violent image in the mass media. Conway (2006a) found that Hizbollah used its collection of websites to publish details of its military operations against Israeli forces. For example, one website features a 'military operations' section, which provides a detailed account of all Hizbollah operations since 1997 (p. 110). While this information may be targeted at the Israeli media, as well as a potential global audience, it also serves another critical group objective. Commentators suggest that the Hizbollah Web presence is very important for the morale of its 'resistance fighters', as it informs them of the support they receive from around the globe (Whine, 1999: 233). A recent study also suggested that Hamas uses one of its websites, www.palestine-info. net, to encourage acts of terrorism. Research commissioned by the Center for Special Studies found that this website encouraged terrorism against Israeli targets, affirming the movement's 'commitment not to disarm and to continue its terrorist attacks on Israel until its destruction' (Intelligence and Terrorism Information Center, 2005). What is clear from the studies conducted so far is that active terrorist organisations in the Middle East, that is to say those who remain engaged in politically motivated violence, tend to use their websites to justify their military activities rather than to deny responsibility for them.

The Northern Irish conflict is pertinent to the discussion of terrorist soft power, due to the paramilitary ceasefires which facilitated the Good Friday Agreement (1998). This book will analyse how terrorists in the region frame their positions regarding the acceptability of political violence during a period of conflict transformation. In order to analyse online communications in post-conflict Northern Ireland, it is necessary to develop an understanding and appreciation of the nuances of the Northern Irish conflict and the actors, both state and non-state, that have been party to this conflict. The Conflict Archive on the Internet (CAIN) provides one of the most comprehensive chronologies of the Northern Irish conflict, often referred to as the Troubles. The Northern Irish conflict can be characterised as the clash of two strands of ethnic nationalism.[23] Since the creation of Northern Ireland in 1921, Protestant and Catholic communities have failed to agree upon a common identity to which they both can subscribe. Catholic and Protestant social identities remain predominantly tied to their external 'ethno-guarantors', the Republic of Ireland and Great Britain respectively (Byrne, 2001: 341). Catholics typically identify themselves as Irish, while Protestants regard themselves as British. Bryan (2000) asserts that the terms 'Protestant', 'Unionist' and 'Loyalist' are used in some discourses 'almost interchangeably', as are the terms 'Catholic' and 'nationalist' (p. 15). These social identities directly influence the political aspirations of these ethnic communities. The majority of Catholics vote for Nationalist or Republican political parties who wish to see Northern Ireland reunite with the Republic of Ireland. The Social Democratic and Labour Party (SDLP) has been the largest nationalist party in the region for over three decades, with its leader John Hume playing a key role in the preliminary talks that led to the inclusion of the Republican movement in the peace process. Committed to achieving a united Ireland through peaceful means, the SDLP was the largest constitutional party in the reconstituted Stormont Assembly after the inaugural Assembly elections in 1998, with deputy leader Seamus Mallon elected to the post of Deputy First Minister of Northern Ireland.

Republicans are traditionally differentiated from nationalists by virtue of their support for political violence. Probably the most well-known Republican paramilitary organisation is the Provisional IRA, which was active between 1969 and 1997 before announcing a permanent end to its military activities in July 2005. The Republican movement adopted a dual strategy during the Northern Irish conflict, using its terrorist organisation to attack both military and civilian targets in the United Kingdom, while its political front, Sinn Fein, competed in local and national elections. Cochrane (2007) argues that the soft power of strategies of Irish-American groups played a pivotal role in convincing the leadership of the Provisional IRA to end its armed campaign and engage in the peace process. Previously a key constituency of support for the military strategy of the Republican movement, Irish-American groups helped to internationalise the Northern Irish conflict and raise its importance as a key priority of US foreign policy during the Clinton administration of the mid-1990s. Subject to extensive censorship during the Troubles, courtesy of legislation such as the UK Broadcasting Ban (1988), Sinn Fein became a permanent feature on the daily news by virtue of its participation in the negotiations that led to the Good Friday Agreement and its subsequent electoral success (Cooke, 2003). Since the Belfast Agreement the party has overtaken the SDLP to become the largest Nationalist/Republican party in the region and has taken several ministerial portfolios within the power-sharing executive. Meanwhile, dissident Republican terrorists and their political affiliates have remained committed to the use of violence for political advantage. Republican splinter groups such as the Continuity IRA and the Real IRA have continued to commit sporadic acts of political violence with often lethal consequences, as demonstrated by the Omagh bomb in August 1998. The murders of Constable Steven Carroll in Lurgan and two army sappers at Massereene barracks near Antrim in March 2009 have served to demonstrate the continued threat posed by dissident Republicans towards the peace process.[24]

The majority of Protestants in Northern Ireland vote for Unionist or Loyalist political parties who support the existing union with Great Britain. The Ulster Unionist Party (UUP) was the largest pro-union political party in terms of electoral support prior to the Good Friday Agreement, with its leader David Trimble becoming the First Minister of Northern Ireland after the inaugural elections to the Northern Ireland Assembly in July 1998. However, the UUP has seen a reduction in its electoral base as the Democratic Unionist Party (DUP), one of the most fervent opponents of the Belfast Agreement, has started to attract the support of Unionists who have grown disenchanted with the peace process. Led by Dr Ian Paisley, the Loyalist party has overtaken the UUP to become the largest pro-union party in the Northern Ireland Assembly since 2005. Both Paisley and his successor, Peter Robinson, have held the post of First Minister in the Northern Ireland Executive alongside Sinn Fein's Martin McGuinness who has served as Deputy First Minister during this period. The shift in attitudes towards the Belfast Agreement within the Unionist community has led voters to desert smaller parties such as the Northern Ireland Unionist Party and the United Kingdom Unionist Party (UKUP) in favour of the DUP. Moderates such as the Alliance Party of Northern Ireland, who are supportive of the union but draw greater support from both communities than their Unionist counterparts, have also suffered a downturn in their election fortunes as the DUP and Sinn Fein have dominated the electoral landscape after 2005.

While Republican groups formerly committed to political violence have gained both legitimacy and support since the Belfast Agreement, Loyalist paramilitaries and their political affiliates have struggled to make an impact in local and national elections since 1998. Despite their commitment to the peace process, both the Ulster Defence Association (UDA) and its sister organisation the Ulster Volunteer Force (UVF) have continued to engage in sporadic acts of paramilitarism since the Good Friday Agreement. Dissident Loyalist groups such as the LVF have also sought to derail the peace process through the targeting of Catholic civilians during the mid-1990s, and even attacked members of the UVF before they announced that they were standing down their military units in October 2005.[25] In contrast to Sinn Fein, Loyalist political parties remain peripheral political actors with limited electoral support. The two most well-known Loyalist parties, the Progressive Unionist Party (PUP) and the Ulster Democratic Party (UDP), have received less than 5 percent of the vote in each of the elections post 1998, with the latter disbanding in 2001. After the dissolution of the UDP, the Ulster Political Research Group (UPRG) has provided political counsel to the UDA and has maintained a relatively low media profile much in the same vein as its predecessor. One explanation for the relative anonymity of Loyalist political parties may be that members of the Protestant community no longer feel they need protection from the threat of attack by the Provisional IRA. Ulster Loyalism is based upon a 'narrative of violence', with 'pro-state' terrorists claiming that they exist purely to protect the province from Republican attacks (Graham, 2004: 488). While Sinn Fein has successfully rebranded itself to occupy the same electoral ground as the SDLP, fringe Loyalists have struggled to break the DUP's dominance within the Protestant community.

The Good Friday Agreement: conflict transformed?

This book presents an analysis of how these actors used their websites to generate soft power during a period of conflict transformation. The Good Friday Agreement sought to deconstruct the siege mentality within both communities that had caused the collapse of the Sunningdale institutions two decades earlier. This was to be achieved through the reconceptualisation of the role of the external 'ethno-guarantors' in Northern Ireland (Byrne, 2001: 341). Britain and the Republic of Ireland were to become the 'trustees' of the Northern Irish peace process, rather than antagonists involved in a power struggle over the disputed province. In addition, a series of political concessions were made to the Unionist and Nationalist political parties that had been involved in the negotiations that led to the Good Friday Agreement. Cross-border bodies, a long-term aspiration for Nationalists since the ill-fated Council of Ireland, were a key component of the Belfast Agreement. Increased cooperation with the Republic of Ireland implied that Northern Ireland was no longer an 'internal' British concern (Williams and Jesse, 2001: 572). The constitution of the Republic of Ireland (1936) was amended to ease the security concerns of the Unionist community. Articles 2 and 3 of the Irish constitution had originally asserted the jurisdiction of the government of the Republic of Ireland over the six counties of Northern Ireland. This territorial 'claim' was removed under the terms of the Good Friday Agreement. Moreover, the 'principle of consent' was designed to alleviate Protestant and Catholic concerns regarding the sustenance of their ethnic identity. Protestants could console themselves with the fact that the status quo would remain, due to their greater numbers. Catholics could look forward to the prospect of a united Ireland once they became the largest community in Northern Ireland. Demographic studies suggested that this would happen soon, perhaps within a few generations. The number of people defining themselves as Protestant had declined since the start of the Troubles, from 63.2 percent in 1961 to 50.6 percent in 1991. By 1991, 38.4 percent of the population of Northern Ireland defined themselves as Catholic (McGarry, 2002: 460). In sum, the Belfast Agreement provided incentives to persuade political representatives from both communities to participate in a power-sharing executive. The siege mentality of both communities was to be alleviated through constitutional reform in both the United Kingdom and the Republic of Ireland.

Whereas previously, terrorist-linked parties faced heavy censorship in both Northern Ireland and the Republic of Ireland, they now enjoy routine access to the news media. While these terrorist organisations remain committed to their ceasefires, soft power has arguably become vital to the achievement of their objectives, with political parties the primary vehicle for these aspirations. As Sinn Fein has adopted an agenda that is broadly similar to that of the nationalist SDLP, this raises questions as to the frames employed on its website. These groups may be using their websites to demonstrate their commitment to democracy and to differentiate themselves from the activities of their terrorist sponsors. Yet, not all Northern Irish terrorist organisations have called a permanent cessation to their military activities. Dissidents on both sides have continued to use both political parties and acts of terrorism to communicate with target audiences. These groups may be using militaristic language on their websites to suggest they are freedom fighters motivated by a just cause. This book will compare and contrast how these actors frame their positions regarding the use of political violence and consider the extent to which these websites might generate soft power for both current and former terrorists.

Coding scheme

In terms of a quantitative approach, each website examined in this book was scored with reference to a coding scheme (Table 1.1). This allowed a direct comparison between the websites of political fronts and constitutional political parties. It also enabled the websites to be ranked in terms of their interactivity, presentation, organisational linkage

Table 1.1 Coding scheme

Interactivity
  Email newsletter (1)
  Bulletin board/chatroom (1)
  Correspondence address (postal) (1)
  Telephone/fax Number (1)
  Email webmaster (1)
  Email individual members (1)
  Donations (1)
  Maximum score available: 7
Online recruitment
  Members only section (1)
  Full membership advertised (1)
  Full membership available (1)
  Public relations 'paraphernalia' available for download (poster, placards) (1)
  Maximum score available: 4
Organisational linkage
  Solidarity organisations/websites (1)
  International terrorist organisations/websites (1)
  Educational websites (universities, external news media) (1)
  Commercial/non-political links (1)
  Number of links >15 (1)
  Maximum score available: 5
Presentation
  Graphics (1)
  Frames (1)
  Sound (1)
  Video/live streaming (1)
  Pages available in PDF/alternative format (1)
  Maximum score available: 5

and online recruitment. The coding scheme was similar to the coding framework devised by Rachel Gibson and Stephen Ward to analyse the function and effectiveness of party websites (Gibson and Ward, 2000). This scheme had features that measured the level of interactivity, networking, presentation and transparency visible on the websites of political parties. Baseline data such as the frequency of updates on a particular website and the availability of a foreign-language translation service were also provided to compare the website strategies of political parties. Previous research into terrorist websites has also drawn heavily upon this coding scheme. Conway (2006b) used a similar coding framework to measure the effectiveness of English-language websites maintained by 'old' terrorist groups such as Hamas, Hizbollah and the Revolutionary Armed Forces of Columbia. This coding scheme was used to compare ten terrorist websites in terms of information and communication flows and the delivery of content. The analysis suggested that the primary function of these websites was to provide information about the terrorist group to Internet users, although there was evidence to suggest that these groups were trying to mobilise supporters online. This study seeks to develop an understanding of Northern Irish terrorist website strategy using a coding scheme to analyse the functionality of their respective homepages. Information and communication flows will be analysed in order to determine whether these actors are also using their websites primarily for information provision or to mobilise supporters.

A point was given to a website if it included one of the features identified in the coding scheme. These points were then compiled to give an overall score in each of the four categories measuring website function, namely, interactivity, target audience, organisational linkage and presentation. Certain features that specifically applied to party websites were not included within the study. For example, it was considered highly unlikely that solidarity actors or residents' groups would use their websites to provide electoral information such as manifestos or to call on their supporters to engage in an online Q & A session with their respective organisations. The presentation, interactivity and target audience categories provided evidence of how these groups used their website to communicate with target audiences. The organisational linkage category provided an insight into how these organisations used the Web to link with like-minded groups online. A website received a point if it provided links pointing towards the websites of external institutions, such as the news media and government agencies. For the purposes of the study, solidarity websites were defined as those that expressed support for the ideology of the actor under analysis. This did not include websites dedicated to the Irish language or the Orange Order, as these were considered cultural rather than political projections of the two traditions in Northern Ireland. International terrorist websites were those that offered support for an international ethno-nationalist movement, such as ETA. This feature was included to determine whether Loyalists and Republicans exposed their links to international terrorist organisations on their websites. A point was also awarded to organisations that provided a large number of links on their websites, defined here as a minimum of 15 links. It was anticipated that these features would provide some insight into the effectiveness of the website strategy of the actors under analysis.

Sample

A total of 65 websites were selected to investigate the framing and functionality of both civil and uncivil Northern Irish actors in May 2004 and April 2005. This was a period in which the UK and Irish governments attempted to restore the power-sharing institutions in the Province. The Northern Ireland Executive had been suspended in October 2002 in the wake of the discovery of an alleged IRA spy operation within the Assembly and the threatened resignation of First Minister David Trimble and his UUP colleagues in the Executive if the Provisional IRA did not formally disband by January 2003.[26] Discussions between the two Prime Ministers, Bertie Ahern and Tony Blair, and the leaders of the political parties continued throughout the period of data collection as they sought to restore devolution to Northern Ireland.[27] However, these talks were often overshadowed by political events elsewhere, both in Northern Ireland and further afield. Hopes for the restoration of the power-sharing institutions appeared bleak after the Provisional IRA was linked to the £26 million Northern Bank robbery in Belfast in December 2004. Unionists suggested that the robbery showed that the Republican movement was not fully committed to the use of exclusively peaceful means to achieve its objectives. The Republican movement also faced international condemnation after its members were linked to murder of Robert McCartney in Belfast in January 2005 (CAIN).[28] The subsequent campaign by the McCartney family to hold the Provisional IRA accountable for the killing saw pressure build on Sinn Fein to deliver a permanent cessation to the Provisional IRA's activities. The Republican movement was to announce an end to its military campaign on 28 July 2005, while talks continued to restore the Northern Ireland Executive that culminated in the restoration of devolution in May 2007.

It should be noted that 27 of these websites have been shutdown since the period of data collection (see Appendix 2). In terms of political parties, both the UKUP and the Northern Ireland Women's Coalition disbanded shortly after the period of data collection and their domain names were available for purchase in November 2009. All of the other parties continued to maintain websites in 2009, although the Green Party of Northern Ireland and the Workers Party have changed their web addresses since the study.[29] A similar pattern emerged from the political fronts, with only the 32 County Sovereignty Movement (32CSM) changing its web address since 2004. There was a much higher turnover of websites maintained by solidarity actors and residents' groups. A total of 15 Loyalist solidarity websites were no longer available in November 2009. Only three Loyalist solidarity websites

(Liverpool UDA, The British Ulster Alliance, and The Volunteer) ana-lysed in the study were still available at the same universal resource locator (URL), while both the Birches Guerrilla Movement (BGM) and the Loyalist Network were available as Bebo profiles. This was a much higher turnover than seen in the study of Republican solidarity websites. A total of 12 Republican websites were available at the same URL that had been analysed during the study. Seven websites, includ-ing Australian Aid for Ireland and Cairde Sinn Fein were no longer available in November 2009, while the Friends of Irish Freedom had developed a Bebo profile to replace its website.[30] In terms of residents' groups, the Short Strand Under Siege website was the only one that was still accessible in November 2009. A Cluan Place Bebo profile was available, although there was no evidence to suggest that it had been created by the webmaster responsible for the original website. While there was no evidence to suggest that community groups such as the Lower Ormeau Concerned Community had ceased to function, they appeared to have abandoned the website strategies of the early 2000s that will be analysed in this book.

Notes

1 Social capital will be discussed in greater detail in Chapter 5.
2 Moveon is an advocacy group that has raised money for the Democratic Party in the United States and taken a prominent role in campaigns against the Iraq War and Republican politicians, including President George Bush and Arnold Schwarznegger, the Republican candidate in the Californian gubernatorial election in 2003.
3 The Chiapas insurrection will be discussed in greater detail in Chapter 5.
4 Internet World Statistics. www.internetworldstats.com/stats (accessed 10 September 2009). The Digital Divide will be discussed in more detail in Chapter 4.
5 The Minnesota E-Democracy project was created in 1994 to promote the use of the Internet to improve citizen participation in politics through information and knowledge exchange. The initial project saw 1,834 people subscribe to the four specially created email lists.
6 There was no publicly available data detailing the age and gender of Northern Irish Internet users in 2005.
7 Ofcom. 2009. 'The Communications Market: Nations and Regions 2008: Northern Ireland'. www.ofcom.org.uk/research/cm/cmrnr08/nireland/nireland.pdf (accessed 1 September 2009).
8 See Radio B92. www.b92.net/doc/aboutus.phtml (accessed 10 July 2007). B92 came to prominence during the NATO air raids on Belgrade in April 1999. In an effort to limit dissent, Milosevic ordered that the station be

closed and its premises occupied by government troops. ANEM was a federation of independent media organisations operating in Yugoslavia during this period.

9 Reporters Without Borders. 2009. 'The 15 Enemies of the Internet and Other Countries To Watch'. www.rsf.org/spip.php?page=article&id_article=15613 (accessed 10 October 2009).

10 Addley, Esther. 2009. 'Twitter: Iran's Voice of Dissent'. *Mail and Guardian Online*, www.mg.co.za/article/2009-06-20-twitter-irans-voice-of-dissent (accessed 2 October 2009).

11 Schechtman, Joel. 2009. 'Iran's Twitter Revolution? Maybe Not Yet'. *Business Week*, 17 June. www.businessweek.com/technology/content/jun2009/tc20090617_803990.htm (accessed 10 October 2009).

12 The Serb Black Hand was alleged to have hacked into an ethnic Albanian website. The UNITY hackers launched a denial of service attack on a range of Israeli websites, in response to an attack on the Hizbollah website.

13 Shachtman, N. 2008. 'How Gadgets Helped Mumbai Attackers'. Wired Blog Network, http://blog.wired.com/defense/2008/12/the-gagdets-of.html (accessed 31 January 2009).

14 Euskal Herria Journal, 'Navarre: A Basque Journal'. www.contrast.org/mirros/ehj/ (accessed 20 June 2004).

15 The video, entitled 'The Slaughter of the Spy-Journalist, the Jew Daniel Pearl', was also sent to FBI and Pakistani officials on February 2002. See CNN. 2002. 'U.S. Journalist Daniel Pearl Is Dead, Officials Confirm'. www.archives.cnn.com/2002/WORLD/asiapcf/south/02/21/missing.reporter/index.html (accessed 10 June 2007).

16 M. Ansari. 2004. 'Daniel Pearl "refused to be sedated before his throat was cut"'. *The Daily Telegraph*. www.telegraph.co.uk/core/Content/displayPrintable.jhtml?xml=/news/2004/05 (accessed 10 August 2007).

17 In 1999, a story emanating from a Hizbollah website claimed that a single coffin had been returned to Israel from Lebanon containing the body parts of several murdered Israeli marines. This caused a row between IDF officials and the families of the deceased.

18 *Belfast Telegraph*. 2001. 'New Internet Terror Fear: Loyalists Are Using Web to Pick Targets' (15 March).

19 Ulster Loyalist Information Service. www.ulisnet.com/main.htm (accessed 2 March 2003). Note that this website is no longer available online. The organisation also asked Internet users to forward information about the Ulster Volunteer Force and Progressive Unionist Party, two paramilitary groups who were involved in a feud with the LVF during this period.

20 The website was no longer available as of November 2004. The domain name remains available for purchase. It is reasonable to speculate that this website was shut down by the ISP for violating the norms of acceptable behaviour online, as defined under the UK Terrorism Act (2000).

21 McCullagh, D. 2003. 'Military Worried about Web Leaks'. *C/Net News*. http://news.com.com/2100-1023-981057.html (accessed 10 June 2007).

22 The links between the Saudi leadership and Osama bin Laden were first brought into the news discourse in articles written by Seymour Hersh (2002) and Thomas Friedman (2001). He provided evidence that the Saudi leadership had provided resources to Islamic terrorists.

23 Ethnic nationalist movements seek to 'politicise' an ethnic group through the exploitation of its history and culture that distinguishes it from other ethnic groups. Invariably, these groups will reject political assimilation and cultural accommodation in multi-ethnic states (O'Sullivan See, 1986: 148).

24 McDonald, H. 2009. 'Northern Irish Teenager Charged with Murder of Policeman'. *Guardian* (24 March). www.guardian.co.uk/uk/2009/mar/24/teenager-charged-murder-policeman.

25 Conflict Archive on the Internet (CAIN). 2009. 'Abstract of Organisations-I'. http://cain.ulst.ac.uk/othelem/organ/iorgan.htm.

26 *Guardian*. 2009. 'Northern Ireland Timeline January 2003–December 2004'. www.guardian.co.uk/northernireland/page/0,12494,908880,00.html (accessed 30 October 2009).

27 A selected chronology of the peace process can be found in Appendix 1.

28 http://cain.ulst.ac.uk.

29 The Green Party website can now be found at www.greenpartyni.org/. The Workers Party website is now part of the Workers Party Ireland portal www.workerspartyireland.net/ni.html.

30 The other Republican websites that are no longer available are Coiste na n-Iarchimi, Give Ireland Back to the Irish, Hardline IRA, Ireland 4 the Irish, Na Gael and New Republican Forum.

2

The peace frame? Comparing the websites of Northern Irish political fronts and political parties

Introduction

Goffman (1974) asserts that frames are the 'schemata of interpretation that enable individuals to locate, perceive, identify, and label occurrences or information' (p. 21). Some commentators suggest that the Northern Irish media helped to build cross-community support for the Good Friday Agreement (1998) through their adoption of a 'peace frame'. This peace frame created a bond between pro-peace groups from both camps, making a clear distinction between the political fronts that were engaged in the process and the violence associated with their terrorist sponsors (Wolfsfeld, 2001: 36). In this chapter the peace frame will be analysed through the lens of Loyalist and Republican political fronts, defined here as organisations 'for and under the control of a terrorist group' (Richards, 2001: 73). The master frames adopted by Northern Irish political parties on their websites in May 2004 will be examined to assess the extent to which they have been influenced by the peace frame employed by the Northern Irish media in the late 1990s. In addition, the websites of political fronts and constitutional political parties are analysed to determine the extent to which these groups were realising the potential of the Web as a tool for mobilisation and organisational linkage. The study suggests that the websites of organisations closely linked to Northern Irish terrorist groups not only do not differ markedly from those of 'civil' groups, but also do not seem to offer any new dimension of terrorist threat. All political fronts use language on their websites that suggests they are cultural democrats, as opposed to the public relations departments of terrorist organisations.

The peace frame

In this section the evolution of the peace frame will be traced from three perspectives, namely the mass media, the two (British and Irish) governments, and Northern Irish terrorist organisations. Levin (2005) defines a frame as a 'publicly presented definition of a situation containing three elements, a problem, protagonist and a solution' (p. 84). For Northern Ireland's two communities the problem and protagonists have remained unchanged since the beginning of the Northern Irish Troubles in 1968. Nationalists remain committed to securing both a British withdrawal from Northern Ireland and the creation of a socialist 32-county Irish Republic. Meanwhile, Unionists remain fervent supporters of the Union with Great Britain and oppose integration into a 32-county Irish Republic. However, the solutions identified by some terrorist organisations have altered by virtue of their support for the Good Friday Agreement. Paramilitaries on both sides, who had previously been committed to armed struggle, agreed to use exclusively democratic means in pursuit of their group objectives and to oppose 'any use or threat of force by others for any political purpose'.[1] In turn, political parties linked to pro-Agreement terrorist groups have altered their frames. These groups have sought to differentiate themselves from the violence associated with their terrorist sponsors.

Political actors used the peace frame to build cross-community support for the Good Friday Agreement. Supporters of the Belfast Agreement differentiated political fronts from the violence associated with their respective terrorist organisations, portraying parties such as Sinn Fein as 'cultural democrats, committed to democracy come what may' (Richards, 2001: 83). This was necessary to convince sceptics within both communities that these terrorist organisations were sincere in their commitment to using exclusively peaceful means. Critics of the Belfast Agreement had claimed that it allowed terrorist organisations to participate in elected bodies while retaining the option to return to political violence should they grow frustrated with the peace process. In the opinion of anti-Agreement Unionists, political fronts were only functional democrats, their support for the Good Friday Agreement perceived as instrumental and even opportunistic (Pridham, 1990: 14). Clearly, if the electorate shared this view it would be harder to mobilise support for the inclusion of these political fronts in the newly constituted Stormont Assembly. Pro-peace groups from both communities had to be convinced that the Good Friday Agreement was the only means of securing permanent peace in the province.

The media and the peace frame
The media environment within Northern Ireland helped to expose both communities to this peace frame. The master frame of each media organisation reflected its support for the Belfast Agreement and, by implication, the inclusion of terrorist-linked groups in the newly

created power-sharing institutions. Between July 1997 and April 1999, newspapers on both sides of the sectarian divide published editorials urging their readership to support the peace process. For example, the *Belfast Telegraph* published 62 editorials in favour of the peace process during this period.[2] The *Irish News*, traditionally considered a nationalist newspaper in favour of a united Ireland, published 64 editorials in support of the peace process during this same period (p. 34). Elsewhere, national and international news media organisations conformed to the framing of the Northern Irish media, even in the aftermath of the Omagh bombing in August 1998. Wolfsfeld (2001) suggests that the media 'amplified' the peace frame after an atrocity that could have been a major setback for the peace process (p. 36).

It is too simplistic to suggest that the framing of the Northern Irish mass media alone united pro-peace groups in both communities, or convinced them that terrorist-linked groups should be included in the Stormont Assembly. Chong and Druckman (2007) argue that the critical determinants of framing effect include not just the strength and prevalence of the frame, but also the knowledge and motivation of its recipients (p. 110). Evidently, the media were responsible for the strength and prevalence of the peace frame between 1997 and 1999, as illustrated by the number of 'pro-peace' editorials in newspapers such as the *Irish News*. The media did not deploy an alternative frame in their editorials during this period, leading to accusations from anti-Agreement Unionists that they had stifled any serious debate about the risks associated with the peace process (Wolfsfeld, 2001: 31). Yet, the Northern Irish media's peace frame also reflected public opinion within the Province. If these media organisations were to retain their audience share, their editorials had to adopt a political perspective that was acceptable to both communities (p. 36). There was sufficient evidence to suggest that the majority of people within Northern Ireland favoured the peace process, particularly after May 1998, when 71.1 percent voted 'yes' in the referendum on the Good Friday Agreement.[3] Moreover, the media routinely projected the peace frame through their coverage of political actors that actively supported the inclusion of political fronts in the peace process, such as the UK and Irish governments. Many pro-peace groups, such as the Northern Ireland Women's Coalition, had already adopted this master frame during the peace negotiations, and in the referendum campaign that followed the Good Friday Agreement.

Megaphone diplomacy: antecedent for the peace frame?
Richards (2001) suggests that the two (UK and Irish) governments 'legitimised' the IRA, its political front and its armed struggle through

their support for the Good Friday Agreement (p. 77). The use of demilitarisation as a quid pro quo for decommissioning had reinforced 'Republican impressions that they had been right all along' (p. 77). Irrespective of the choreography that lay behind efforts to secure IRA decommissioning, it would appear that the two governments viewed the Troubles through the lens of the peace frame and wished others to do the same. Both governments favoured an all-inclusive peace process, one in which terrorists were encouraged to abandon political violence and work towards their objectives through their political affiliates. This process arguably began with the 'megaphone diplomacy' that facilitated the clarification of the Downing Street Declaration (1993).[4] Megaphone diplomacy is the 'practice of engaging in dialogue and sending messages via the media to other parties in a conflict, in a situation where it is not possible or desirable to conduct formal negotiations for whatever reason' (Sparre, 2001: 89). Both governments issued a series of strategic statements designed to persuade paramilitaries on both sides to call ceasefires and create a context in which negotiations could take place with the mainstream political parties. For example, the Declaration called for an end to all forms of paramilitary violence, stating that only democratically mandated parties, who were committed to 'exclusively peaceful methods', could participate in negotiations regarding the future of Northern Ireland. This marked the first time that the two governments had talked publicly about the inclusion of terrorist-linked groups in the peace process. The frame adopted by the UK and Irish governments reflected a change in their approach to the management of the Northern Irish conflict. After all, the political fronts invited to join the peace negotiations were the same organisations that had been denied the 'oxygen of publicity' during the previous two decades.

Newspaper columns became the arena for the clarification of the Declaration, as there was no channel of communication open between the British government and Sinn Fein during this period. UK government ministers presented information to journalists in 'newsworthy formats', such as public speeches and press conferences, in the expectation that they would be picked up by Sinn Fein representatives in the press (Sparre, 2001: 90). The UK government issued a number of statements to the media suggesting that the Republican movement would gain entry into the political process if it declared a permanent ceasefire, even if it did not accept the terms of the Declaration (p. 102). Simultaneously, Sinn Fein used its press releases to call for face-to-face meetings with UK government ministers to clarify the Declaration (p. 97). The subsequent Loyalist and Republican ceasefires (1994) paved the way for a 'normalisation of relations' between parties such as Sinn Fein and the UK and Irish governments (Cooke, 2003: 84). From 1994 onwards terrorist-linked groups were given regular access to the news media, in contrast to the censorship associated with the Broadcasting Ban a few years earlier. These political fronts had become 'woven into the tapestry of daily news' through their contact with the White House, regular meetings with the British prime minister, and their participation in negotiations over the future of Northern Ireland (p. 83).

Terrorist frames after the Good Friday Agreement
The frames adopted by Loyalist and Republican terrorists altered by virtue of their support for the peace process. The nexus between pro-Agreement terrorist organisations and their political fronts had arguably shifted in favour of the latter in 2001. Richards (2001) asserts that the 9/11 attacks on Washington and New York led to a transfer of power within the Republican movement, Sinn Fein becoming the 'driving force of the movement', in place of the Provisional IRA Army Council (p. 84). Concurrently, Sinn Fein received an unprecedented level of popular support. The Republican Party received 17.3 percent of the vote in the Northern Ireland Assembly elections (June 1998) and gained two ministerial portfolios in the new Stormont Executive.[5] One explanation for this electoral success was that Sinn Fein had adopted a political agenda closely modelled on that of the largest Nationalist party, the Social and Democratic Labour Party (SDLP). Sinn Fein was no longer a subservient organisation projecting a 'war frame' that justified acts of political violence. Equality, human rights and democracy had become central planks of Sinn Fein political manifestos since the Belfast Agreement (McGovern, 2004: 623). Bruce (2001) asserts that Sinn Fein was able to compete with the SDLP by 'not just be wanting some different things but also by wanting the same things more aggressively' (p. 40). In order to appeal to Nationalist voters, the party differentiated itself from the Provisional IRA. Sinn Fein claimed that it had a legitimate right to be involved in the political process 'purely on the strength of the party's electoral mandate', rather than as a negotiator acting on behalf of the Provisional IRA (O'Docherty, 1998: 158).

The pro-Agreement PUP, a political affiliate of the UVF, also altered its political discourse after the Good Friday Agreement. The PUP presented a liberal political agenda that was critical of Unionists who opposed the Belfast Agreement. The party claimed that these groups had a lack of confidence in the power of Unionism, and that they should follow the lead of the PUP in dealing with its opponents within the Stormont Assembly (Bruce, 2001: 45). However, the PUP and the other Loyalist political parties have failed to match the electoral performance of Sinn Fein since 1998. For example, the PUP has received no more than 1.4 percent of the votes cast in elections since 1998 (McAuley, 2004: 537). The UDP, political affiliate of the UDA and the UFF, failed to win a single seat in the 1998 Assembly elections (Cooke, 2003: 89). These parties were arguably unable to emulate Sinn Fein's relationship with the SDLP, as the DUP was already established within the Unionist community as the primary opposition to the UUP (p. 40). Overall, Loyalist terrorist organisations have struggled to find a satisfactory role in the new political landscape ushered in by the Good Friday Agreement. Bruce (2004) asserts that in the wake of the Belfast Agreement the intended supporting population for Loyalist terrorist organisations have felt less of a need to create a range of institutions outside or against those of the state (p. 505). The Provisional IRA ceasefire may have removed the need for Loyalist terrorist organisations to protect their communities.

Anti-Agreement groups and the peace frame
The peace frame has not been projected by all political organisations in Northern Ireland since 1998. Dissidents on both sides of the sectarian divide have rejected the Good Friday Agreement. These groups disagree with the solution put forward in the peace frame, namely that terrorist organisations should pursue their objectives through exclusively democratic means in the new power-sharing institutions. On the Republican side, groups such as the Real IRA formed, due to discontent at concessions made by Sinn Fein during the peace process. The Real IRA claimed that the Sinn Fein leadership had jettisoned a number of core Republican principles by abandoning the 'armed struggle' (Institute for Counter-Terrorism, 2004). However, these groups have failed to mobilise support amongst the Northern Irish electorate for their master frame. For example, a poll conducted for the BBC Northern Ireland television programme *Hearts and Minds* (October 2002) found that only 7.1 percent of respondents in the West Belfast constituency supported dissident Republican organisations, such as Republican Sinn Fein (RSF). In the same poll, a clear majority of respondents (49.8 percent) stated that Sinn Fein 'best represented' the view of the West Belfast electorate (Tonge, 2004: 688).

The peace frame has done little to convince anti-Agreement Unionists that terrorist-linked groups should be involved in power-sharing institutions. The release of paramilitary prisoners, police reform and the involvement of Sinn Fein in the Northern Ireland Executive have proved particularly contentious for anti-Agreement Unionists. The DUP has probably been the most vociferous opponent of the Good Friday Agreement. DUP leader Ian Paisley claimed that it was a 'complete and total sell-out of the province'.[6] Loyalist terrorist organisations have also grown increasingly disenchanted with the peace process. Nearly all of the Loyalist terrorist organisations that initially supported the Belfast Agreement have been 'specified' as 'active' terrorist organisations at one time or another since 1998. For example, the UVF was specified in October 2001, as the UK Home Office believed that the terror group had once again been engaged in violence.[7] Nevertheless, the PUP has remained a fervent supporter of the peace process, despite its military organisation returning to violence. In sum, the peace frame has not become the master frame for all political actors involved in the Northern Irish Troubles. Dissident terrorist organisations on both sides do not support the power-sharing institutions, nor have committed to using exclusively peaceful means to achieve their objectives. In addition, the DUP rejects the terms of the Good Friday Agreement, as it opposes the participation of terrorist-linked groups in the power-sharing institutions. These groups frame the Northern Irish conflict with reference to their own values, as opposed to the peace frame projected by the two governments and the Northern Irish media in the late 1990s. This chapter now turns to a consideration of how these different frames are projected online.

The civil web: political fronts and political parties online

Sample

The material posted on the websites of political parties and political fronts was analysed in May 2004 to determine the strength of the peace frame. This was a period in which the two main Unionist parties, the UUP and the DUP, refused to sit in government with Sinn Fein until the Provisional IRA had fully decommissioned its arms and renounced its campaign of violence once and for all. The recent European election had seen the DUP and Sinn Fein consolidate their positions as the largest Unionist and Nationalist parties in the region.[8] For the purposes of the study, constitutional political parties were defined as those parties that have always been against the use of political violence (Cooke, 2003: 83). This category included not just Unionist and Nationalist political parties, but also left-wing political organisations such as the Socialist Environmental Alliance. Of the 13 constitutional political parties that participated in the Assembly elections, the Independent Labour Party and the Northern Ireland Unionist Party were the only organisations

Table 2.1 Northern Irish political parties, Northern Ireland Assembly election (November 2003)

Political party	Website
Alliance Party of Northern Ireland	www.allianceparty.org/
Conservative Party of Northern Ireland	www.conservativesni.com/main_main.htm
Democratic Unionist Party	www.dup.org.uk/
Green Party of Northern Ireland	www.greens-in.org/tiki-index.php
Independent Labour Party	N/A
Northern Ireland Unionist Party	N/A
Northern Ireland Women's Coalition[a]	www.niwc.org/
Social and Democratic Labour Party	www.sdlp.ie/
Socialist Environmental Alliance	http://socialistenvironmentalalliance.org/cgi-bin/sea/index.pl
Socialist Workers Party	www.swp.ie/html/home.htm
Ulster Unionist Party	www.uup.org/
United Kingdom Unionist Party*	www.ukup.org/
Workers Party	www.workers-party.org/wphome.htm

Note: [a] Website no longer available (8 February 2007).

that did not maintain an official web presence during the period of data collection (Table 2.1).

Six political fronts – two Loyalist and four Republican – were identified by reference to both the First Report of the Independent Monitoring Commission (IMC) (April 2004) and the CAIN (Table 2.2). Many of the organisations defined in the study as political 'fronts' have publicly denied their complicity in the military activities of proscribed terrorist organisations, despite compelling evidence to the contrary. Sinn Fein's inclusion as the Provisional IRA's political front was based upon evidence presented by the ICM, a body formed to assess paramilitary activity in the Province. The IMC report states that with regard to the link between Sinn Fein and the Provisional IRA, 'senior members of Sinn Fein are in a position to exercise considerable influence on PIRA's major policy decisions' (Independent Monitoring Commission, 2004).

The Irish Republican Socialist Party (IRSP) was included as it was the political front of the Irish National Liberation Army (INLA). The IMC report states that the INLA is the 'paramilitary wing of the Irish Republican Socialist Party' (Independent Monitoring Commission, 2004). The other Republican political fronts had links to dissident Republican terrorist organisations such as the Continuity IRA. RSF was

Table 2.2 Northern Irish terrorist organisations and political fronts

Terrorist organisation	Political front organisation
Continuity Army Council	Republican Sinn Fein
Cumann na mBan	None
Fianna na hEireann	None
Irish National Liberation Army	Irish Republican Socialist Party
Irish People's Liberation Organisation	None
Irish Republican Army	Sinn Fein
Loyalist Volunteer Force	None
Orange Volunteers	None
Real Irish Republican Army	32 County Sovereignty Movement
Red Hand Commandos/	Progressive Unionist Party
Ulster Volunteer Force	Progressive Unionist Party
Red Hand Defenders	None
Saor Eire	None
Ulster Defence Association/	Ulster Political Research Group
Ulster Freedom Fighters	Ulster Political Research Group

Sources: Independent Monitoring Commission. 2004. *First Report of the Independent Monitoring Commission*; Conflict Archive on the Internet. 2005. 'Loyalist and Republican Groups', http://cain.ulst.ac.uk/othelem/organ/azorgan.htm.

included, due to its links with the Continuity Army Council, widely believed to be a synonym for the proscribed Continuity IRA. According to security sources, the Continuity IRA is in effect the 'military wing' of RSF.[9] Despite its repeated denials to the contrary, the 32CSM was included in the study as it was the 'political wing' of the Real IRA[10] (Conflict Archive on the Internet, 2005). The Real IRA, although not listed as a terrorist organisation in the UK Terrorism Act (2000),[11] had claimed responsibility for a number of high-profile atrocities, such as the Omagh bombing in August 1998.

The two Loyalist political fronts identified in the study had links to four of the seven pro-union terrorist organisations currently proscribed in the United Kingdom. Since the dissolution of the UDP in November 2001, the UDA has received political counsel from an alternative Loyalist advisory body, the UPRG. The IMC report asserts that the UDA is 'associated' with the UPRG and 'operates through other paramilitary organisations such as the Ulster Freedom Fighters' (Independent Monitoring Commission, 2004). The Tullycarnet UPRG was included as it was the only branch of the UPRG to maintain a website during the period of data collection. The PUP was the other Loyalist political front included in the study. The IMC report states that the PUP exerts 'appreciable influence' upon the activities of both the UVF and Red Hand Commandos (Independent Monitoring Commission, 2004).

Website registration data

The majority of the websites under analysis were registered with Internet hosts based in the United Kingdom or the Republic of Ireland (see Appendix 3, Table 1). For example, a subsidiary of a local television station, UTV Internet, hosted the websites of the Northern Ireland Women's Coalition and the Workers Party. However, it should be noted that companies based in Canada hosted the websites of two political fronts, the 32CSM and the PUP.[12] Irrespective of where these websites were hosted, the webmasters tended not to provide personal information on domain registration websites such as Nominet (www.nominet.co.uk) and Whois (www.whois.net). The Green Party proved exceptional, providing extensive information on Whois.net as to how Internet users could contact its webmaster, such as a registered postal address in Germany.[13] Yet the omission of this information was not in and of itself evidence of the webmasters' complicity in illegal activity. Both civil and uncivil actors may request that domain registration companies, such as Whois, refrain from publishing their contact details online. Furthermore, as these websites were registered in Europe and North America they were not expected to incite political violence or solicit resources on behalf of proscribed terrorist groups. These webmasters were expected to self-regulate online, due to the anti-terrorist regime governing the behaviour of pro-terrorist webmasters (see Reilly, 2008). It should be noted that all of these websites remained available in November 2009, with the exception of the UKUP and the Northern Ireland Women's Coalition sites.[14]

Research design: website function

The framing and function of websites maintained by Northern Irish political parties was analysed during the study. Data were collected during May 2004 to enable a comparison of material posted online by these groups. Interviews with the webmasters were not possible during the study due, to a poor response rate amongst the organisations responsible for these websites.[15] Website function was analysed to determine how these groups used their websites to mobilise supporters. Cyberoptimists suggest that the Internet can have a critical multiplier effect for civil society organisations via improvement in organisational linkage, bureaucratic efficiency and the advertisement of group values to a potential global audience. The study assessed whether Northern

Irish political parties and political fronts were realising this potential, particularly in terms of organisational linkage and mobilisation. Irish Republicans have received support from diaspora communities since the beginning of the Northern Irish conflict, particularly from Irish-Catholic communities in the United States (O'Dochartaigh, 2003: 1). Conversely, Northern Ireland's Loyalist and Unionist communities have been unable to mobilise a similar emigrant population, despite a large number of people with Ulster Protestant ancestry residing in North America (p. 1). The study assessed whether the Internet enabled Loyalist political fronts to create international support networks similar to those established by their Republican counterparts in the late 1960s. It also analysed whether Republican political fronts used the Web to mobilise their established support networks. This was determined through an analysis of the links available on each website. Finally, the study determined how terrorist-linked groups and constitutional political parties present their frames online. It was anticipated that only political parties with large financial resources would be able to afford innovations such as video streaming on their websites.

Online framing
The study also used qualitative frames to analyse the websites of political parties and political fronts. Online framing was analysed by examining the language and images used by these groups on their websites. The quotations provided from each website were considered to be representative of the most common theme on each website and were used to illustrate whether the respective actor supported the peace process. It was anticipated that some terrorist-linked parties – such as Sinn Fein – would purposely remove references to their terrorist sponsors, to suggest that they were cultural democrats. This reflected their support for the power-sharing institutions created under the terms of the Belfast Agreement. However, the study was also designed to test the hypothesis that the Internet provided a space for dissidents to oppose this peace frame. As such, political fronts and constitutional political parties that opposed the Belfast Agreement were expected to use their websites to criticise its supporters, albeit for different reasons. The Tullycarnet UPRG and the DUP would reject the peace frame because they believed that Sinn Fein was only functionally democratic, with the Republican movement likely to return to armed struggle if it failed to achieve its objectives through politics. Dissident Republicans were also expected to reject the peace frame on their websites. Groups such as RSF would claim Sinn Fein had abandoned core Republican principles, and use their website to justify the use of political violence to achieve a united Ireland.

Results

Online framing

The majority of political actors under analysis used frames that were similar to the peace frame projected by the mass media in the late 1990s. Themes such as 'equality' and 'shared responsibility' were prevalent on the websites of many political fronts and constitutional political parties. These themes evoked comparison with the editorials of the *Belfast Telegraph* in 1999, which had attempted to create a bond between pro-peace groups in the Protestant and Catholic communities. The SDLP and Sinn Fein employed virtually identical frames on their respective websites, stressing their support for both the equality agenda and a 32-county Irish Republic. The SDLP asserted on its website that it was committed to building new agreed Ireland based on 'equality for all, partnership and respect for difference' (Figure 2.1). Simultaneously, the headline on the Sinn Fein website stated: 'The task of building an Ireland of equals is a huge and exciting challenge for all of us'.[16] This theme of 'equality' resonated with the material posted online by the PUP, the Loyalist political front with links to the UVF. Its website detailed how the PUP supported both the 'principle of consent' and a 'sharing of responsibility' between Unionists and Nationalists.[17] Similar themes were evident on the websites of all pro-Agreement political parties. For example, the Alliance Party of Northern Ireland asserted on its website that 'cultural participation and self-expression should be developed in the context of respect and understanding of our own and others' heritage'.[18]

Anti-agreement frames

The peace frame did not influence the framing of all Northern Irish political groups online. Two constitutional political parties, the DUP and the UKUP, used their websites to criticise the Belfast Agreement. Both parties supported the exclusion of Sinn Fein from the Northern Ireland Executive until the Provisional IRA had decommissioned all its arms and declared a permanent end to its terrorist campaign. For example, the DUP's Seven Principles stated, 'terrorist structures and weaponry must be removed before the bar to the Stormont Executive can be opened' (Figure 2.2). The UKUP also stated on its homepage that it was opposed to the 'immoral provisions of the Belfast Agreement that have violated the basic principles of democracy by installing the front men for terror into Government'.[19] Anti-Agreement Unionists used their websites to suggest that Sinn Fein should be removed from the peace process as it was functionally democratic, its commitment to democracy

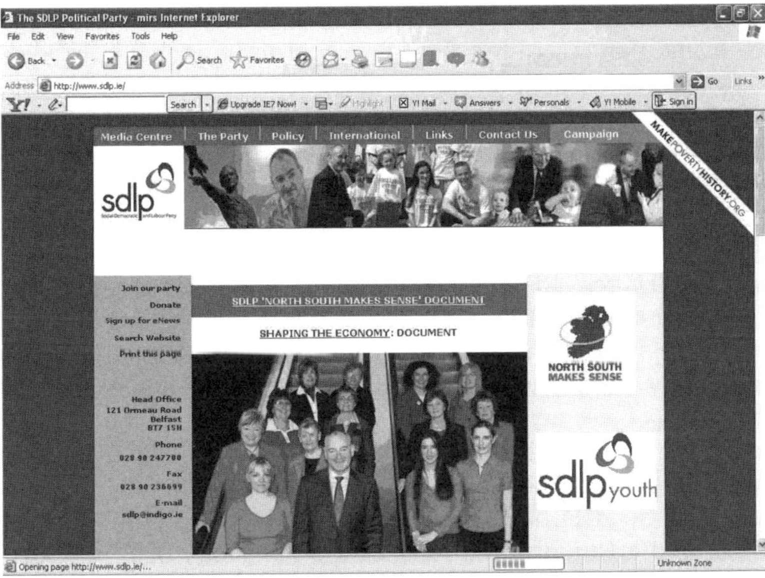

Figure 2.1 Screenshot of Social Democratic and Labour Party website

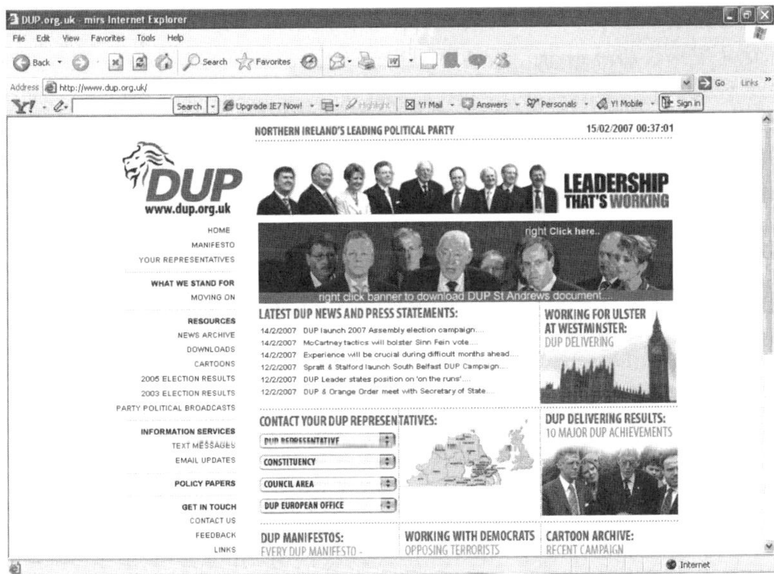

Figure 2.2 Screenshot of Democratic Unionist Party website

both opportunistic and ephemeral. This was in total contrast to the peace frame that suggested Sinn Fein had to be included in a peace process that represented all shades of political opinion.

Dissident Republican political fronts also attacked the peace frame on their websites. These groups rarely referred to the political entity of Northern Ireland on their websites. For example, the IRSP website repeatedly referred to Northern Ireland as a 'colonial statelet' or the 'occupied six counties', thus denying the legitimacy of its position within the United Kingdom.[20] Dissident Republicans used frames that justified the use of armed struggle to achieve the reunification of Ireland. RSF's president, Ruairí Ó Brádaigh, asserted on its website, 'All necessary means must be used to restore Ireland and her resources to the Irish people, not precluding as a last resort the use of physical force against the British Army of Occupation.'[21] The 32CSM also used its website to attack the Good Friday Agreement. The 32CSM website stated, 'The Good Friday Agreement, built as it is around continuing partition and a Unionist veto, makes the possibility of Britain declaring their intention to withdraw even less likely.'[22] These political fronts attacked Sinn Fein for participating in the peace process, claiming that they had abandoned core Republican principles for a peace agreement that fell far short of achieving their objectives.

Political fronts and grass-roots politics
There was little to differentiate between constitutional political parties and the terrorist-linked parties in terms of their discussion of local politics. Indeed, grass-roots politics appeared to be the primary focus for all of the political parties under analysis. Political parties such as the UUP posted policy documents on their websites for public consumption, covering issues as diverse as Provisional IRA decommissioning and the proposed location of a John Lewis store near Lisburn.[23] A similar pattern emerged from the analysis of the websites of the Alliance Party and the DUP, both of which focused on the activities of their elected representatives in their local communities. Terrorist-linked parties also used their websites to discuss local political issues. The Sinn Fein website provided an archive for Internet users to access policy documents, conference speeches and party election manifestos. RSF also highlighted the work of its local councillors on its website (Figure 2.3). One of the headline stories on the website highlighted an RSF councillor's efforts to create more effective rubbish disposal systems in County Wicklow.

The PUP used its website to detail a list of policies that addressed the interests of its voters, including proposals to reintroduce student

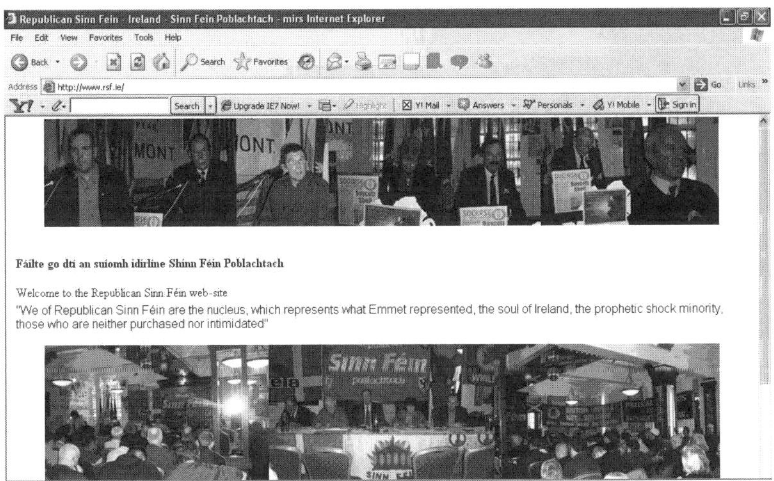

Figure 2.3 Screenshot of Republican Sinn Fein website

grants and tackle homelessness.[24] The Tullycarnet UPRG was the only actor in the study that did not clarify its position on whether Northern Ireland should remain part of the United Kingdom. Although the use of the Union Jack on the homepage suggested the organisation was pro-union, the website did not include a section that detailed the strategic objectives of the UPRG (Figure 2.4). The website focused the attention of Internet users upon issues affecting the Tullycarnet district in Belfast, in effect demonstrating the UPRG's role as a community group. For example, plans for the redevelopment of a local playground were published on the UPRG website, with local residents invited to post their views on this development.[25] The focus on local politics on these websites appeared to suggest that these actors were cultural democrats rather than organisations that were subservient to the will of terrorist organisations.

Self-identification
Pro-Agreement political fronts did not disclose their links to terrorist organisations on their websites. The Provisional IRA appeared little more than a historical footnote on the Sinn Fein website. The Republican organisation was only referred to in the 'History' section of the website, in which the Republican 'armed struggle' in 1969 was justified due to Unionist political discrimination and British military aggression against Catholics in the region.[26] The two Loyalist political fronts, the Tullycarnet UPRG and the PUP, also omitted references to their respective terrorist organisations from their websites. For example, the

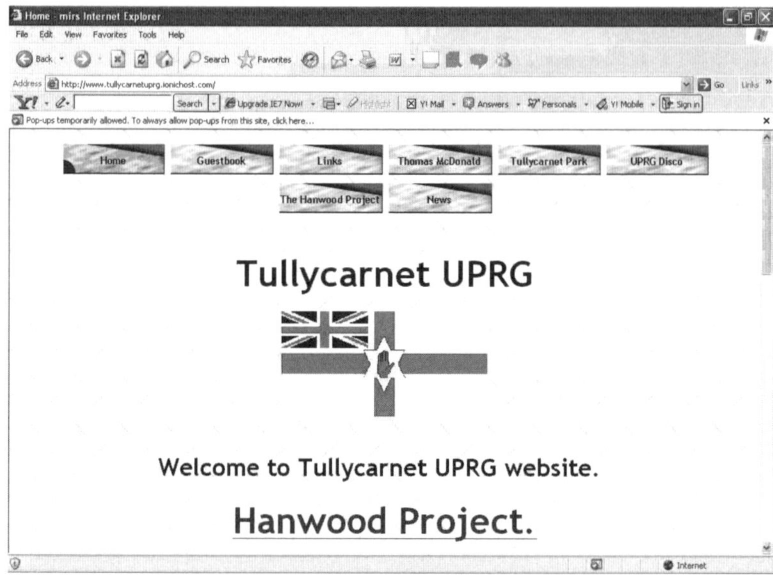

Figure 2.4 Screenshot of Ulster Political Research Group website

PUP used its website to respond to an ICM report that alleged it had close ties with the UVF. This was the only reference to the UVF throughout the entire website.

The images used by political fronts on their websites appeared to have been chosen to demonstrate their credentials as cultural democrats. None of these websites featured paramilitary emblems, despite the linkages between these political fronts and proscribed terrorist organisations. For example, Sinn Fein's homepage featured pictures of its elected representatives framed against a distinctive blue background.[27] This was somewhat surprising, as blue is a colour traditionally associated with the mainstream Unionist parties in the region, while Nationalist and Republican parties have traditionally favoured green and red on their political manifestos. While the Sinn Fein web page did contain numerous images of the island of Ireland that evoked comparison with images found on the SDLP website, there were few visual cues to suggest that this website was maintained by an Irish Republican party. The two Loyalist political fronts also used colours and emblems on their websites that were not traditionally associated with their respective terrorist organisations. The PUP homepage framed its then leader, David Ervine, against a white background rather than the blue associated with Unionist and Loyalist political parties. The Union Jack, a key emblem of the party in its election manifestos, was conspicuous by its absence from this website. Although the Tullycarnet UPRG website did feature the Union Jack on its homepage, it was notable that no paramilitary insignias were present. A picture of a local park that had been the focus of a recent UPRG campaign was the focal point of this website.

Dissident Republicans referred to their terrorist organisations on their websites and often used language that revealed their support for political violence. For example, the IRSP website carried a number of statements from its military wing, the proscribed INLA. One statement referred to an assault on an alleged police informer, warning that 'if his family think he is above any responsibility to the local community for his actions, let this be a salutary lesson'.[28] This website also depicted members of the movement as 'comrades', reflecting not just the military ambitions of the movement but also its Marxist principles.[29] The 32CSM also revealed its links to its terrorist sponsors, the Real IRA, on its website. The constitution and membership rules of the party indicated that, at the very least, there were cross-cutting cleavages between the 32CSM and the Real IRA. The constitution asserted that the 32CSM was not interested in participating in elections and intended to 'build a movement that can one day convince Britain' to withdraw from Ireland.[30]

Despite these thinly veiled references to paramilitarism, dissident Republicans used images on their homepages that suggested they were cultural democrats. For example, the RSF homepage featured a series of photographs of its elected representatives, alongside the party emblem. The 32CSM did not feature any images on its website. However, the colour scheme did reflect the ideological position of the group, the use of green text against a white background evoking comparison with the green, white and gold flag of the Republic of Ireland. The IRSP proved exceptional amongst the political fronts under analysis. Its website used 'militaristic' images that suggested it was aligned with a proscribed terrorist organisation. The 'Roll of Honour' section provided an image of two hooded gunmen flanked by the names of every (INLA) 'volunteer' that had lost their life during the Troubles.[31] In sum, the content analysis suggested that anti-Agreement political fronts were more likely to reveal their terrorist sponsors than pro-Agreement groups such as Sinn Fein.

Website function

Organisational linkage

Overall, constitutional political parties demonstrated a greater range of organisational linkages on their websites than Loyalist and Republican political fronts (Table 2.3). The Green Party and the SDLP were the only political parties to achieve the maximum score in this category. The Green Party of Northern Ireland website provided links not only to the websites of environmental pressure groups such as Greenpeace (www.greenpeace.org), but also to a number of non-political websites, such as Amazon (www.amazon.co.uk).[32] The SDLP provided links on its website not only to the sites of ideologically similar political parties, such as Fianna Fail (www.fiannafail.ie), but also to civil society organisations such as the Ulster Scots Agency (www.ulsterscotsagency.com).[33] However, a number of political parties, including the Alliance Party of Northern Ireland and the Workers Party, did not provide any links on their websites.

Republican political fronts did not use their websites to network with terrorist groups who shared their left-wing political ideologies. This was an unexpected observation, given the historic links between the Republican movement and ethno-nationalist terrorist groups such as ETA (Institute for Counter-Terrorism, 2004). Instead, Sinn Fein provided links to the websites of community groups such as the Bloody Sunday Trust (www.bloodysundaytrust.org) and British–Irish Rights Watch (www.birw.org). The 32CSM provided no links on its website. The IRSP proved exceptional in the study, providing links to such diverse international groups as the PFLP (www.pflp-pal.org), Jaleo (www.geocities.com.independentistas) and the Kurdish Workers Party (http://pkk.org/pkk).[34]

There was little to differentiate between Loyalist and Republican parties in terms of the organisational linkages visible on their websites. However, there was no evidence to suggest that Loyalist parties were using the Internet to mobilise support from diaspora communities. The PUP was the political front that achieved the highest score in this category, providing links to the websites of external news media organisations, such as the *Belfast Telegraph* (www.belfasttelegraph.co.uk), and government websites such as the Northern Ireland Assembly (www.ni-assembly.gov.uk).[35] Although the website provided a large number of links, none of these pointed towards the websites of diaspora communities that expressed support for Loyalist paramilitaries. The other Loyalist political front included in the study, the Tullycarnet UPRG, did not provide any links on its website. In sum, the study suggested

Table 2.3 Organisational linkages exhibited on official Northern Irish political websites

Website	Soli-darity links	Inter-national terrorist links	Educa-tional links	Com-mercial/non-political links	Number of links >15	Score (/5)
Alliance Party of Northern Ireland	0	0	0	0	0	0
Conservative Party of Northern Ireland	1	0	0	0	0	1
Democratic Unionist Party	0	0	0	0	0	0
Green Party of Northern Ireland	1	1	1	1	1	5
Irish Republican Socialist Party	1	1	0	1	1	4
Northern Ireland Women's Coalition	0	0	0	0	0	0
Progressive Unionist Party	1	0	1	1	1	4
Republican Sinn Fein	1	0	0	1	0	2
Sinn Fein	1	0	0	0	1	2
Social and Democratic Labour Party	1	1	1	1	1	5
Socialist Environmental Alliance	0	0	0	0	0	0
Socialist Workers Party	1	1	0	0	1	3
32 County Sovereignty Movement	0	0	0	0	0	0

Table 2.3   (continued)

Website	Soli-darity links	Inter-national terrorist links	Educa-tional links	Com-mercial/ non-political links	Number of links >15	Score (/5)
Tullycarnet Ulster Political Research Group	0	0	0	0	0	0
Ulster Unionist Party	0	0	1	0	1	2
United Kingdom Unionist Party	0	0	1	0	1	2
Workers Party	0	0	0	0	0	0
Mean	0.5	0.29	0.29	0.24	0.47	2.14

that constitutional political parties in Northern Ireland have been more effective than political fronts in harnessing the 'interconnectedness' offered by the Internet, using their websites to connect with external political, cultural and media organisations online.

Interactivity

Constitutional political parties offered a high degree of interactivity on their websites (Table 2.4). In some cases, smaller political parties provided more interactive features on their websites than did those with greater human and financial resources. This was demonstrated by the access given to political leaders on these websites. While the UUP website provided the telephone number of the constituency office of leader David Trimble, the Green Party of Northern Ireland provided personal email addresses and mobile telephone numbers for their co-leaders Dr John Barry and Lindsay Whitcroft on its website.[36] However, the SDLP, one of the largest political parties in the region, achieved the same score in this category as the Green Party of Northern Ireland. The SDLP website provided the telephone numbers and correspondence addresses for each of its constituency offices in the region.[37] Elsewhere, the study found that only one political party, the Socialist Workers Party, provided a bulletin board on its website.

Republican political fronts also provided a large number of interactive features on their websites, the IRSP and the 32CMS being amongst

Table 2.4 Interactive features available on official Northern Irish websites

Website	Email newsletter	Bulletin board	Postal address	Telephone/ fax number	Email webmaster	Email members	Resource solicitation	Score (/7)
Alliance Party of Northern Ireland	1	0	1	1	1	1	0	5
Conservative Party of Northern Ireland	0	0	1	0	0	0	1	2
Democratic Unionist Party	1	0	1	1	1	1	0	5
Green Party of Northern Ireland	1	0	1	1	1	1	1	6
Irish Republican Socialist Party	1	1	1	1	1	0	1	6
Northern Ireland Women's Coalition	0	0	1	1	1	1	1	5
Progressive Unionist Party	0	0	1	1	1	1	0	4
Republican Sinn Fein	1	1	1	1	1	0	0	5
Sinn Fein	1	0	1	1	1	0	1	5
Social and Democratic Labour Party	1	0	1	1	1	1	1	6

Table 2.4   (continued)

Website	Email newsletter	Bulletin board	Postal address	Telephone/ fax number	Email webmaster	Email members	Resource solicitation	Score (/7)
Socialist Environmental Alliance	1	0	1	1	1	1	1	6
Socialist Workers Party	0	1	1	1	1	1	1	6
32 County Sovereignty Movement	0	1	1	1	1	1	1	6
Tullycarnet Ulster Political Research Group	0	0	0	0	1	0	0	1
Ulster Unionist Party	0	0	1	1	1	1	0	4
United Kingdom Unionist Party	0	0	1	1	1	0	0	3
Workers Party	0	0	1	1	1	1	0	4
Mean	0.47	0.24	0.94	0.88	0.94	0.65	0.53	4.65

the parties that achieved the highest score in this category. Each of the Republican groups examined provided correspondence details for their organisations on their websites, although only the 32CSM published the email addresses of individual members on its website.[38] Republican organisations were more likely to encourage Internet users to subscribe to email newsletters on their websites than were the constitutional political parties. For example, Sinn Fein advertised its email newsletter, *The Irish Republican Media*, on its website. This service granted the subscriber access to video and audio clips, exclusive interviews with the leadership of the party and downloadable copies of the Sinn Fein newspaper, *An Phoblacht/Republican News*.[39] The study also found that Republican political fronts used their websites to solicit resources from sympathetic constituencies. For example, the 32CSM used its website to sell merchandise such as T-shirts to Internet users.[40]

In sharp contrast to the Republican organisations, neither of the Loyalist political fronts used their websites to solicit resources from sympathisers. This was indicative of the lower levels of interactivity available on the websites of the Tullycarnet UPRG and PUP. Neither of these websites provided interactive features such as an email newsletter or a bulletin board for its membership, although the PUP did publish personal email addresses for both its leader, David Ervine, and its chief electoral officer on its website.[41] The Tullycarnet UPRG website was the least interactive of the websites analysed during the study. Interaction between Internet users and the organisation was only possible via an email to an anonymous webmaster.[42] While constitutional political parties and Republican groups used their websites to encourage interaction with Internet users, Loyalists provided no such opportunity for visitors to their websites.

Recruitment resources

The study suggested that the majority of Northern Irish political parties favour face-to-face recruitment strategies, rather than allowing prospective members to apply online. Almost all of the groups included in the study – with the exception of the Alliance Party of Northern Ireland – used their websites to advertise for new members (Table 2.5). Yet few of these organisations provided an online application form for prospective new members. For example, the UKUP asked those interested in joining the party to email the webmaster for further information.[43] In a similar vein to the UKUP, the Workers Party asked Internet users to apply for membership at local branches.[44] The DUP proved exceptional amongst the constitutional political parties, asking potential new members to submit personal details and a £12 subscription fee on

Table 2.5 Online recruitment resources of official Northern Irish political websites

Website	Members only section	Full member-ship advertised	Full member-ship available via online application	Download-able public relations material	Score (/4)
Alliance Party of Northern Ireland	0	0	0	0	0
Conservative Party of Northern Ireland	0	1	0	0	1
Democratic Unionist Party	0	1	1	1	3
Green Party of Northern Ireland	1	1	1	1	4
Irish Republican Socialist Party	0	1	0	1	2
Northern Ireland Women's Coalition	0	1	1	0	2
Progressive Unionist Party	0	1	0	0	1
Republican Sinn Fein	0	1	0	0	1
Sinn Fein	0	1	0	1	2
Social and Democratic Labour Party	0	1	1	0	2
Socialist Environmental Alliance	0	1	1	0	2
Socialist Workers Party	0	1	1	1	3
32 County Sovereignty Movement	0	1	0	0	1
Mean	0.08	0.92	0.46	0.38	1.85

its website.[45] Few Northern Irish political groups used the Internet to disseminate downloadable public relations material, defined here as election posters that could be downloaded and displayed by supporters. Once again, the DUP was a notable exception, providing downloadable desktop backgrounds bearing election slogans such as 'Time for a Fair Deal' on its website.[46]

A similar pattern emerged from the analysis of Loyalist and Republican websites. The IRSP and Sinn Fein were the only political fronts to provide downloadable public relations material on their websites. Although each political front provided information on how Internet users could become members of their respective organisation, potential recruits invariably had to contact the webmaster for further information. For example, the PUP website invited potential members to phone or email the webmaster in order to get an application form.[47] In a similar fashion to the PUP website, the IRSP invited Internet users to submit an electronic form with their email address and telephone number, presumably in order that the organisation could vet potential new members.[48] Nonetheless, a clear majority of political fronts used their websites to attract support from around the globe. For example, Sinn Fein devoted space on its website specifically to detail how supporters in the United States could donate resources to the Republican movement.[49] RSF proved exceptional in the study, asserting that 'Members must live in Ireland, Wales, Scotland or England.'[50] Overall, the study suggested that both civil and 'uncivil' Northern Irish political actors have chosen to rely upon traditional methods of recruiting new members and disseminating propaganda.

Presentation

Both constitutional political parties and political fronts maintained static web pages, devoid of multimedia facilities (Table 2.6). The DUP website was the exception to this rule, providing video footage of leader Dr Ian Paisley and copies of manifestos as downloadable files.[51] The other constitutional political parties did not provide sound or video facilities on their websites. For example, the Northern Ireland Women's Coalition provided only text and a few images of its politicians, such as leader Monica McWilliams, on its website.[52] In a similar vein, the Alliance Party of Northern Ireland provided a text-based web page, illustrated only by a few pictures of party members such as Eileen Bell and Naomi Long.[53]

Republican political fronts achieved scores that were well above the mean score for this category. Sinn Fein in particular appeared to have invested heavily in its official website. This was illustrated by the

Table 2.6 Presentation and delivery of official Northern Irish political websites

Website	Graphics	Frames	Sound	Video streaming	Pages available in alternative format e.g. PDF	Score (/5)
Alliance Party of Northern Ireland	1	1	0	0	0	2
Conservative Party of Northern Ireland	1	1	0	0	1	3
Democratic Unionist Party	1	1	1	1	1	5
Green Party of Northern Ireland	1	1	0	0	1	3
Irish Republican Socialist Party	1	0	0	1	1	3
Northern Ireland Women's Coalition	1	0	0	0	1	2
Progressive Unionist Party	1	0	0	0	1	2
Republican Sinn Fein	1	1	0	0	1	3
Sinn Fein	1	0	0	1	1	3
Social and Democratic Labour Party	1	1	0	0	0	2
Socialist Environmental Alliance	1	0	1	1	1	4
Socialist Workers Party	1	0	0	0	1	2
32 County Sovereignty Movement	1	1	0	0	1	3

Table 2.6 (continued)

Website	Graphics	Frames	Sound	Video streaming	Pages available in alternative format e.g. PDF	Score (/5)
Tullycarnet Ulster Political Research Group	1	1	0	0	0	2
Ulster Unionist Party	1	1	0	0	1	3
United Kingdom Unionist Party	1	1	0	0	1	3
Workers Party	1	0	0	0	1	2
Mean	1.00	0.59	0.12	0.24	0.82	2.76

layout of the Sinn Fein homepage, a series of clear navigation menus enabling Internet users to view the history of the organisation, contact local constituency offices, donate resources to the Republican movement, and subscribe to electronic publications such as 'sinnfeinnews. com'. Upon visiting the website, Internet users were drawn towards a banner suggesting that the website was available in multiple languages such as French and German. Although the message 'Welcome' appeared in a number of different languages on the homepage, the website was only available in English. Sinn Fein was also one of the few political fronts to use video streaming on its website. Both members and non-members could download video footage of speeches made by its leader, Gerry Adams.[54] The IRSP was the only other political front to use video streaming on its website. The IRSP website enabled Internet users to download video footage of an Irish Republican Easter commemoration service.[55]

Loyalist political fronts employed far less sophisticated presentation methods on their websites as compared to the other political parties analysed in the study. The PUP did not employ frames, sound or video streaming on its website.[56] There were no clear menus for navigation on this site, although the postal address and contact telephone number of the organisation were clearly displayed on the PUP homepage. The Tullycarnet UPRG also maintained a basic website devoid of multimedia facilities. This was a text-based website punctuated by pictures of the UPRG's proposals for the development of a local park. Although Republican political fronts achieved higher than average scores in this category, the study suggested that both political fronts and political parties favour static websites over sophisticated presentation methods such as video streaming.

Discussion

Tactical frames

The study suggested that each Northern Irish political party, irrespective of its links to terrorism, used tactical frames to articulate its position on the peace process. Levin (2005) asserts that social organisations use tactical frames to demonstrate to the public that their master frame is the 'best definition of the reality that society is facing' (p. 85). Northern Irish political parties used end-run, denial and incorporation frames on their websites to express their opinions about the peace process. End-run frames are used by political actors to convince people that 'new considerations are necessary for decision-making' (p. 86). Constitutional political parties such as the UUP appeared to employ end-run frames on their websites to reach out to potential supporters. For example, the UUP 'Disarmament for Peace' policy document called for the completion of Provisional IRA decommissioning before the restoration of the power-sharing institutions. This reflected growing concern within the Unionist community about the Provisional IRA's capacity to resume its terrorist campaign. Incorporation frames tend to be used by political actors to 'cut off support for others by absorbing their values' (p. 87). There were indications in the study that both Loyalists and Republicans who supported the Belfast Agreement were trying to 'mainstream' their organisations through the adoption of policies that were identical to those of constitutional political parties in the region. For example, the Sinn Fein website referred repeatedly to the equality agenda traditionally associated with the SDLP. On the Loyalist side, the PUP used its website to promote what it saw as a new strand of 'liberal' Unionism. This could be interpreted as the PUP's attempt to appeal to the moderate Unionist voters who had previously voted for either the Alliance Party of Northern Ireland or the UUP.

The peace frame did not influence the framing of all Northern Irish political parties. Denial frames, which are used by political actors to claim that the values of the other side are 'invalid', permeated the websites of anti-Agreement Unionists and dissident Republicans, albeit for different reasons (p. 86). While the DUP condemned the Belfast Agreement for allowing 'unreconstructed' terrorist organisations into government, dissident Republicans criticised Sinn Fein for abandoning its armed struggle. One interpretation of these denial frames might be that it reflects the growth in opposition to the Belfast Agreement since 1998, particularly amongst the Unionist community. Anti-Agreement Unionists have used incidents such as the Northern Bank robbery in December 2004 to cast doubt upon the validity of the Provisional IRA's commitment to exclusively peaceful means.[57] This has resonated with the Unionist community, with the anti-Agreement DUP becoming the largest Unionist party after the Northern Ireland Assembly elections (November 2003).[58] However, an alternative explanation might be that the Internet has provided a platform for anti-Agreement groups to choose their own frames, one that was not available to them in the period leading up to the Good Friday Agreement. Essentially, the political opponents of the Belfast Agreement have remained the same, with dissident Republicans and anti-Agreement Unionists having opposed the peace process since 1998. The media's adoption of the peace frame in the late 1990s arguably left little space for these groups to voice their opposition to the Belfast Agreement. The study suggests that these groups have used their websites to choose their own frames, free from the editorial constraints of the mass media.

Online framing and public opinion
Online framing may only affect attitudes towards the peace process if the master frame is publicised heavily and resonates with the values of a large audience. Individuals tend to favour frames that are consistent with their own values (Chong and Druckman, 2007). Campaigns with greater resources will be able to identify frames that appeal most to the public, and advertise these themes more frequently than groups who project opposing frames (p. 102). The study found that the Internet provided political fronts, such as Sinn Fein and the PUP, with a space in which they could demonstrate their democratic credentials – irrespective of their sincerity – to a potential global audience. For example, Sinn Fein published policies on its website that appealed not just to Republicans but also to the broader Nationalist community. However, this online framing has not created public support for the master frame of Sinn Fein in and of itself. Rather, the Sinn Fein website holds a mirror to its political activism and electoral success in the offline world. The party has achieved unprecedented electoral success by adopting policies traditionally associated with the SDLP, such as the equality agenda. Sinn Fein has publicised these policies via a number of media platforms, including television, newspapers and the Internet.

The offline world also determines how the frames adopted by

anti-Agreement groups affect public opinion. The DUP's framing has become increasingly influential as it has made significant gains in consecutive elections at the expense of other pro-union political parties, such as the UUP. In contrast, dissident Republicans remain 'politically marginalised, short of weaponry and lacking in popular support' (Tonge, 2004: 678). Therefore, these groups arguably require a large audience for their websites if their online framing is to affect public opinion towards the peace process, given their relative obscurity in the mass media. Yet, this proposition is based upon the assumption that these groups wish to influence public opinion using their websites. These groups remain committed to their 'military' campaigns to further their political objectives, a strategy that inevitably brings them into conflict with the majority of public opinion. In contrast to Sinn Fein, they do not need to convince the public that they are cultural democrats, nor seek to influence public opinion using their websites and the mass media. Therefore, dissident Republicans may be using their websites primarily for intra-group communication, rather than to generate soft power amongst Internet users who have no links to their respective organisations. In sum, online frames reinforce attitudes towards the Northern Irish peace process, leaving marginalised political groups outside the triangle of political communication that includes the government, the media and the public.

Information vs interaction
Northern Irish political parties use their websites to modernise their bureaucracies, as opposed to create a space for genuine political deliberation amongst its membership. This was similar to the findings of previous studies such as the Gibson and Ward analysis of Australian political party websites (2003). Gibson and Ward characterised the level of web activity amongst Australian political parties as 'patchy', some parties lacking an official web presence while other party websites were hard to locate on the Internet (p. 152). The Internet enabled Australian political parties to 'feed information to the mass media, rather than promote a 'transparent, interconnected and interactive face' (p. 152). In a similar vein to Australian parties, Northern Irish political parties used their websites primarily for top-down political communication and providing statements to the mass media. The study found that most political parties – irrespective of their terrorist linkages – favoured face-to-face recruitment strategies and traditional methods of disseminating propaganda. Many political parties chose to remain anonymous on their official websites, directing potential supporters towards local constituency offices if they wished to join the organisation. Although

groups such as the Socialist Workers Party did provide bulletin boards on their websites, the study produced insufficient evidence to suggest that minority political groups provide higher degrees of interactivity online than larger political parties do.

Several of the political fronts arguably had no interest in promoting political deliberation on their websites. Political fronts such as the Tullycarnet IPRG do not compete in local or national elections, and therefore have no need to attract voters on their websites. Moreover, the groups themselves may not wish to interact with Internet users. Dissident Republicans such as the 32CSM do not support democracy nor possess internal democratic structures, as demonstrated by the material posted on their websites. For example, the 32CSM rules out the adoption of 'constitutional parliamentary sovereignty' to achieve its aims, as it might 'alienate' them from the people on whose behalf it is organising.[59] The 32CSM remains committed to using armed struggle to achieve its political objectives, setting itself in opposition to the majority of public opinion that favour the peace process. Interaction with anonymous Internet users online might compromise the security of its members, thus hindering the future military operations of its respective terrorist organisation. Instead, these groups use their websites to issue statements to the conventional mass media. Internet users are invited to contact the organisation via telephone to obtain information about membership. Overall, Northern Irish political groups use their websites for top-down communication rather than encouraging interaction between their members and Internet users.

Organisational linkage: critical multiplier effect?
The cyberoptimist model suggests that small sub-state groups may experience a critical multiplier effect in terms of their organisational linkage if they use ICTs. The study of constitutional political parties online provided limited evidence to support this proposition. There was no divergence between the large and small parties in terms of the scores received in this category. For example, both the Green Party of Northern Ireland and the Social Democratic and Labour Party shared the highest score in this category. Despite the Green Party's low media profile and lack of electoral success, there was little to differentiate between these two websites in the analysis of their 'links' section. In addition, the study found that political parties of all sizes were likely to provide no links on their websites, with the DUP and Alliance Party of Northern Ireland receiving no score in this category.

Political fronts also demonstrated variable levels of organisational linkage on their websites. The study found no evidence to suggest that

Loyalist political fronts were using their websites to mobilise diaspora communities in North America, the Tullycarnet UPRG providing no links whatsoever on its website. Republican websites also achieved relatively low scores in this category in comparison to the constitutional political parties. The IRSP proved exceptional, as it was the only political front to provide links pointing towards the websites of international terrorist organisations. One interpretation of these results might be that these groups do not wish to publicise their links to ethno-nationalist terrorist groups such as ETA. Political fronts such as Sinn Fein have adopted frames on their websites that suggest they are cultural democrats rather than the propaganda wing of a terrorist organisation. The disclosure of links to groups that remain engaged in political violence would seem to be at odds with Sinn Fein's commitment to the peace process, potentially souring relations with the influential Irish-American lobby. Alternatively, these groups may be experiencing a critical multiplier effect in terms of organisational linkage via other 'less public' aspects of the Internet, such as email. This would allow these groups to network with other terrorists without the risk of compromising the security of their members. In sum, the study would appear to cast doubt upon the enabling potential of ICTs, as detailed in the cyberoptimist model. None of the groups appears to be experiencing a critical multiplier effect via its website, although, this conclusion is based upon the organisational linkage that each group is willing to disclose on its website.

Conclusion

The study suggests that there is little to differentiate between terrorist-linked groups and constitutional political parties in terms of both website function and online framing. All Northern Irish political parties have yet to realise the potential of the Web as a tool for organisational linkage and mobilisation. These groups use their websites primarily to disseminate information about their grass-roots political activism to the mass media rather than to encourage interaction between Internet users and the organisations themselves. All Northern Irish political parties, irrespective of their links to terrorists, appeared to use tactical frames to define their position vis-à-vis the peace process. Terrorist-linked parties such as Sinn Fein used their Web presence to define themselves as cultural democrats rather than as the propaganda machine of a terrorist organisation. Themes such as equality and shared responsibility permeated the websites of these groups, with little or no reference made to their terrorist linkages. This framing has an antecedent in the peace frame projected by the mass media in the mid-1990s, which sought to build public support for a political process that included the political representatives of Loyalist and Republican terrorists. However, not all political parties subscribe to the peace frame. Anti-Agreement Unionists and dissident Republicans used their websites to attack the peace process and its supporters, albeit for different reasons. The DUP argued that Sinn Fein should be excluded from the power-sharing institutions as it was not fully committed to using exclusively democratic means to achieve it aims. Meanwhile, dissident Republicans criticised Sinn Fein for abandoning Republican principles. They believed that armed struggle was still necessary to remove British troops from the province. However, these denial frames were only likely to affect public opinion vis-à-vis the peace process if they featured prominently in the mass media and resonated with the values of a large audience. Although the DUP message did appear to be resonating with large sections of the Unionist community, there was no evidence that dissident Republicans were challenging Sinn Fein's electoral hegemony amongst the Nationalist community in Northern Ireland. Yet, dissident Republicans did not rely solely upon the soft power generated by their websites to further their objectives in 2004. These groups continued to use hard power during this period, perpetrating atrocities to maximise publicity for their organisations and their goals. Therefore, it is perhaps no surprise that they made no effort to portray themselves as cultural democrats on their websites.

Notes

1 The Good Friday Agreement, 1998. See www.hsmo.gov.uk for electronic version.
2 The *Belfast Telegraph* has traditionally been considered a 'pro-Union' newspaper, but has been read by both communities since the 1980s.
3 CAIN. 'The 1998 Referendums'. http://cain.ulst.ac.uk (accessed 10 May 2007).
4 CAIN. 'Joint Declaration on Peace: The Downing Street Declaration'. http://cain.ulst.ac.uk/events/peace/docs/dsd151293.htm (accessed 19 January 2006). The Downing Street Declaration represented a milestone in the Northern Irish peace process as it sett out the conditions under which Sinn Fein could enter the all-party talks on the future of the Province.
5 CAIN. 'Elections: Assembly Election (NI) Thursday 25 June 1998'. http://cain.ulst.ac.uk/issues/politics/election/ra1998.htm (accessed 19 January 2006).
6 BBC. 1998. 'The People Decide'. http://news.bbc.co.uk/1/hi/events/northern_ireland/latest_news/78618.stm (accessed 10 April 2007).
7 CAIN. 2005. 'Violence – Loyalist and Republican Groups'. http://cain.

ulst.ac.uk/issues/violence/paramilitary.htm Online. Available (accessed 10/03/06). Please note that specification did not mean that the UK government publicly declared that the ceasefire of these organisations was over.

 8 See Appendix 1 for a selected chronology of Northern Irish peace process.
 9 CAIN, http://cain.ulst.ac.uk.
10 CAIN, http://cain.ulst.ac.uk.
11 The UK Terrorism Act extended the definition of terrorism to include the 'support network' of organisations proscribed by the UK government. Amongst its most controversial clauses was the extension of 'stop and search' powers held by the police.
12 Netfirms hosted the 32CSM website, while the Tullycarnet UPRG was hosted by Hyperspace communications.
13 A telephone number and the postal address of the Green Party headquarters were provided on Whois.net.
14 The Northern Ireland Women's Coalition formally disbanded in May 2006. The United Kingdom Unionist Party remains involved in local politics but has no website.
15 An email was sent to each webmaster informing them that their website was to be analysed in this book. Only two responses were received from the webmasters responsible for the websites in this chapter.
16 Sinn Fein. www.sinnfein.ie (accessed 16 May 2004).
17 Progressive Unionist Party. www.pup-ni.org.uk (accessed 16 May 2004).
18 Alliance Party of Northern Ireland. www.allianceparty.org (accessed 16 May 2004).
19 United Kingdom Unionist Party. www.ukup.org (accessed 16 May 2004).
20 Irish Republican Socialist Movement. 2004. 'Thirty Years of Struggle'. www.irsm.org/general/history/irsm20yr.htm (accessed 16 May 2004).
21 Ó Brádaigh, R. 2004. 'What is Republicanism? Republican Sinn Fein'. www.rsf.ie (accessed 16 May 2004).
22 32 County Sovereignty Movement. http://32csm.netfirms.com/code/home.html (accessed 16 May 2004).
23 Ulster Unionist Party. www.uup.org (accessed 16 May 2004).
24 Progressive Unionist Party. www.pup-ni.org.uk (accessed 16 May 2004).
25 Tullycarnet Ulster Political Research Group. www.tullycarnetuprg.ionichost.com (accessed 16 May 2004).
26 Sinn Fein. 2004. 'History of the Conflict 1968–1992'. www.sinnfein.ie (accessed 16 May 2004).
27 Sinn Fein. www.sinnfein.ie/fosf/usa (accessed 16 May 2004).
28 Irish Republican Socialist Party. 2004. 'Action Taken against Ardoyne Thug Necessary – INLA'. www.irsm.org (accessed 16 May 2004). Eamonn Clarke, an alleged PSNI informer was attacked by the INLA in January 2004. The IRSP website carried a statement in which the INLA justified its 'punitive' sanctions.
29 Irish Republican Socialist Party. www.irsm.org (accessed 16 May 2004).

30 32 County Sovereignty Movement. http://32csm.netfirms.com/code/ home.html (accessed 16 May 2004).
31 Irish Republican Socialist Party. www.irsm.org (accessed 16 May 2004).
32 Green Party of Northern Ireland. www.greens-in.org/tiki-index.php (accessed 16 May 2004).
33 Social and Democratic Labour Party. www.sdlp.ie (accessed 16 May 2004).
34 Irish Republican Socialist Movement. 2004. 'Links in Solidarity'. www. irsm.org/general/links (accessed 16 May 2004). Note: Tupac Amaru linked to Peruvian terrorist organisation MRTA. Jaleo is a group of Andaluscian Socialists.
35 Progressive Unionist Party. www.pup-ni.org.uk (accessed 16 May 2004).
36 Green Party of Northern Ireland. www.greens-in.org/tiki-index.php (accessed 16 May 2004).
37 Social and Democratic Labour Party. www.sdlp.ie (accessed 16 May 2004).
38 32 County Sovereignty Movement. http://32csm.netfirms.com/code/ home.html (accessed 16 May 2004).
39 Sinn Fein. www.sinnfein.ie (accessed 16 May 2004).
40 32 County Sovereignty Movement. http://32csm.netfirms/com/code/ home/html (accessed 16 May 2004).
41 Progressive Unionist Party. www.pup-ni.org.uk (accessed 16 May 2004).
42 Tullycarnet UPRG. www.tullycarnetuprg.ionichost.com (accessed 16 May 2004).
43 United Kingdom Unionist Party. www.ukup.org (accessed 16 May 2004, no longer available).
44 Workers Party. www.workers-party.org/wphome.htm (accessed 16 May 2004).
45 Democratic Unionist Party. www.dup.org.uk (accessed 16 May 2004).
46 Democratic Unionist Party. www.dup.org.uk (accessed 16 May 2004).
47 Tullycarnet UPRG. 2004. www.tullycarnetuprg.ionichost.com (accessed 16 May 2004).
48 Irish Republican Socialist Party. www.irsm.org (accessed 16 May 2004).
49 Sinn Fein. www.sinnfein.ie/fosf/usa (accessed 16 May 2004).
50 Republican Sinn Fein. www.rsf.ie (accessed 16 May 2004).
51 Democratic Unionist Party. www.dup.org.uk/ (accessed 16 May 2004).
52 Northern Ireland Women's Coalition. www.niwc.org (accessed 16 May 2004).
53 Alliance Party of Northern Ireland. www.allianceparty.org (accessed 16 May 2004).
54 Sinn Fein. www.sinnfein.ie/news/av/34 (accessed 16 May 2004).
55 Irish Republican Socialist Party. www.irsm.org (accessed 16 May 2004).
56 Progressive Unionist Party. www.pup-ni.org.uk (accessed 16 May 2004).
57 An estimated £22 million was stolen from a Northern Bank branch in Belfast city centre in December 2004. The robbery has been linked to the Provisional IRA.

58 The Democratic Unionist Party became the largest political party in the Northern Ireland Assembly, polling 177,470 votes (25.6 percent of total vote). See www.ark.ac.uk/elections for more details.

59 32 County Sovereignty Movement, http://32csm.netfirms/com/code/home/html (accessed 16/05/04).

3

Terrorist superfans? Loyalist and Republican solidarity actors online

Introduction

Sandvoss (2005) argues that fan communities should be viewed as groups of people whose differing interpretations of the object of their fandom are influenced by personal experiences and identity. This chapter presents an analysis of how 'terrorist superfans' frame conflict on their websites, using Loyalist and Republican solidarity websites as its case study. Solidarity websites are defined here as websites that project messages of support for Loyalist or Republican terrorist groups but reveal no formal link between the webmaster and these organisations. The function and framing of solidarity websites will be examined in this chapter. Website function will be analysed to determine whether these groups have realised the potential of the Internet as a tool for organisational linkage and mobilisation. The study will assess whether dissident Republicans were more likely to justify political violence on their websites than were their respective political fronts. It will also examine to what extent the peace frame, which differentiates parties such as Sinn Fein from their terrorist organisations, influences the content of Loyalist and Republican solidarity websites. The study suggests that there is little differentiation between the online framing of 'terrorist superfans' and political fronts. These sites express facets of the webmaster's identity and in many cases this corresponds with the framing of their terrorist organisation of choice. However, there is limited evidence on these websites to suggest their webmasters have links to 'official' terrorist organisations. These webmasters appear to use their websites to repost propaganda associated with their most favoured terrorist group rather than to provide a new dimension of terrorist threat themselves.

Solidarity websites as a manifestation of social netwar

In *Fans: The Mirror of Consumption*, Sandvoss suggests that fandom is essentially an 'extension of the self', in which fan texts act like mirrors that reflect back a wide range of personal meanings to each individual viewer. The Internet is a communicative space that allows individuals to use terrorist propaganda to express facets of their identity irrespective of whether they support the use of political violence in the real world. This chapter will consider how the framing of Loyalist and Republican supporters in cyberspace compares to the frames utilised by the 'objects of their fandom'. Cyber enthusiasts as far back as Spears and Lea (1994) have argued that the Internet enables new forms of mobilisation that undermine unequal power relations within liberal democracies. The analysis presented in this chapter will determine what function, if any, solidarity websites serve for the campaigns of Loyalists and Republicans in Northern Ireland. Conceivably, these websites might be a manifestation of a social netwar strategy designed to build support for Loyalist or Republican terrorists in 2005. Social netwar refers to a form of 'conflict and crime at societal level, short of traditional military warfare, in which the protagonists use network forms of organisation and related doctrines, strategies and technologies attuned to the information age' (Arquilla and Ronfeldt, 2001: 6). The Ejercito Zapatista de Liberacion National (EZLN) in Mexico were the subject of the first successful social netwar. Curiously, the Zapatista netwar occurred with little or no premeditation on the part of the EZLN insurgents. Initially, there was little to differentiate between the EZLN military campaign in Chiapas and other traditional Maoist insurgencies of the period (Ronfeldt and Arquilla, 2001: 177). On 1 January 1994, a group of guerrillas seized control of several towns in the Chiapas region to highlight the Mexican government's discrimination against the indigenous people of the Chiapas province. The clashes between the insurgents and the Mexican army lasted for 11 days before both sides agreed to cease military operations in the region. During the fighting and the subsequent peace negotiations, support for the Zapatistas began to mobilise on Internet newsgroups such as Chiapas-1 and other sympathetic websites hosted by American universities such as the University of Texas (Cleaver, 1998).

The dispersed 'nodes' that mobilised in favour of Subcommandante Marcos and the Zapatistas included activist non-governmental organisations and individuals from five continents, aligned together via a network structure rather than under a traditional top-down hierarchy (Cleaver, 1997: 2). Arquilla and Ronfeldt use the term 'swarm networks' to describe these non-governmental organisations, reflecting the speed with which they descended upon the Chiapas region during the mid-1990s (Arquilla and Ronfeldt, 2001: 177). These 'swarm networks' raised the international profile of the EZLN insurgents within days of the first military skirmishes in January 1994, leading ultimately to a jointly agreed ceasefire and a three-year period of protracted peace negotiations. This online mobilisation led to increased international scrutiny of the Mexican government and a number of strategic gains for the Zapatistas and their supporters. The netwar led to two successive Mexican presidents, Carlos Salinas de Gortari and Ernest Zedillo, halting military operations in Chiapas and engaging in political negotiations with the insurgents (Ronfeldt and Arquilla, 2001: 188).

The context in which sub-state actors operate determines whether netwar is a suitable vehicle for achieving their political or military objectives. The EZLN insurgents had no access to the Internet during their insurrection in January 1994.[1] The activities of non-governmental organisations drew the attention of the global media towards the Chiapas region of Mexico, highlighting the grievances of the EZLN insurgents in the process. Clearly, Northern Irish terrorists and their political fronts operate in a much different political context than the EZLN insurgents. While Subcommandante Marcos had to rely upon 'swarm networks' to convey EZLN propaganda to international audiences, Northern Irish terrorists face fewer restrictions on their use of the conventional mass media. Irish terrorism has created international headlines since the outbreak of the Troubles in the late 1960s, primarily as a result of the activities of influential Irish diasporas scattered around the globe. Irish-American support groups have lobbied in favour of the Republican movement for over three decades, achieving some degree of influence over US policy vis-à-vis Northern Ireland. Furthermore, Loyalist and Republican political fronts have become regular fixtures in the conventional mass media since the late 1990s, due to their support for the peace process. In contrast to the EZLN insurgents, some political fronts now have the ability to influence government policy in the region. Sinn Fein in particular has grown increasingly influential as a result of the peace process, the party receiving two ministeral portfolios in the power-sharing institutions that were set up in 1998. During the period of data collection, Sinn Fein made frequent media appearances, as the party was involved in negotiations to break the impasse over Provisional IRA decommissioning and to help restore devolution in Northern Ireland. Therefore, in some cases, Northern Irish terrorists might not have needed social netwar as they already possessed the means to turn government policy in their favour.

Dissident terrorists such as the Real IRA would be very likely to benefit from social netwar, given their lack of electoral support and political clout both during and after the study. Yet, dissident terrorists and their supporters are unlikely to attract the support of 'swarm networks', a prerequisite for a social netwar. While these groups continue to use political violence, they are likely to remain a minority interest with limited ability to mobilise supporters around the globe. Political violence is now considered less permissible in the region, even amongst the Irish-American groups that provided logistical support to the Republican movement during the Troubles. Opposition towards dissident Republicans stirred after the Omagh bombing (August 1998), which was condemned by groups such as the Irish American Unity Conference on their websites.[2] Dissident Loyalist groups, such as the LVF, are even less likely to persuade global non-governmental organisations to act on their behalf. To date, Loyalist terrorists have been able to develop only 'weak and thin' support networks outside the United Kingdom, despite several million Americans having Ulster Protestant ancestry (O'Dochartaigh, 2003). The analysis presented in this chapter will determine the extent to which the websites of solidarity actors might be contributing towards a social netwar on behalf of dissident terrorists in Northern Ireland. In doing so, the study will provide further insight into the role that solidarity actors play in the campaigns of Loyalists and Republicans who remain committed to armed struggle.

Solidarity websites as manifestation of amateur terrorism
An alternative hypothesis was that the Internet was being used by individuals to promote dissident terrorism in Northern Ireland during the period of data collection. Tucker (2001) suggests that there has been a 'proliferation of amateur terrorists' since the early 1990s, many of whom have used the Internet to network with like-minded actors (p. 2). The label 'amateur terrorist' is applied to lone individuals 'who have little or no formal connection to an existing terrorist group' (Hoffman, 1998: 185). Theodore Kaczynski and Timothy McVeigh can be classified as amateur terrorists, according to the above definition. Kaczynski, a University of California mathematician, declared war on society as a whole. This was evident in the 'Unabomber manifesto', which described the Industrial Revolution as a 'disaster' for the human race.[3] During his 17-year campaign, Kaczynski sent homemade bombs to people associated with universities or the airline industry, killing three people and wounding 23 others (Hoffman, 1998: 155). In contrast to Kaczynski, Timothy McVeigh was responsible for only one lethal act of terrorism. The US army veteran perpetrated the attack on the Alfred P. Murrah building in Oklahoma City in April 1995, which resulted in 168 fatalities. He had been a member of the American Christian Patriots, who believed that a secretive elite was planning world domination through institutions such as the United Nations. The Alfred P. Murrah building

was targeted because McVeigh believed it to be a processing centre for detention camps in the region.[4]

Both Kaczynski and McVeigh were engaged in terrorist campaigns before the advent of the Information Age. The rapid pace of computer-mediated communication has made it much easier for individuals to mobilise in favour of terrorist organisations. There is already some evidence to suggest that webmasters responsible for jihadist websites are disseminating propaganda on behalf of terrorist organisations and encouraging others to commit acts of terrorism (see Eid, 2006; Conway, 2006a). For example, Younes Tsouli was sentenced to 16 years in prison for using the Internet to incite acts of terrorism in July 2007. The 23-year-old IT technician from North London was found to have used websites and bulletin boards to distribute videos of beheadings and bomb-making instructions to would be jihadists. His trial also revealed that Tsouli had been asked by an Al Qaida affiliate to translate one of their training manuals into English.[5] Yet, there was no evidence to suggest that he had become a member of an Al Qaida group, at least not in an official capacity. Nevertheless, he was convicted of conspiracy to cause murder and providing material support to a proscribed terrorist organisation under the terms of the UK Terrorism Act (2000). The Tsouli case demonstrates how the distinction between terrorist and supporter may have become increasingly blurred, due to the ability of lone individuals to network with established terrorist groups in cyberspace.

According to the UK Terrorism Acts (2000 and 2006), terrorist offences now include the use of the Internet to invite support for a proscribed organisation and to glorify acts of terrorism.[6] This legislation also prohibits the provision of resources to those responsible for terrorist atrocities, albeit that individuals will only face prosecution if they are knowingly complicit in these terrorist activities. A similar definition of terrorist offences is included in the US Patriot Act (2001). This Act prohibits the provision of material support to terrorists 'when it is known and intended that it be used to prepare for, or carry out, certain terrorist related crimes'.[7] There is already some evidence to suggest that solidarity websites are being used to plan and perpetrate atrocities in Northern Ireland. In March 2001, a message posted on an 'Ulster Loyalist' website urged Loyalists to attack a named bar where it claimed members of the IRA visited regularly.[8] As we have seen with the example of ULISNET, solidarity actors have also used their websites to solicit resources on behalf of Loyalist terrorist groups (see Chapter 1). The research presented in this chapter will determine whether other Loyalist and Republican webmasters are using their websites to plan and promote acts of terrorism.

Table 3.1 Loyalist and Republican solidarity websites

Loyalist	Republican
Birches Guerrilla Movement	Australian Aid for Ireland
British Ulster Alliance	Cairde Sinn Fein
Fife Loyalists	Coiste na n-larchimi
Greenock Loyalists	Eire Saor
Larne UVF/YCV/RHC	Fourthwrite
Liverpool UDA	Friends of Irish Freedom
Loyalist Network	Give Ireland Back to the Irish
Loyalist View	Hardline IRA
Loyalistvoice.co.uk	Hungerstrike Commemorative Web Project
Red Hand Land	Ireland for the Irish
Scottish Loyalists	Irelands Own
The Loyalist	Irish American Unity Conference
The Volunteer	Irish Anti-Partition League
Ulster Defence Association	Irish Freedom Committee
United Loyalist Movement	Irish Northern Aid Committee
Ulster Online	Irish Republican Political Prisoners
Ulster Protestant Movement for Justice	Mise Eire
UVF-The Peoples Army	Na Gael
West of Scotland Ratpack	National Irish Freedom Committee
Yorkshire Loyal	New Republican Forum

Loyalist and Republican solidarity websites

Sample

The material posted on Loyalist and Republican solidarity websites was analysed to test these two hypotheses. The term 'solidarity actor' referred to a political actor that expressed support for Loyalist or Republican terrorists. The study determined what role, if any, these websites fulfilled for the campaign of their terrorist patrons. As the total population of 'unofficial' Loyalist and Republican websites is probably undefinable, a sample size of 40 websites – 20 Loyalist and 20 Republican – was selected for the study (Table 3.1). Data were collected during April 2005 to enable a comparison of material posted online by these groups.[9] This was a period in which negotiations between the two governments and the political parties continued to break the impasse over Provisional IRA decommissioning. The Provisional IRA was also coming under increasing pressure from Irish-Americans after the revelation of its involvement in the Northern Bank robbery in December 2004 and the murder of Robert McCartney in January 2005.[10] These websites were located by entering the names of the 14 proscribed Northern Irish terrorist organisations into the basic search facility of the Google and Yahoo Internet search engines.[11] The links generated by the top 25 search engine results were then analysed to locate the websites of Loyalist and Republican solidarity actors.[12] The sample did not include cultural projections of the two traditions in the province, such as websites dedicated to the Orange Order or preservation of the Irish language. It was considered highly unlikely that these actors would express support for a terrorist organisation.

Website registration data
The majority of solidarity websites under analysis were registered with Internet hosts based in the United States (see Appendix 3, Table 2). For example, Freewebs hosted the websites of the UDA and the BGM. Two websites, the UVF-The People's Army and the British Ulster Alliance, were registered to a German Internet Host, Schlund. In a similar vein to the constitutional political parties, few of the Loyalist solidarity websites provided registered postal addresses or telephone numbers for their respective webmasters on Whois.net. Only three Loyalist websites, including the British Ulster Alliance (www.britishulsteralliance.co.uk), provided the name of their respective webmaster. It should be noted that registration details for two Loyalist websites, the West of Scotland Ratpack and Yorkshire Loyal, could not be located on either Nominet or Whois.

The majority of Republican solidarity websites were registered to Internet Hosts based in North America (see Appendix 3, Table 3). This reflected the large number of websites in the sample that were linked to Irish-American political organisations. For example, the Na Gael website (www.nagael.com) was registered via an American subsidiary of Yahoo. Whois.net gave Internet users the name of the webmaster and a postal address in the United States, should they wish to contact the organisation.[13] In contrast to the Loyalist websites, Republican solidarity sites provided extensive information about their webmasters on Whois.net. Five of the Republican websites provided comprehensive contact details such as a registered postal address and personal email address. For example, the Irish American Unity Conference website (www.iauc.org) provided a correspondence address in Washington, D.C. for its webmaster.[14] The analysis suggested that solidarity websites were more likely to be hosted outside the United Kingdom than were websites maintained by constitutional political parties in the region. However, these websites were not expected to offer support for terrorist organisations in a similar fashion to the ill-fated ULISNET website.[15] These websites were expected to comply with the norms of acceptable behaviour online, as they were registered in the United States and Western Europe.

It should be noted that there has been a high turnover of solidarity websites since the period of data collection. A total of eight Republican websites were no longer available in November 2009, including Give Ireland Back to the Irish and Hardline IRA. There were even fewer Loyalist solidarity websites available in November 2009. Only three Loyalist solidarity websites (Liverpool UDA, The British Ulster Alliance and The Volunteer) analysed in the study were still available at the same URL, while both the BGM and the Loyalist Network were available as Bebo profiles.

Research design: framing
Both the social netwar and amateur terrorist models suggest that so-called 'amateur terrorists' might use their websites to advance the campaigns of established terrorist networks, albeit that the former strategy does not involve the use of violence. This study assessed whether solidarity websites were being used to reproduce the frames of their terrorist sponsors, and what function, if any, these websites fulfilled for the campaigns of official Loyalist and Republican groups. Online framing was analysed by examining how each actor used language and images on their websites. The information provided by each webmaster on their website was scrutinised to determine whether they had any links with a proscribed terrorist organisation. The study also examined to what extent the peace frame influenced the online framing of Loyalist and Republican supporters. It was anticipated that the framing of each solidarity website would reflect its webmaster's support for one of the 14 proscribed Northern Irish terrorist groups. For example, actors that aligned themselves with the Provisional IRA would project the peace frame espoused by Sinn Fein, its political front. Conversely, opponents of the Belfast Agreement on both sides would use their websites to criticise its supporters. Dissident Republicans would use their websites to attack Sinn Fein for abandoning the armed struggle and participating in the power-sharing institutions. These frames would be virtually indistinguishable from those employed by dissident Republican parties, such as RSF. Loyalist amateurs were expected to use identical frames to the DUP, highlighting the links between Sinn Fein and the Provisional IRA on their websites (see Chapter 2). In contrast to political fronts, it was anticipated that solidarity websites would refer to the military campaigns of their nominated terrorist organisations. These actors would not have to demonstrate their democratic credentials by removing all references to terrorism from their websites.

Research design: function
In order to assess their function, each website was scored with reference to the coding scheme used earlier in this book (see Chapter 1). It enabled the websites to be ranked in terms of their interactivity, presentation, organisational linkage and online recruitment. It also enabled a direct comparison between the websites of political fronts, amateur terrorists and other Northern Irish societal groups. The study assessed whether Loyalist and Republican solidarity actors have realised the potential of the Internet as a tool for organisational linkage and mobilisation. As we have seen in Chapter 2, none of the political parties in Northern Ireland appears to be experiencing a critical multiplier effect via its website, particularly in terms of organisational linkage. Cyberoptimists suggest that the Internet can provide a degree of organisational coherence to political actors that ordinarily are incapble of 'punching above their weight' in the international community. This research was designed to assess whether these websites might be considered a manifestation of a social netwar on behalf of dissidents who had yet to realise the potential of the Internet as a communication tool.

Results

Online framing: pro-Agreement frames
Few solidarity actors projected the peace frame on their websites, although a sampling error could not be ruled out, due to the difficulty in estimating the total population of solidarity websites. Cairde Sinn Fein was the only Republican actor to express support for the peace process on its website. This group used identical online frames to Sinn Fein, its patron, calling for a United Ireland 'based on internationally accepted democratic principles'.[16] A similar pattern emerged from the analysis of Loyalist solidarity websites. Only two Loyalist actors expressed support for the peace process on their websites. The Red Hand Land website called on Loyalists to engage in the political process. Accordingly, the webmaster urged Loyalists to abandon their military campaigns and 'use the Internet fully to spread our argument'.[17] Similar sentiments featured on the Liverpool UDA website, although it adopted a more pragmatic approach towards the peace process. This group declared its continued support for the peace process, although its webmaster warned that the group 'would defend Ulster if and when the need arises'.[18] Overall, it appeared that only groups with close ties to political fronts used their websites to express their support for the peace process.

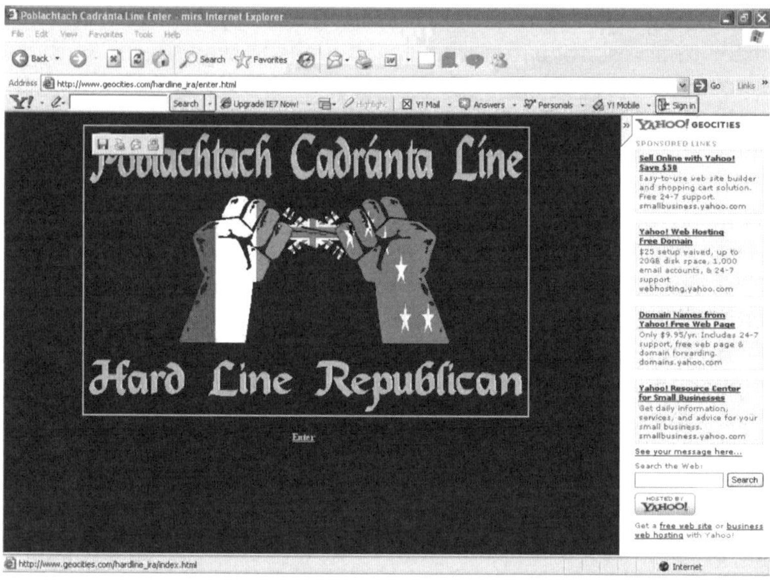

Figure 3.1 Screenshot of Hardline IRA website

Anti-Agreement frames

The majority of Republicans used their websites to reject the peace frame. These actors tended to use their websites to focus on how Sinn Fein had 'sold out' the Republican movement. Dissident Republicans criticised Sinn Fein for abandoning core Republican values and 'administering British rule in Ireland'.[19] In the opinion of these actors, the Provisional IRA ceasefire had left the Catholic community at greater risk of attack from Loyalist paramilitaries, and had failed to remove the 'British imperialists' from Ireland. These groups often referred to themselves as 'Fenians' on their websites, reinforcing the perception that Catholics still faced discrimination from the Unionist community in Northern Ireland.[20] For example, the New Republican Forum asserted on its website that it would have to 'chart a course for the future of the republican struggle due to the Provisionals' collaboration with the London and Dublin governments'.[21] These anti-Agreement sentiments were repeated on the Hardline IRA website (Figure 3.1). On this website, the webmaster declared that the Provisional IRA ceasefire had 'nullified the defense of catholics and nationalists, and left them vulnerable to brutal attacks from Loyalist paramilitaries'.[22]

Loyalist solidarity actors sought to unite the 'Protestant/Loyalist people' against the 'farce' of a Good Friday Agreement.[23] In a similar

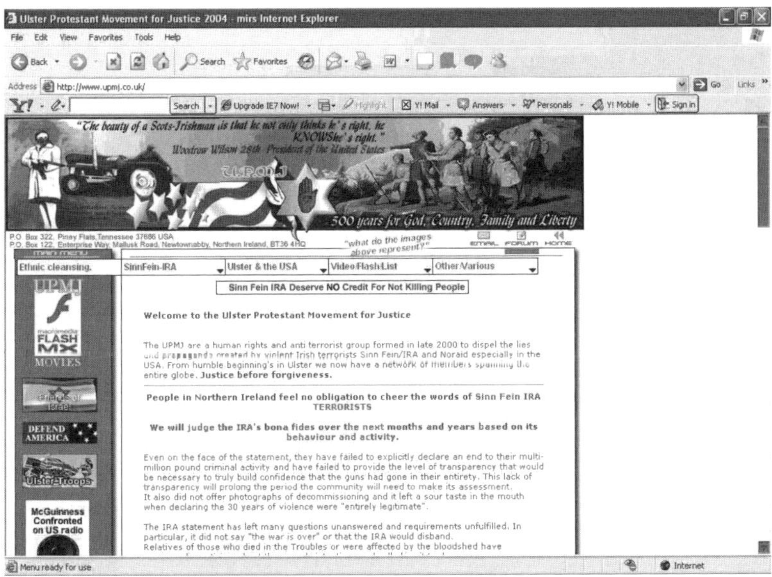

Figure 3.2 Screenshot of Ulster Protestant Movement for Justice website

vein to anti-Agreement Unionists, these actors rejected the notion that political fronts should be differentiated from their respective terrorist organisations. Groups such as the British Ulster Alliance used their websites to highlight the links between Sinn Fein and the Provisional IRA, often referring to them as one and the same organisation, 'Sinn Fein/IRA'.[24] These actors also used their websites to criticise Unionists who supported the Belfast Agreement. For example, the webmaster responsible for the Loyalist Network website declared: 'the sooner we are rid of Trimble and his followers the better for Ulster'.[25] Pro-Agreement Unionists were criticised for allowing Sinn Fein to enter government before the completion of Provisional IRA decommissioning. The Ulster Protestant Movement for Justice encapsulated this sentiment in its slogan, 'No Guns, No Government' (Figure 3.2). The Belfast Agreement was also rejected on the basis that it did little to reassure 'besieged' Protestant communities in Northern Ireland. This was particularly evident in the use of the term 'ethnic cleansing' on Loyalist websites, such as the West of Scotland Ratpack. In one article on this website, it was alleged that 'Sinn Fein/IRA' were engaged in a campaign of intimidation, designed to force Protestants out of the Glenbryn district in North Belfast.[26] In sum, Loyalist and Republicans used their websites to suggest that the Belfast Agreement has left their communities at greater risk from one another.

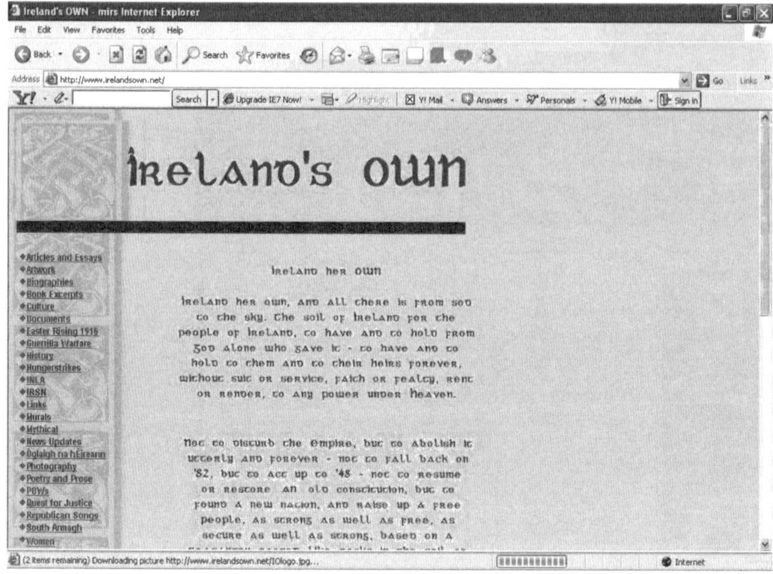

Figure 3.3 Screenshot of Ireland's Own website

Justification of political violence
Loyalists and Republicans did not tend to justify contemporary political violence on their websites. Only three Republican solidarity actors provided a rationale for 'armed struggle' on their websites. For example, the webmaster who maintained the Ireland's Own website did little to hide his or her support for the continued military activity of dissident Republican organisation the Real IRA (Figure 3.3). In an article entitled 'Guerrilla Warfare', the webmaster justified the Real IRA military campaign, asserting that Britain 'has never left any of its so-called colonies without an armed struggle'.[27] The support for terrorists was often implicit in statements posted on Republican websites, such as Eire Saor. The webmaster responsible for this website pledged to 'support to any organisation fighting for a 32-County Irish Republic free of British imperialism'.[28] Similar language was used on the website of the Hardline IRA, the organisation stating its desire to 'drive out the British army in a war of attrition'.[29] In general, none of the Republican websites carried statements on behalf of proscribed terrorist organisations, such as the Real IRA. This was perhaps to be expected, given that Republican terrorists issued press releases through the websites of their political fronts (see Chapter 2).

Loyalist groups also used language on their websites that implied they supported the use of political violence. Only three Loyalist actors

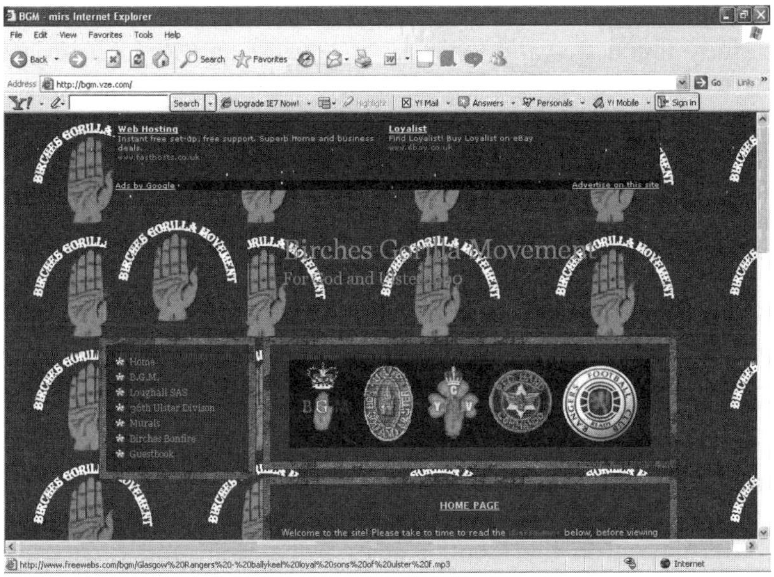

Figure 3.4 Screenshot of Birches Gorrilla Movement website

provided a justification for political violence on their websites. For example, the Birches Guerrilla Movement (BGM) used its website to respond to the growing numbers of Catholics who wished to reside in their area (Figure 3.4). In one statement, the BGM asserted that it would do its utmost to ensure that 'Robinsonstown has not a single Catholic in its dwelling and shall never have either'.[30] Two Loyalist solidarity actors appeared to act as intermediaries between the paramilitaries and the mass media. The Volunteer website carried a number of statements from the North Antrim Brigade of the UVF. In one of these statements, the Brigade warned that 'members [of the UVF] caught dealing drugs would be court-martialed and severely dealt with'.[31] This resonated with the material posted on the Loyalist Voice website, which reproduced statements from the Orange Volunteers. In one such article, entitled 'We will kill freed IRA, says group', the Orange Volunteers threatened to kill Republican prisoners who had been granted early release under the terms of the Belfast Agreement.[32] In sum, the material posted on Loyalist and Republican websites did not appear to contravene the terms of anti-terrorist legislation, such as the UK Terrorism Act. Accordingly, few of these webmasters justified contemporary terrorist atrocities on their websites, or encouraged Internet users to perpetrate political violence themselves.

Self-identification

The study found that the majority of Loyalist and Republican actors chose to remain anonymous online. Only Irish-American groups, such as the Friends of Irish Freedom, provided extensive information regarding their leadership on their website. This organisation, based in New York City, provided the names of all of its high-ranking officials, such as National Co-Chairmen John Hurley and Charles McLoughlin.[33] The Irish Freedom Committee website also named all of its senior figures, including National Chairman Joe Dillon.[34] Elsewhere, webmasters appeared reluctant to reveal their true identities on their websites. Most of the websites under analysis contained a disclaimer, possibly to prevent the webmaster from prosecution under the terms of anti-terrorist legislation, such as the US Patriot Act (2001). For example, the West of Scotland Ratpack website contained numerous references to the LVF, including pictures of hooded gunmen that were allegedly members of the proscribed terrorist organisation. Yet the website did not provide any information on the identity of its webmaster, and carried a disclaimer stating that it did 'not speak for the Loyalist Volunteer Force'.[35]

A number of websites in the study purported to be the official web presence of a proscribed Northern Irish terrorist organisation, or had URLs that contained the names of these groups. Yet, upon further investigation, many of these websites contained disclaimers stating that they were not linked to proscribed terrorist organisations. On the Republican side, the Eire Saor website appeared to have no links to the terrorist organisation from which it took its name. This was apparent in the first line on the homepage, which described Eire Saor as a 'web-based project dedicated to the traditional Irish Republican goal of a 32-County Irish Republic free of British imperialism'.[36] There was also little evidence to suggest the Hardline IRA was a terrorist organisation. This webmaster appeared to support any Republican organisation that opposed the Belfast Agreement, providing links to a variety of dissident Republican political fronts, including RSF and the IRSP.

Four Loyalist actors in the study shared the name of a proscribed terrorist organisation. In a similar vein to the Republican websites, there was little evidence on these websites to verify their credentials as terrorist organisations. These websites tended to carry legal disclaimers stating that the webmaster was not a member of a proscribed terrorist organisation. For example, the UDA disclaimer stated that its webmaster 'did not support any terrorist organisation'.[37] The UVF website also contained a disclaimer that denied any links between the webmaster and its subject matter.[38] In the case of the Fife Loyalists website, the webmaster appeared to have accidentally exposed himself as an 'amateur terrorist'. This website was alleged to be the official web presence of the UVF's West Fife battalion. Yet, upon further inspection, the website turned out to be the personal webpage of a Fife teenager known simply as 'Euan'. This was revealed through analysis of the photograph section of the website, in which 'Euan' was seen posing with a group of teenagers at a Glasgow Rangers FC football match.[39] The Liverpool UDA proved exceptional amongst the websites that shared the title of a terrorist organisation. There was no evidence on this website to refute the organisation's claims that it was linked to the UDA.[40] Overall, it appeared that Loyalist and Republican actors made a conscious effort to remain anonymous on their websites. Although few solidarity sites justified contemporary political violence, the majority of webmasters nevertheless chose to conceal their identities online.

Images

The images used on solidarity websites illustrated whether their webmasters supported or opposed the Good Friday Agreement. Pro-Agreement Republicans, such as Cairde Sinn Fein, used similar images to those employed on the Sinn Fein website. Pictures of gunmen and the national flag of Ireland were conspicuous by their absence from this website, which featured pictures of Cairde Sinn Fein officials at fund-raising dinners on its homepage.[41] Nevertheless, the majority of Republican actors used 'militaristic' images on their websites to demonstrate their opposition to the peace process. For example, the Irish Freedom Committee used a recurring motif of a baseball bat on its website, a weapon associated with paramilitary 'punishment beatings'.[42] The Hardline IRA website also projected a violent image of Republicanism, the centrepiece of its homepage featuring a Union Jack flag being torn apart by two clenched fists.[43] Elsewhere, Republican actors used iconic Republican propaganda to demonstrate their opposition to the Belfast Agreement. For example, the Ireland For the Irish homepage was dominated by a mural of Margaret Thatcher sneezing across the island of Ireland, entitled, 'Get the Brits Out'.[44] Republicans also used their websites to laud fallen 'comrades', such as the 10 Republican prisoners who died on hunger strike in the Maze prison in 1981. The Hungerstrike Commemorative Web Project provided pictures of each of the 'ten men who died on the doorstep of the British government' during the hunger strike.[45] Although this might suggest that these actors supported a particular terrorist group, none of the Republican websites contained paramilitary emblems, or pictures of hooded gunmen.

Loyalists used more militaristic images on their websites than did their Republican counterparts. Paramilitary insignias were prominent on all of the Loyalist websites under analysis, such as the Red Hand Land. This website displayed a UVF badge on its homepage, leaving Internet users with little doubt that the webmaster supported the proscribed Loyalist group. The UVF and the Orange Volunteers were also lauded on many of the Loyalist websites under analysis. For example, the West of Scotland Ratpack homepage was dominated by a flag, with the UVF emblem as its centrepiece.[46] Eulogies for 'fallen comrades' were also common on the Loyalist websites under analysis. For example, the Liverpool UDA provided a UDA roll of honour on its website, featuring pictures of members such as John McMichael, who had been killed during the Troubles.[47] In a similar vein, the Scottish Loyalists website provided articles on a host of slain Loyalist leaders, such as UDA Brigadier John Gregg and LVF leader Billy Wright.[48] Loyalist opposition to the peace process was also conveyed through the images of hooded gunmen that permeated their websites. This was particularly evident on the Loyalist Voice website, which carried statements from the Orange Volunteers. These press releases were listed below a picture of six hooded gunmen, all of whom were allegedly members of the Loyalist terror group.[49] In a similar vein to Republicans, Loyalists turned to murals to demonstrate their opposition to the Belfast Agreement. The Greenock Loyalist website was in effect an archive of Loyalist murals in East Belfast. This homepage was dominated by a of picture of two gunmen beneath the slogan 'Prepared for Peace, Ready for War'.[50] In sum, Loyalist and Republican amateurs employed more violent images on their websites than did their respective political fronts. However, Loyalists were more likely to be use paramilitary emblems on their websites, perhaps to suggest that they were actual members of these organisations.

Website function

Organisational linkage

The study found that Republicans demonstrated the greatest range of organisational linkages on their websites. Five Republican websites received the maximum score in this category (Table 3.2). For example, the Irish Anti-Partition League website not only provided links to other Republican websites such as the Sovereign Nation (www.members. aol.com/ir32s), but also to the websites of media organisations such as Reuters (www.reuters.com).[51] Republican solidarity actors were also noteworthy for their reciprocation of links with actors engaged in 'armed struggle' elseswhere. For example, Coiste na n-larchimi was

Table 3.2 Organisational linkages exhibited on Republican solidarity websites

Website	Soli-darity links	Inter-national terrorist links	Educa-tional links	Com-mercial/ non-political links	Number of links >15	Score (/5)
Coiste na n-larchimi	1	1	0	0	0	2
Eire Saor	1	1	1	0	1	4
Fourthwrite	0	0	0	0	0	0
Friends of Irish Freedom	1	0	0	0	0	1
Give Ireland Back to the Irish	1	1	0	0	0	2
Hardline IRA	1	0	0	0	0	1
Hungerstrike Comm-emorative Web Project	1	1	1	1	1	5
Ireland for the Irish	0	0	1	0	0	1
Irelands Own	1	1	0	1	1	4
Irish American Unity Conference	1	1	1	1	1	5
Irish Anti-Partition League	1	1	1	1	1	5
Irish Freedom Committee	1	1	1	1	1	5
Irish Northern Aid Committee	0	0	0	0	0	0
Irish Republican Political Prisoners	1	1	1	0	0	3
Mise Eire	1	1	1	1	1	5
Na Gael	1	0	0	0	0	1
National Irish Freedom Committee	1	0	1	1	0	3
New Republican Forum	1	1	1	0	1	4
Mean	0.85	0.6	0.55	0.4	0.45	2.85

an umbrella organisation for groups and individuals who worked with former Republican prisoners. Reflecting the long-established links between the Republican movement and ETA, the Coiste na n-Iarchimi website provided links to the websites of Basque separatist prisoner groups such as Senideak (www.senideak.org).[52] Yet not all of the Republican solidarity websites provided such an array of links on their websites. Two Republican solidarity actors – Fourthwrite and the Irish Northern Aid Committee – did not provide any links on their respective websites.

Loyalist actors also reciprocated links with like-minded groups online (Table 3.3). For example, the Scottish Loyalists website provided links to the websites of the West of Scotland Ratpack, UDA and Greenock Loyalists.[53] However, none of the Loyalist solidarity websites provided links to the websites of groups engaged in campaigns of political violence outside the United Kingdom. Loyalist websites also not tended not to provide links to the websites of universities or external agencies. Nevertheless, a few Loyalist websites did achieve high scores in this section of the coding scheme. The Loyalist Network received the highest score of all the Loyalist websites included in the study. This website provided links pointing towards a diverse set of websites, including The Ulster Loyalist, the Northern Ireland Executive, and the *Belfast Telegraph*.[54] Furthermore, the study found that there was little to differentiate between Loyalists and Republicans in terms of the number of links on their websites. This was illustrated by the analysis of the Scottish Loyalists website, which revealed that it provided the greatest number of links (142) in the study. In sum, solidarity actors on both sides do not appear to have realised the potential of the Internet as a tool for organisational linkage. As was the case in the analysis of political front websites, Republicans were the most likely to provide links to the websites of external agencies and diaspora communities. However, there was limited evidence to suggest that these actors were experiencing a critical multiplier effect in terms of organisational linkage.

Interactivity

Both Loyalist and Republican solidarity actors offered a relatively low degree of interactivity on their websites. The study found that Republicans provided a higher degree of interactivity on their websites than did their Loyalist counterparts. The Irish American Unity Conference received the highest score in this section of the coding scheme (Table 3.4). This website enabled Internet users not just to send correspondence to a registered postal address, but also to email individual members of the organisation.[55] It also provided an innovative way

Table 3.3 Organisational linkages exhibited on Loyalist solidarity websites

Website	Soli-darity links	Inter-national terrorist links	Educa-tional links	Com-mercial/ non-political links	Number of links (>15)	Score (/5)
Birches Guerrilla Movement	1	0	0	0	0	1
British Ulster Alliance	1	0	0	1	1	3
Fife Loyalists	1	0	0	0	1	2
Greenock Loyalists	1	0	0	0	0	1
Larne UVF/ YCV/RHC	0	0	0	0	0	0
Liverpool UDA	1	0	0	0	1	2
Loyalist Network	1	0	1	1	1	4
Loyalist View	1	0	0	0	0	1
Loyalistvoice. co.uk	1	0	1	1	0	3
Red Hand Land	1	0	0	0	0	1
Scottish Loyalists	1	0	0	1	1	3
The Loyalist	0	0	0	1	0	1
The Volunteer	1	0	0	0	0	1
Ulster Defence Association	1	0	0	0	0	1
United Loyalist Movement	0	0	0	0	0	0
Ulster Online	0	0	0	0	0	0
Ulster Protestant Movement for Justice	1	0	1	0	1	3
UVF-The Peoples Army	1	0	1	0	1	3
West of Scotland Ratpack	1	0	1	1	1	4
Yorkshire Loyal	1	0	0	0	1	2
Mean	0.8	0	0.25	0.3	0.45	1.8

Table 3.4 Interactive features available on Republican solidarity websites

Website	Email newsletter	Bulletin board	Postal address	Telephone/ fax number	Email webmaster	Email individual members	Resource solicitation	Score (/7)
Australian Aid for Ireland	0	0	0	0	0	0	0	0
Cairde Sinn Fein	0	0	1	0	1	0	1	3
Coiste na n-Iarchimi	0	0	1	1	1	1	0	4
Eire Saor	0	0	0	0	1	0	0	1
Fourthwrite	0	0	1	1	1	1	1	5
Friends of Irish Freedom	0	0	1	0	1	0	0	2
Give Ireland Back to the Irish	0	1	0	0	0	0	0	1
Hardline IRA	0	0	0	0	1	0	0	1
Hungerstrike Commemorative Web Project	0	0	0	0	1	0	1	2
Ireland for the Irish	0	1	0	0	1	0	0	2
Irelands Own	1	0	0	0	1	0	0	2
Irish American Unity Conference	1	0	1	1	1	1	1	6

Table 3.4   (continued)

Irish Anti-Partition League	1	0	0	0	1	0	0	2
Irish Freedom Committee	1	0	1	0	1	1	0	4
Irish Northern Aid Committee	0	1	1	1	1	0	1	5
Irish Republican Political Prisoners	0	0	0	0	1	0	1	2
Mise Eire	0	0	0	0	0	0	0	0
Na Gael	0	0	0	0	1	0	0	1
National Irish Freedom Committee	0	0	1	0	1	1	1	4
New Republican Forum	0	0	1	0	1	0	1	3
Mean	0.2	0.15	0.45	0.2	0.85	0.25	0.4	2.5

for people to express their 'solidarity' with the organisation. Internet users were invited to add their personal details to a standard email in support of the Irish American Unity Conference. Once submitted, this email would be sent to the editors of over 400 daily newspapers in the United States.[56] The Fourthwrite website also encouraged interaction between Internet users and its members, the Republican magazine inviting people to contribute to the latest edition of its online journal, and providing postal addresses and telephone numbers for its editorial staff.[57] However, it should be noted that two of the Republican websites under analysis – Mise Eire and Australian Aid for Ireland – received no score in this category.

Republicans were more likely to solicit resources from Internet users who visited their websites than were Loyalists. In this respect, the research findings were similar to the pattern that emerged from the study of Loyalist and Republican political fronts (see Chapter 2). The results suggested that some of the Republican solidarity actors were closely connected with their respective political fronts. These websites often had titles that drew the attention of the viewer to the link between the solidarity actor and its nominated terrorist organisation. Consequently, it was perhaps no surprise that groups such as Cairde Sinn Fein would use their websites to directly solicit resources for the Republican movement. This organisation declared on its homepage that it was 'a support group for Sinn Fein, the Irish political party striving for the acheivement of a united Ireland'.[58] This group appealed for assistance from both the United Kingdom and North America on its website. The other Republican solidarity websites solicited resources on behalf of Republican prisoners and their families. For example, the Irish Republican Political Prisoners website provided links to a number of websites dedicated to Irish Republican 'Prisoners of War'. This website raised funds for these prisoners through the the sale of Republican merchandise like books and audio cassettes.[59] The Irish Northern Aid Committee also sold merchandise to raise funds for Republican prisoners. A range of videos and books were available for purchase on this website, along with a T-shirt with the slogan 'Sniper at Work'.[60]

Few of the Loyalist actors in the study provided interactive features like email newsletters, postal addresses or telephone numbers on their websites (Table 3.5). Interaction with most Loyalist actors was limited to an email to an anonymous webmaster, as was the case on the BGM website.[61] The West of Scotland Ratpack and UDA websites provided even less opportunity for Internet users to interact with their respective webmasters. On both websites an email webmaster function was listed as 'under construction'.[62] However, these results arguably

Table 3.5 Interactive features available on Loyalist solidarity websites

Website	Email newsletter	Bulletin board	Postal address	Telephone/ fax number	Email webmaster	Email individual members	Resource solicitation	Score (/7)
Birches Guerrilla Movement	0	0	0	0	1	0	0	1
British Ulster Alliance	0	1	1	0	1	0	1	4
Fife Loyalists	0	1	0	0	1	0	0	2
Greenock Loyalists	0	0	0	0	0	0	0	0
Larne UVF/YCV/ RHC	0	0	0	0	1	0	0	1
Liverpool UDA	0	0	1	0	1	0	0	2
Loyalist Network	0	1	0	0	1	0	0	2
Loyalist View	0	1	0	0	1	0	0	2
Loyalistvoice. co.uk	0	0	1	0	0	0	1	2
Red Hand Land	0	0	0	0	1	0	0	1
Scottish Loyalists	0	1	0	0	1	0	0	2
The Loyalist	0	1	1	0	1	0	0	3
The Volunteer	0	0	0	0	1	0	0	1

Table 3.5 (continued)

Website	Email newsletter	Bulletin board	Postal address	Telephone/ fax number	Email webmaster	Email individual members	Resource solicitation	Score (/7)
Ulster Defence Association	0	0	0	0	0	0	0	0
United Loyalist Movement	0	1	0	0	1	0	0	2
Ulster Online	0	0	0	0	1	0	0	1
Ulster Protestant Movement for Justice	1	0	0	0	1	0	0	2
UVF-The Peoples Army	0	0	0	0	1	0	0	1
West of Scotland Ratpack	0	0	0	0	0	0	0	0
Yorkshire Loyal	0	1	0	0	1	0	0	2
Mean	0.05	0.4	0.2	0	0.8	0	0.15	1.55

demonstrated the extent to which these actors were fans of terrorism rather than amateur terrorists themselves. Many Loyalist actors purported to be terrorist organisations, despite compelling evidence on their websites that suggested they were private individuals. Thus, a website such as Fife Loyalists would be unlikely to provide email addresses for its members, as its membership was probably limited to one private individual, namely a Fife teenager known as Euan.[63]

Loyalist solidarity actors used their websites for the dissemination of propaganda rather than to generate new revenue streams. Only two of the Loyalist solidarity actors under analysis sought to solicit resources from their supporters online. For example, the British Ulster Alliance sought to generate revenue through the sale of Loyalist memorabilia. A range of T-shirts, mugs, ties and mousemats – all emblazoned with the Union Jack – could be purchased from the British Ulster Alliance, although these items could not be obtained direct from the website.[64] In a similar vein to the Republican websites, Loyalist Voice solicited resources on behalf of prisoners and their families. This website provided a postal address for Internet users to make a donation to the Dissident Loyalist Prisoners' Aid.[65] In sum, the analysis suggested that Republican websites offered more interactive features than did their Loyalist counterparts. However, both Loyalist and Republican solidarity actors did not appear to use their websites to increase the transparency of their respective organisations.

Online recruitment resources
Few of the websites under analysis allowed prospective members to apply for membership online. The Ulster Protestant Movement for Justice website received the highest score in this category, although it did not provide an online application form for prospective members (Table 3.6). This website provided a correspondence address for those who wished to apply for membership. It was also the only Loyalist solidarity website to provide a 'members only' section, in which members could submit a password to gain access to restricted material. A large number (14) of Loyalist solidarity websites received no score in this section of the coding scheme. As discussed above, it appeared that the majority of Loyalist solidarity actors were private individuals who purported to be terrorist organisations. For example, Loyalist View did not provide any information regarding its membership on its website. Instead, the disclaimer on this website asserted that it was for 'informational and research purposes only'.[66] In addition, Loyalist solidarity actors did not provide downloadable propaganda on their websites. The Liverpool UDA was one of the few Loyalist solidarity actors to enable

Table 3.6 Online recruitment resources on Loyalist solidarity websites

Website	Members only section	Full member-ship advertised	Full member-ship available via online application	Download-able public relations material	Score (/4)
Birches Guerrilla Movement	0	0	0	0	0
British Ulster Alliance	0	0	0	1	1
Fife Loyalists	0	0	0	0	0
Greenock Loyalists	0	0	0	0	0
Larne UVF/ YCV/RHC	0	0	0	0	0
Liverpool UDA	0	0	0	1	1
Loyalist Network	0	0	0	0	0
Loyalist View	0	0	0	0	0
Loyalistvoice. co.uk	0	0	0	1	1
Red Hand Land	0	0	0	0	0
Scottish Loyalists	0	0	0	0	0
The Loyalist	0	0	0	0	0
The Volunteer	0	0	0	0	0
Ulster Defence Association	0	0	0	0	0
United Loyalist Movement	0	1	0	0	1
Ulster Online	0	0	0	0	0
Ulster Protestant Movement for Justice	1	1	0	1	3
UVF-The Peoples Army	0	0	0	0	0
West of Scotland Ratpack	0	0	0	0	0
Yorkshire Loyal	0	0	0	0	1
Mean	0.05	0.1	0	0.2	0.4

Internet users to download posters from its website. This website enabled Internet users to download a number of desktop backgrounds, one of which featured a group of masked Loyalist gunmen engaged in a paramilitary 'show of strength'.[67]

There was little to differentiate between Loyalists and Republicans in terms of their online recruitment strategies. A total of 12 Republican solidarity websites received no score in this section of the coding scheme (Table 3.7). However, Republican solidarity actors such as the Irish Anti-Partition League did use their websites to advertise the benefits available to those who joined their respective organisations. This Derry- based organisation invited Internet users to apply for one of three categories of association with the organisation, namely registered societies, associate members and external correspondents.[68] The Irish Northern Aid Committee also sought to attract new members using its website. Internet users were able to join the organisation for as little as $25, with an online application form provided on its website.[69] Republican websites were also unlikely to provide posters for Internet users to download and display in their homes. The Irish Freedom Committee was one of the few websites under analysis to provide downloadable propaganda. This website enabled Internet users to download a number of articles expressing sympathy for dissident Republican terrorists, as well as a list of correspondence addresses for 'Republican P.O.Ws' who remained in British and Irish prisons.[70] Overall, the results suggested that Loyalist and Republicans prefer face-to-face recruitment strategies. However, an alternative interpretation of the results might be that these 'online terrorists' may have no organisation to sustain. These webmasters may be 'superfans' masquerading as terrorist organisations online.

Presentation
Both Loyalist and Republican solidarity actors used plain text and still photographs on their websites. This was in contrast to the more sophisticated presentation methods used by Northern Ireland's mainstream political parties on their websites (see Chapter 2). Only a few of the Republican solidarity actors under analysis provided audio and video streaming on their websites. The Irish Freedom Committee website received the highest score of all the websites under analysis (Table 3.8). This website provided a number of streaming videos including footage of the trial of Real IRA leader Michael McKevitt and a controversial Fox News report on the death of the hunger striker Bobby Sands.[71] The National Irish Freedom Committee website also received a high score in this category. This website provided audio downloads of

Table 3.7   Online recruitment resources on Republican solidarity websites

Website	Members only section	Full member-ship advertised	Full member-ship available via online application	Download-able public relations material	Score (/4)
Australian Aid for Ireland	0	0	0	0	0
Cairde Sinn Fein	0	1	1	0	2
Coiste na n-larchimi	0	0	0	0	0
Eire Saor	0	0	0	0	0
Fourthwrite	0	0	0	0	0
Friends of Irish Freedom	0	0	0	0	0
Give Ireland Back to the Irish	0	0	0	0	0
Hardline IRA	0	0	0	0	0
Hungerstrike Commemorative Web Project	0	0	0	0	0
Ireland for the Irish	0	0	0	0	0
Irelands Own	0	0	0	0	0
Irish American Unity Conference	0	1	0	1	2
Irish Anti-Partition League	0	1	0	0	1
Irish Freedom Committee	0	1	0	1	2
Irish Northern Aid Committee	1	1	1	0	3
Irish Republican Political Prisoners	0	0	0	0	0
Mise Eire	0	0	0	0	0
Na Gael	0	0	0	1	1
National Irish Freedom Committee	0	1	0	1	2
New Republican Forum	0	0	0	0	0
Mean	0.05	0.3	0.1	0.2	0.6

Table 3.8 Presentation methods used on Republican solidarity websites

Website	Graphics	Frames	Sound	Video streaming	Pages available in alternative format e.g. PDF	Score (/5)
Australian Aid for Ireland	1	0	0	0	0	1
Cairde Sinn Fein	1	0	0	0	0	1
Coiste na n-Iarchimi	1	0	0	0	1	2
Eire Saor	1	0	0	0	0	1
Fourthwrite	1	0	0	0	0	1
Friends of Irish Freedom	1	1	0	0	0	2
Give Ireland Back to the Irish	1	0	0	0	0	1
Hardline IRA	1	0	0	0	0	1
Hungerstrike Commemorative Web Project	1	0	0	0	0	1
Ireland for the Irish	1	0	0	0	0	1
Irelands Own	1	1	0	0	0	2
Irish American Unity Conference	1	1	0	0	0	2
Irish Anti-Partition League	1	1	0	0	0	2
Irish Freedom Committee	1	0	1	1	1	4
Irish Northern Aid Committee	1	0	0	0	0	1
Irish Republican Political Prisoners	1	0	0	0	0	1
Mise Eire	1	0	0	0	0	1
Na Gael	1	0	0	0	0	1
National Irish Freedom Committee	1	0	1	0	1	3
New Republican Forum	1	0	0	0	1	2
Mean	1	0.2	0.1	0.05	0.2	1.55

Radio Free Eireann broadcasts, one of which analysed the events surrounding Bloody Sunday.[72] The other Republican solidarity actors did not provide audio or video facilities on their websites. For example, the Australia Aid for Ireland website consisted mainly of plain text punctuated by a few photographs such as a picture of a Republican memorial outside Sydney.[73] The Ireland for the Irish website also provided a basic website that limited visual cues about their Republican sympathies to a few grainy pictures of Provisional IRA gunmen.[74]

A similar set of results was generated by the analysis of Loyalist solidarity websites (Table 3.9). Loyalist solidarity actors did not provide audio or video facilities on their websites. The United Loyalist Movement website was notable, as it was the only website to receive no score in this category. This was partly explained by the fact that this website was in effect a Loyalist chat forum in which Internet users could network with fellow Loyalists and discuss pertinent issues.[75] The Ulster Protestant Movement for Justice was the only Loyalist website under review to allow Internet users to download music and images. This website enabled Internet users to sample music from Loyalist bands and download images of Republican atrocities, one of which showed the aftermath of the Omagh bomb in August 1998.[76] However, the other Loyalist actors tended to provide only still images on their websites. For example, only a few photographs of Loyalist 'P.O.Ws' punctuated the plain text on the UDA website.[77] In sum, the study suggested that Loyalist and Republican solidarity actors were more likely to use static text-based websites over sophisticated methods like audio and video streaming.

Discussion

The Zapatista effect?

The study found limited evidence to suggest that this form of web activism constituted a social netwar on behalf of Loyalist or Republican terrorists. Although these websites are being used to reproduce the framing of their terrorist sponsors, it is unclear whether they will have an impact upon international public attitudes towards their subject matter.[78] As discussed in the previous chapter, dissidents on both sides may struggle to attract the support of international audiences who remain opposed to their violent campaigns. Therefore, it is perhaps unrealistic to expect that the website strategies of solidarity actors will generate a critical multiplier effect for groups that remain outside the triangle of political communication. Moreover, these websites might not be a suitable vehicle for reproducing the international mobilisation that propelled

Table 3.9 Presentation methods used on Loyalist solidarity websites

Website	Graphics	Frames	Sound	Video streaming	Pages available in alternative format e.g. PDF	Score (/5)
Birches Guerrilla Movement	1	1	0	0	0	2
British Ulster Alliance	1	1	0	0	0	2
Fife Loyalists	1	0	0	0	0	1
Greenock Loyalists	1	0	0	0	0	1
Larne UVF/ YCV/RHC	1	0	0	0	0	1
Liverpool UDA	1	0	0	0	0	1
Loyalist Network	1	0	1	0	0	2
Loyalist View	1	0	0	0	0	1
Loyalistvoice. co.uk	1	0	0	0	0	1
Red Hand Land	1	0	0	0	0	1
Scottish Loyalists	1	1	0	0	0	2
The Loyalist	1	1	0	0	0	2
The Volunteer	1	1	0	0	0	2
Ulster Defence Association	1	0	0	0	0	1
United Loyalist Movement	0	0	0	0	0	0
Ulster Online	1	1	0	0	0	2
Ulster Protestant Movement for Justice	1	1	1	0	0	3
UVF-The Peoples Army	1	1	0	0	0	2
West of Scotland Ratpack	1	1	0	0	0	2
Yorkshire Loyal	1	1	0	0	0	2
Mean	0.95	0.5	0.1	0	0	1.55

the Zapatista netwar. It might be easier for a non-governmental organisation (NGO) to mobilise its supporters via email rather than to rely upon them to search for information on their websites. It should be remembered that the mobilisation on behalf of the Zapatistas was facilitated by newsgroups rather than websites. Newsgroups such as Chiapas-95 facilitated the rapid transfer of information between groups that had moblised in favour of Marcos and the EZLN insurgents. Global campaigns such as Make Poverty History (MPH) have also sought to mobilise supporters through the use of rapid communication such as text messaging and email. For example, 30 million texts were sent by supporters of MPH in July 2005, urging members of the G8 to act to end global poverty.[79] Both MPH and the Zapatistas used ICTs to mobilise an audience that was broadly receptive to their core objectives.

Nevertheless, social netwar might be better understood as a description of events surrounding the the Zapatista insurgency in 1994, which marked the first occasion that the Internet had facilitated mobilisation on a global scale. The 'coordinated anarchy' that characterised the pro-Zapatista mobilisation reflected the diverse NGOs that took an interest in the Chiapas region of Mexico. For many activists, the Chiapas insurrection was a way of gaining greater media exposure for their own broad political objectives. Many of the swarm networks used the Chiapas insurrection to voice their opposition to the North American Free Trade Agreement (NAFTA) treaty. In addition, groups that supported the rights of indigenous peoples in Latin America used the Zapatistas to highlight their own campaigns. Chiapas encapsulated many of the problems identified by NGOs that were already active in the region, highlighting the potential detrimental effect of the NAFTA treaty upon indigenous people in Latin America. As the Zapatistas had struck a particular chord with these groups, they were more likely to use all forms of media – including the Internet – to project messages of support for Marcos and his insurgent army. Therefore, the Zapatista case study suggests that a successful netwar is contingent upon securing support amongst geographically dispersed groups, many of whom coalesce around high-profile international issues. If a sub-state actor fails to secure support amongst such influential international actors, its netwar campaign is less likely to generate strategic gains. The prospects for dissident Loyalists and Republicans achieving such prominence would appear remote, given their continued support for armed struggle.

Terrorist superfans?
The study also suggests that it may become increasingly difficult for nation-states to remove pro-terrorist content from the Internet. The

webmasters responsible for these websites were able to show their support for proscribed terrorist organisations without contravening the norms of acceptable behaviour online. Private individuals may purport to be terrorists online despite compelling evidence to the contrary on their websites. Yet this research perhaps illustrates the distinction that should made between terrorist 'superfans' and amateur terrorists in terms of their website strategy. The Tsouli case demonstrates how private individuals may use the Internet to further the campaigns of terrorists without becoming absorbed into their organisational structure. During Tsouli's trial, evidence emerged showing that the young IT technician was in direct contact with members of Al Qaida and had encouraged people to perpetrate acts of terrorism on a number of bulletin boards. This form of web activism is qualitatively different from the activities of Loyalist and Republican solidarity actors that have been analysed in this chapter.

In terms of website function, there was little to differentiate between these solidarity actors and political fronts such as Sinn Fein. The Internet provided a communicative space in which Loyalist and Republican solidarity actors could define their political ideologies and provide their own history of the Northern Irish conflict. However, there were some differences between solidarity actors and political fronts in terms of their online framing. Clearly, the peace frame had a negligible influence upon the online framing of many Loyalist and Republican actors. These solidarity actors used their websites to claim the peace process had left them at greater risk of attack from the 'other' community. Moreover, the analysis suggested that the relative anonymity offered by the Internet allowed these actors to say things that their sponsors were often unable to say on their own websites. In contrast to political fronts, these actors did not have to convince Internet users of their democratic credentials and could openly refer to the activities of terrorist organisations on their websites. Thus, images of hooded gunmen and paramilitary insignias were frequently used on the websites of Loyalist and Republican supporters. In some cases, solidarity actors provided a justification for political violence and paid tribute to dissident terrorist organisations on their websites. The study suggested that the Internet had liberated these actors from their offline identities insofar as they would probably have been either unable or unwilling to use these frames publicly in the offline world.

However, there was no evidence on these websites to suggest that many of the dissident solidarity actors were engaged in paramilitary activity on behalf of a proscribed terrorist organisation. There was no website comparable with the ULISNET example discussed earlier in this book. Indeed, most of the websites under analysis did not focus upon the current activities of Loyalist and Republican terrorist groups. Websites dedicated to 'Prisoners Of Wars', with titles such as the Irish Republican Political Prisoners, focused upon proving resources to the families of paramilitaries rather than promoting terrorism. In other cases the webmaster used legal disclaimers to inform Internet users that they had no complicity in acts of terrorism. Yet, the results of the study are based upon the evidence that each webmaster is willing to disclose on his or her website. While the study suggested many webmasters were fraudulently claiming to be members of terrorist organisations, it did not rule out the possibility that these actors may be supporting terrorism in the offline world. It is conceivable that some of these actors are using less public forms of computer-mediated communication, such as email, to provide resources for dissident terrorists in the region. However, it is fair to say that the website strategy of solidarity actors does not appear to pose a new dimension of terrorist threat in and of itself. An audience will still need to locate these websites in cyberspace in order for their online framing to affect public attitudes towards their subject matter.

Sandvoss (2005) suggests that fandom is based around self-constitution and the expression of facets of each fan's own identity. He suggests that fandom undermines the role of class as a vector of social change and that each fan will interpret texts about their favoured subject in accordance with their own personal experiences. What the analysis above suggests is that many Loyalist and Republican fans may be using the Internet not only to network with like-minded individuals but also to express their own identities using the language and symbolism of the Northern Irish conflict. However, it is not clear whether these actors have any tangible links to the objects of their fandom. Take, for example, the case of the Fife Loyalist website that appeared to be run by a Fife teenager. It is conceivable that the webmaster's fandom was influenced by contact with other Loyalist supporters, possibly even at the Glasgow Rangers FC match at which he was photographed wearing a Union Jack. What is not clear is whether he has had any actual contact with Loyalist paramilitaries or has encouraged acts of terrorism in the real world. An Internet user would have to unconditionally accept the frames evident on these websites to believe that many of these solidarity actors have been complicit in acts of terrorism. Moreover, it cannot be assumed that the existence of pro-terrorist websites in cyberspace will lead to an increased terrorist threat in the real world. While Sandvoss argues that fandom has the potential to prompt social change through its ability to link people from different socio-economic classes, a caveat must be applied to his thesis that is evident in the above research. While fan communities may critically analyse the object of their fandom, they invariably do not seek to promote change or collective action. The analysis above suggested that these Loyalist and Republican solidarity actors used their websites to criticise the Belfast Agreement and reproduce the frames of their favoured terrorist organisations. These actors stopped short of justifying political violence on their websites and did not appear to be organising their own campaigns of political violence online. However, it is possible that these actors have real-world involvement with terrorism that is not apparent on these websites.

Conclusion

The evidence presented in this chapter suggested that these actors were terrorist 'fans' rather than amateur terrorists. Although many of these webmasters used paramiliary insignias and pictures of hooded gunmen on their websites, there was no evidence to suggest that they were engaged in terrorism themselves. Many of these websites appeared to have no links to the terrorist organisations from which they took their names. Yet one cannot assume that these webmasters have no links to terrorism whatsoever. Conceivably, they may be using more anonymous forms of computer-mediated communication, such as email, to support terrorist organisations. Irrespective of their links to terrorism, these actors did not appear to have realised the potential of the Web as a tool for organisational linkage and political communication. These websites did not in and of themselves constitute a new dimension of terrorist threat in the region. This form of web activism fell far short of constituting a mobilisation on the scale of the Zapatista social netwar. Yet, this study does tell us something about the nature of fandom in cyberspace. The rapid communication and networking available to fan communities online will not necessarily lead to collective action in the real world. While these terrorist fans used their websites to reproduce the political ideologies of their most favoured terrorist organistions, there was limited evidence to suggest that these actors had become actively involved in dissident terrorist campaigns, nor that they were encouraging others to do so. However, this conclusion is based upon the evidence that each webmaster is prepared to reveal online and it is conceivable that these fans are using less public forms of computer-mediated communication to support terrorism.

Notes

1 The EZLN now maintains a website. www.ezln.org.
2 The Omagh bombing in August 1998 drew international condemnation for

its perpetrators, the Real IRA. The atrocity saw 29 people lose their lives, one of the most lethal attacks perpetrated in Northern Ireland since the late 1960s.

3 Laqueur, W. 1999. *The New Terrorism: Fanaticism and the Arms of Mass Destruction*. London: Phoenix, p. 206. The Unabomber manifesto was printed in the *Washington Post* and *New York Times* in accordance with Kaczynski's demands.

4 Rotten. 2005. 'The Turner Diaries'. www.rotten.com/library/culture/turner-diaries/ (accessed 1 October 2005).

5 BBC. 2007. 'Trio linked to terrorist films'. http://news.bbc.co.uk/1/hi/uk/6592537.stm (accessed 10 May 2009).

6 UK Home Office. 2004. *Counter-Terrorism Powers: Reconciling Security and Liberty in an Open Society*. London: Hme Office, p. 24.

7 The full title of this Act is the Uniting and Strengthening America by Providing Appropriate Tools Required to Intercept and Obstruct Terrorism Act. Electronic version of the Act can be viewed here: www.fincen.gov/statutes_regs/patriot/index.html (accessed 10 May 2009).

8 *Belfast Telegraph*. 2001. 'New Internet Terror Fear: Loyalists are Using Web to Pick Targets'. (15 March).

9 An email was sent to each webmaster informing them that their website was to be analysed in this book. Only two responses were received from the webmasters responsible for the websites in this chapter.

10 A selected chronology of the events is provided in Appendix 1.

11 www.google.co.uk and www.yahoo.co.uk were used in the study.

12 The total number of links generated by search engines can be viewed in Chapter 4, Tables 4.2 and 4.3.

13 Whois.net. www.whois.net (accessed 10 June 2005).

14 Whois.net. www.whois.net (accessed 10 June 2005).

15 ULISNET was shut down in late 2004. As discussed in the Introduction, it is reasonable to speculate that this was due to its contravention of anti-terrorist legislation. The website solicited resources and information on behalf of the Loyalist Volunteer Force, a proscribed Northern Irish terrorist organisation.

16 Cairde Sinn Fein. www.cairde.com (accessed 10 April 2005).

17 Red Hand Land. http://mysite.freeserve.com/Redhandland (accessed 10 April 2005).

18 Liverpool UDA. www.liverpooluda.co.uk (accessed 10 April 2005).

19 New Republican Forum. www.newrepublicanforum.ie (accessed 10 April 2005).

20 The term 'Fenian' refers to the Fenian Brotherhood, an Irish Republican organisation active in the nineteenth century. It has been used as a term of sectarian abuse in Northern Ireland in recent times, to depict a member of the Catholic community.

21 New Republican Forum. www.newrepublicanforum.ie (accessed 10 April 2005).

22 Hardline IRA. www.geocities.com/hardline_ira/enter.html (accessed 10 April 2005).

23 United Loyalist Movement. www.unitedloyalistmovement.bravepages.com (accessed 10 April 2005).

24 British Ulster Alliance. www.britishulsteralliance.co.uk (accessed 10 April 2005).

25 Loyalist Network. www.houstonpk.freeserve.co.uk/2ndindex.htm (accessed 10 April 2005).

26 West of Scotland Ratpack. www.westofscotlandratpack.co.uk (accessed 10 April 2005).

27 Ireland's Own. www.irelandsown.net (accessed 10 April 2005).

28 Eire Saor. www.morrigan.net/eireshaor (accessed 10 April 2005).

29 Hardline IRA. www.geocities.com/hardline_ira/enter.html (accessed 10 April 2005).

30 Birches Guerrilla Movement. http://bgm.vze.com (accessed 10 April 2005).

31 The Volunteer. www.thevolunteer.8m.com (accessed 10 April 2005).

32 Loyalistvoice.co.uk. www.loyalistvoice.co.uk (accessed 10 April 2005).

33 Friends of Irish Freedom. www.geocities.com/foif_usa (accessed 10 April 2005).

34 Irish Freedom Committee. http://members.freespeech.org/irishpows/ bb3// (accessed 10 April 2005).

35 West of Scotland Ratpack. www.westofscotlandratpack.co.uk (accessed 10 April 2005).

36 Eire Saor. www.morrigan.net/eireshaor (accessed 10 April 2005).

37 Ulster Defence Association. www.freewebs.com/ulsterdefenceassociation (accessed 10 April 2005).

38 Ulster Volunteer Force. www.theuvf.2ya.com (accessed 10 April 2005).

39 Fife Loyalists www.fifeloyalists.co.uk (accessed 10 April 2005).

40 Liverpool UDA. www.liverpooluda.co.uk (accessed 10 April 2005).

41 Cairde Sinn Fein. www.cairde.com (accessed 10 April 2005).

42 Irish Freedom Committee. http://members.freespeech.org/irishpows/ bb3// (accessed 10 April 2005). The term 'punishment beating' refers to attacks by Republican paramilitaries upon members of their local communities. Republican paramilitaries often cite anti-social behaviour as the justification for these attacks, or local opposition to the police.

43 Hardline IRA. www.geocities.com/hardline_ira/enter.html (accessed 10 April 2005).

44 Ireland for the Irish www.ireland4theirish.yk (accessed 10 April 2005).

45 Hungerstrike Commemorative Web Project. http://larkspirit.com/hunger-strikes/ (accessed 10 April 2005).

46 West of Scotland Ratpack. www.westofscotlandratpack.co.uk (accessed 10 April 2005).

47 Liverpool UDA. www.liverpooluda.co.uk (accessed 10 April 2005). John McMichael was a leader of the UDA during the late 1980s. In December

1987 he was killed in Lisburn by an Provisional IRA booby trap bomb that had been placed under his car.
48 Scottish Loyalists. www.scottishloyalists.com (accessed 10 April 2005).
49 Loyalistvoice.co.uk. www.loyalistvoice.co.uk (accessed 10 April 2005).
50 Greenock Loyalists. www.greenockloyalists.cjb.net (accessed 10 April 2005).
51 Irish Anti-Partition League. www.ia-pl.org (accessed 10 April 2005).
52 Coiste na n-Iarchimi. www.coiste.ie (accessed 10 April 2005).
53 Scottish Loyalists. www.scottishloyalists.com (accessed 10 April 2005).
54 Loyalist Network. www.houstonpk.freeserve.co.uk/2ndindex.htm (accessed 10 April 2005).
55 Irish-American Unity Conference. www.iauc.org/index3.htm (accessed 10 April 2005).
56 Irish-American Unity Conference. www.iauc.org/index3.htm (accessed 10 April 2005).
57 Fourthwrite. www.fourthwrite.ie (accessed 10 April 2005).
58 Cairde Sinn Fein. www.cairde.com (accessed 10 April 2005).
59 Irish Republican Political Prisoners. www.larkspirit.com/psn (accessed 10 April 2005).
60 Irish Northern Aid Committee. www.inac.org (accessed 10 April 2005).
61 Birches Guerrilla Movement. http://bgm.vze.com (accessed 10 April 2005).
62 West of Scotland Ratpack. www.westofscotlandratpack.co.uk (accessed 10 April 2005).
63 Fife Loyalists. www.fifeloyalists.co.uk (accessed 10 April 2005).
64 British Ulster Alliance. www.britishulsteralliance.co.uk (accessed 10 April 2005). The merchandise could only be purchased by sending a cheque to a registered postal address.
65 Loyalistvoice.co.uk. www.loyalistvoice.co.uk (accessed 10 April 2005).
66 Loyalist View. http://clix.to/loyalistview (accessed 10 April 2005).
67 Liverpool UDA. www.liverpooluda.co.uk (accessed 10 April 2005). A paramilitary 'show of strength' refers to the phenomenon of masked gunmen assembling in their local neighbourhoods and firing their weapons into the air. These events typically have members of the conventional mass media present, usually with the consent of the respective terrorist organisation, in order that the images be transmitted to a larger audience.
68 Irish Anti-Partition League. www.ia-pl.org (accessed 10 April 2005).
69 Irish Northern Aid Committee. www.inac.org (accessed 10 April 2005).
70 Irish Freedom Committee. http://members/freespeech.org/irishpows/bb3// (accessed 10 April 2005).
71 Irish Freedom Committee. http://members/freespeech.org/irishpows/bb3// (accessed 10 April 2005).
72 National Irish Freedom Committee. 2005 www.irishfreedom.net (accessed 10 April 2005). On 30 January 1972, 13 unarmed men were shot dead by the Parachute Regiment during unrest that followed a civil rights rally. These events became known as Bloody Sunday.

73 Australian Aid for Ireland. www.aai.org.au (accessed 10 April 2005).

74 Ireland for the Irish www.ireland4theirish.yk (accessed 10 April 2005).

75 United Loyalist Movement. www.unitedloyalistmovement.bravepages.com (accessed 10 April 2005).

76 Ulster Protestant Movement for Justice. www.upmj.co.uk (accessed 10 April 2005).

77 Ulster Defence Association. www.freewebs.com/ulsterdefenceassociation (accessed 10 April 2005).

78 The audience for these websites will be considered in the next chapter.

79 See Make Poverty History. www.makepovertyhistory.org (accessed 10 June 2007). The self-styled 'UK alliance of charities, trade unions, campaigning groups and celebrities' calls for the G8 to wipe out the debts of the world's poorest countries, and G8 leaders to agree to give 0.7 percent of national income in foreign aid to alleviate poverty in the developing world. The campaign received support from a number of influential politicians, including former South African President Nelson Mandela.

4

Googling terrorism: how visible are Northern Irish terrorists on the Internet?

Introduction

The Internet enables Northern Irish terrorists and their supporters to choose their own frames and circumvent the ideological refractions of the conventional mass media. However, this framing may only affect the attitudes of the public if the master frame is publicised heavily and resonates with the values of a large audience. In this chapter, the online audience for Northern Irish terrorists will be discussed with reference to data already available in the public domain, such as Internet usage patterns and the ranking systems used by Internet search engines. Factors such as the number of Internet users who use the Web for political research will be analysed to determine the potential audience available to Northern Irish terrorists. As a majority of Internet users rely upon search engines for information retrieval, visibility on search engine listings is arguably invaluable to political actors who wish to affect public opinion using their online frames. Internet users are more likely to click on links to the websites listed on the first page of results generated by a search query. Factors that influence the ranking of websites such as the sale of priority retrieval to the highest bidder will be analysed to determine their potential impact upon the audience available to Northern Irish terrorists online. The study suggests that Northern Irish terrorists are only visible on search engines if Internet users select the correct search terms. This limits the audience for Northern Irish terrorists to those Internet users who have prior knowledge about the links between these organisations and political fronts such as Sinn Fein.

Internet usage patterns: the United Kingdom and the United States

In this section, the potential audience for Northern Irish terrorists will be examined using Internet usage patterns. The analysis presented in this book so far suggests that the Internet provides a space in which dissident Loyalists and Republicans can use their own frames to reject the Good Friday Agreement. For their frames to affect public opinion, groups such as RSF require a large number of Internet users to access their websites. This is because people access the Internet in a qualitatively different fashion to the conventional mass media. Media 'literacy' is arguably a universal good in advanced industrialised nation-states. For example, television is a low-cost public medium available in virtually every household in advanced industrialised nation-states. Conversely, ICTs require a new form of media literacy, a literacy that comes with experience in using information technology (Locke, 1999: 219). Media literacy in Northern Ireland might have an impact upon how the online framing of dissident terrorists is processed by domestic audiences. During the period of data collection the majority of people in Northern Ireland did not have access to the Internet. While almost two-thirds of the adult population read at least one paid-for newspaper on a daily basis in 2005, only 48 percent had Internet access at home (see Ofcom 2006). Furthermore, only 10 percent of Internet users in the Province had created online content during the same period. Yet the analysis presented in this book so far has suggested that these websites may be targeted at international audiences rather than at the population of Northern Ireland. North America in particular has been a focus of Republicans' activism as they seek to mobilise Irish-American diaspora communities (see Chapter 2). Therefore, global Internet usage patterns may be more pertinent to the debate over the potential online audience available to Northern Irish terrorists.

Digital divide and Internet access
In order to explore the potential audience for Northern Irish terrorist websites, one must first determine who has access to the Internet. The digital divide refers to the gap between 'those able to benefit from digital technology and those who are not' (International Telecommunication Union, 2007). Clearly, private citizens are more likely to benefit directly from digital technology if they have access to the Internet. People can use the Internet for a variety of activities, including shopping, research, political activism and the pursuit of hobbies and interests. The indications are that Internet consumption is growing rapidly across the globe as more people begin to use the Internet on a regular basis. In September 2009, there were more Internet users (over 738 million) in Asia than in any other continent. This compares to approximately 67 million Internet users in Africa and 57 million in the Middle East during this period (Internet World Statistics, 2009). Europe and, in particular, North America continue to hold a 'strong lead in realising digital

opportunity' (International Telecommunication Union, 2007). Despite having only 5.1 percent of the world's population, North America provides 14.6 percent of the total number of Internet users worldwide. Meanwhile, Internet penetration in Africa remains low, with an estimated 6.8 percent of its population having access to the Internet. Although 14.6 percent of the world's population lives in Africa, it provides only 3.9 percent of the total number of Internet users worldwide (Internet World Statistics, 2009). This First World hegemony is reflected in the predominance of English as the vernacular of cyberspace. This suggests that so-called 'fourth-generation rights' are being denied to developing countries, for whom English is not the common tongue. These rights include the right to information and the right to communicate (Council of Europe, 1997: 39). However, Africa has seen a 1329.4 percent growth in Internet consumption between 2000 and 2009 as broadband services become available in countries such as Ghana (Internet World Statistics, 2009). The digital divide between the West (North America and Europe) and Africa would appear to be narrowing.

Yet, the digital divide remains an issue for all nation-states, irrespective of their prosperity. Take, for example, Internet usage patterns in the United States and the United Kingdom during the period of data collection. In the United States, an estimated 27 percent of people had never accessed the Internet in 2005 (Madden, 2006: 1). This was comparable to research conducted in the United Kingdom shortly afterwards, which found that 36 percent of Britons claimed never to have used the Internet (Shepherd and Bryson, 2007: 8). There was also little to differentiate between men and women in terms of their use of the Internet in these countries during this period. The Oxford Internet Survey (2005) found that 63 percent of men and 57 percent of women claimed to have used the Internet (Di Gennaro and Dutton, 2006: 301). The socio-economic profile of Internet users provides greater insight into the digital divide within advanced industrialised nation-states. For example, only 40 percent of adults in the United States who have less than a high school education claim to use the Internet, compared to 64 percent of adults with a high school education (Madden, 2006: 3). Research from the United Kingdom shows a similar correlation between educational attainment and Internet use during the period of data collection. An estimated 88 percent of people with a degree qualification, or higher, use the Internet in the United Kingdom. The same study suggested that only 22 percent of Britons with no qualifications use the Internet (Shepherd and Bryson, 2007: 13).

Annual income and age also influence whether people are likely to use the Internet. The wealthiest households in both countries are more likely to be online than the poorest households. For example, 80 percent of American households with annual income of between $30,000 and $50,000 per year were online in 2005, compared to 53 percent of households with income less than $30,000 (Madden, 2006: 3). Internet use also varies significantly across different age groups in both countries. While 88 percent of 18- to 29-year-olds in the United States used the Internet, only 32 percent of those aged over 65 went online (Madden, 2006: 3). A recent study also suggested that 84 percent of people in the United Kingdom aged between 16 and 24 years used the Internet, in comparison to 15 percent of those aged 65 and over (Shepherd and Bryson, 2007: 12). In sum, it would appear that the online audience for Loyalists and Republicans is likely to come from Europe, North America and Asia, given their high rates of Internet penetration. With a recent report from the Oxford Internet Institute showing that Internet use has diffused only gradually since 2005, these Internet users are still likely to be educated to at least high school level, wealthy and aged less than 25 years.[1] However, it is conceivable that these groups might attract support from Internet users who do not match this profile, depending on what these people search for online.

Internet usage patterns
The target audience for Loyalist and Republicans is likely to be drawn from the United Kingdom and the United States. There have been long-standing links between the Republican movement and Irish-America since the Northern Irish conflict began in the late 1960s. Cochrane (2007) suggests that Irish-American groups were a key constituency of support for the Republican movement during the Troubles and played a critical role in the internationalisation of the conflict that facilitated the peace process. While Loyalists have had less success in mobilising support from North American communities with Ulster-Scots ancestry, the websites analysed in the previous two chapters suggest that there has been a renewed effort by Loyalists to elicit support from these groups. Internet usage patterns within the two nation-states UK and US suggest that this online audience may be limited to those Internet users who are familiar with Loyalism and Republicanism in the offline world. This is because people invariably use ICTs as a stimulus for 'pursuing existing interests' rather than creating new ones (Selwyn, Gorard and Furlong, 2005: 13). During the period of data collection, Americans and Britons were most likely to check their email or social networking profile when they used the Internet. One survey found that 92 percent of Internet users in the United Kingdom used the Internet to check their

email during this period (Di Gennaro and Dutton, 2006: 303). The next most common online activity was looking up information about products and services, while 61 percent of respondents reported that they used the Internet to look for information on current affairs (p. 303). Only one in five Britons went online to obtain political information, suggesting that the Internet's potential for enhancing political engagement may remain unfulfilled (p. 307).

Moreover, Internet users themselves perceive that the Internet is a means for pursuing their private interests rather than a tool for political engagement. This was illustrated by the share of online Americans who claim that the Internet had greatly improved the way they pursue their hobbies and interests, rising from 20 percent in 2000 to 33 percent in 2005 (Madden, 2006: 2). Some commentators suggest that this is evidence that the Internet may not help to generate social capital in liberal democracies as was suggested in the cyberoptimist model. Shah, Kwak and Holbert (2001) assert that recreational uses of the Internet may 'erode individual level production of social capital, as these activities are generally asocial or anonymous but foster a sense of social interaction' (p. 144).[2] Recent empirical studies have also suggested that the Internet has yet to transform civic engagement as envisaged in the cyberoptimist model. A report from the Pew Internet and American Life Project (2009) suggests that well-to-do and the well-educated are still more likely than those less well-off to participate in online political activism.[3]

Loyalists and Republicans may be able to reach out beyond their grass-roots support to young people who use the Internet for research. Young people, who are under-represented in 'offline' politics, appear more likely to engage in politics online (Di Gennaro and Dutton, 2006). Approximately 58 percent of people aged between 16 and 24 used the Internet to find information for their studies during the period of data collection (Madden, 2006: 48). Young people who study the Northern Irish Troubles may reference online sources, such as the websites of Loyalists and Republican political fronts, in their assignments. Owen (2006) suggests that young people in the United States have a high level of trust in Internet sources and produce political content online that has influenced mainstream media reports (p. 35). This suggests that young people who access the websites of Loyalist and Republican organisations may accept their online framing unconditionally. However, only a minority of young people will turn to the Internet for political information or the latest news stories. The Pew Research Center for the People and the Press (2007) suggested that only 25 percent of Americans aged between 18 and 25 went online to follow news stories (Pew Research

Center for the People and the Press, 2007: 27). The survey respondents were more likely to follow news stories on television or radio rather than on the Internet.

Nevertheless, Internet news consumers may be a potential target audience for Loyalists and Republicans. Recent studies suggest that people are increasingly likely to use the Internet for their political news sources. For example, data gathered from two US mid-term elections showed that the Internet news audience had increased from 7 percent in 2002 to 15 percent in 2006 (Fallows, 2007: 1). Yet Internet news consumers may choose to access the same news sources they rely upon in the offline world. The Pew Research Center for the People and the Press (2007) found that 20 percent of people who get political news online use the websites of international news media organisations, with a further 25 percent favouring state and local government websites (Fallows, 2007: 6). Nonetheless, the survey did find that 25 percent of Internet news consumers would visit issue-oriented websites for an alternative viewpoint on a breaking news story (p. 6). Conceivably, these people might access the websites of 'primary definers', such as Loyalist and Republican political fronts, to follow a news event involving the group in question (Negrine, 1994: 127). This news event would presumably be publicised first in the conventional mass media, prompting people to seek this information in the first place. In other words, Loyalist and Republican websites may attract more Internet news consumers if their subjects receive the 'oxygen of publicity' from the conventional mass media. In sum, there does appear to be an online audience for Loyalist and Republicans websites, one that does not consist solely of supporters and sympathetic diaspora communities. This audience may be receptive to the framing of Loyalist and Republican political fronts if they broadly agree with the values on their websites. This suggests that political fronts must maintain websites that are both visible and accessible on the Internet if they wish to reach out to this audience. At the very least, Internet users should be able to see these websites on search engines when looking for information on their respective organisation.

Search engines: role in computer-mediated communication

The online audience for Northern Irish terrorists may depend upon the visibility of their websites on Internet search engines. In this section, the role of Internet search engines in computer-mediated communication will be discussed. Internet search engines can be best characterised as 'digital librarians', as opposed to the 'gatekeepers' that are employed in the conventional mass media. While Internet search engines index websites, they have little or no direct influence on the tone and content of the websites in question. Nevertheless, the order of websites within a particular search engine directory may be comparable to decisions made by editorial staff in the news media. Editors have to deliberate over which stories are worthy of greater coverage in conventional media products such as television news bulletins or newspapers. On the one hand, they have to ensure that large numbers of media consumers access their products, particularly when advertising revenues are critical to the sustenance of their respective organisations. Advertisers are only likely to invest in media organisations that provide large numbers of readers or viewers that are able to purchase their products (Negrine, 1994: 67). On the other hand, editors have to make the decision to drop news stories, as they have finite resources and space with which to give equal coverage to all events that occur within their jurisdiction. Internet search engines are also unable to give equal attention to the millions of websites contained in their respective directories, nor do they index all of the websites available on the Internet. One study suggested that all of the major search engines combined only covered 16 percent of the total number of 'indexable' websites on the Internet (Bar-Ilan, 1999: 1). Consequently, by virtue of their criteria used to index a website and their popularity with Internet users, search engines direct web traffic towards certain websites rather than to others on the Web.

Internet users, whether expert or non-expert, feel comfortable using Internet search engines as navigational 'tools' on the Internet. They rarely know the exact URL of a website, typically entering 'keywords' into search engines to locate information relevant to their area of interest. Studies suggest that as much as 90 percent of all traffic on the Web comes directly from search engines (Submit Corner, 2004). For example, Internet users around the globe spend a total of 13 million hours per month interacting with the Google search engine alone (Ntoulas, Cho and Olson, 2004: 1). Furthermore, Internet users are unlikely to look beyond the first 25 results generated by a particular search query. Similar to the content of newspapers, the most visible items are likely to receive more 'hits' than those situated on the third or fourth page of links generated by a search term. This suggests that search engines can influence the choices of Internet users in terms of which websites they access in order to pursue their private interests. Overall, the popularity of search engines suggests that the Internet enables new forms of 'mediated interaction', as opposed to the 'unmediated' interaction that might benefit those who receive minimal coverage in the conventional mass media (Wouters and Gerbec, 2003: 4). The multifarious information flows synonymous with the cyberoptimist model must pass through these filters before they reach a potential global audience. The creation of a website will not necessarily lead to greater levels of popular recognition for actors that lack a visible presence in the conventional mass media. Conversely, visibility on Internet search engines appears to be equally as important as visibility in the conventional mass media. The websites of publicity-starved sub-state actors must consistently appear in the top 25 results generated by search engines, if they are to achieve a high degree of visibility online.

How do search engines work?

Updating frequencies

In this section, the factors that determine whether a website is 'visible' on Internet search engines are analysed. Wouters, Helsten and Leydesdorff (2004) characterise Internet search engines as the 'clocks' of cyberspace, representing the updating frequency of both the Web and the underlying Internet (p. 15). The maintenance of search engine directories reflects the closure of websites, changes to the search engine algorithms, and the extent to which 'old' pages remain in their databases (p. 17). Internet search engines have to update their databases constantly, due to the high turnover of websites on the Internet, an estimated 80 percent of websites available today likely to be inaccessible after one year (Ntoulas, Cho and Olson, 2004: 2). Companies such as Yahoo, and even the market leader, Google, do not have the resources to index all available websites on the Internet, or to trawl through these websites in order to generate a list of results in response to a search query. Internet search engines use a combination of automated website crawlers (or 'spiders') and human editors to index websites and update their directories. Directory search engines such as DMOZ (www.dmoz. org) employ as many as 50,000 human editors to decide whether a website should be included in their database and how it should be ranked in comparison to other sites (Search Engine Yearbook, 2003). However, the majority of commercial Internet search engines use browser-like programs to follow the links from one website to another, indexing everything that they find.

Both human editors and automated web crawlers look for the same information on websites before deciding whether, or invariably where, they are to be included within their respective directories. Meta tags, containing information like the name of the webmaster and which 'keywords' best describe the content of the website, are used to determine whether a site should be indexed by an Internet search engine (Webopedia, 2004). In this respect, meta tags arguably perform a similar function to the 'headlines' deployed by conventional news media organisations to boost public consumption of their products. The meta tag description is critical in determining how high a website will be 'ranked' in the results generated by 'keyword' searches on search engines. Meta tags present the content of a website – in no more than 256 characters – in an effort to attract the attention of both human editors and automated web crawlers (Softsteel Solutions, 2003). Consequently, webmasters that seek greater visibility online must market their websites at a target audience that includes not only Internet users but also the browsing programs used by search engines.

Googlearchy vs Googlocracy
Internet search engines do not behave like 'objective, well informed librarians' (Gerhart, 2004: 3). Instead, each individual search engine has its own set of protocols that determine whether a website is included in its directory, and its position vis-à-vis other indexed websites. There is little specific information available on these protocols, which are often referred to as 'algorithms'. This is because the companies behind Internet search engines are reluctant to disclose information about how they rank websites to their competitors. Internet search engines compete not only to secure the patronage of Internet users but also to accrue revenue from companies wishing to place advertisements on their websites. Google remains the only search engine company to have published details of how it ranks websites in its directory. The original Google algorithm 'ranks' a website in its directory through an assessment of the links pointing towards it, and an assessment of the 'standing' of these linking pages themselves (Thelwall, 2001: 3). Google equates a link from one website to another as an endorsement of both websites, attributing an undisclosed value to each website (Walker, 2002: 3). For a website to receive a high ranking in the Google search engine, it clearly pays to reciprocate links with other websites, regardless of whether they share similar themes. This phenomenon, whereby the most heavily linked websites received the highest ranking in the Google directory, is also known as Googlearchy (Hindman, Tsioutliklis and Johnson, 2003). It would appear to militate against the cyberoptimist conception of the Internet as a political communication device open to all sections of society. Small sub-state actors are unlikely to reciprocate links with large numbers of actors online, particularly if they have very few supporters in the offline world.

The Googlearchy model suggests that the websites of these actors are likely to be less 'visible' on search engines than the sites of extensively linked organisations such as government agencies, research institutes and media outlets (Gerhart, 2004: 22). However, an alternative hypothesis has emerged surrounding the effects of Google's Pagerank algorithm. Menczer et al (2006) suggest that search engines contribute towards a Googlocracy rather than Googlearchy. Their study found that Google directed Internet users towards websites that they were unlikely to visit through surfing. However, their research suggested that minority websites had a greater chance of being discovered through search engines so long as they were 'about specific topics that matched the interests of users'. The research presented in this chapter will consider the impact of search engine algorithms for the visibility of Northern Irish terrorists in cyberspace. It will determine whether people who use search engines are more or less likely to visit 'non-establishment' websites, such as those of solidarity actors or minority political interests.

Do search engines 'suppress' information on the Internet?

In this section, the proposition that search engines actively 'suppress' information on the Internet is analysed. As discussed earlier, search engines are more likely to direct Internet users towards the websites of extensively linked organisations than to those of peripheral sub-state actors. Some analysts suggest that there may be an alternative explanation for 'controversial' websites not featuring in the top 25 results generated by Internet search engines. Internet search engines may filter information with reference to many of the norms that inform the behaviour of the conventional mass media. Media models permit government censorship of the conventional mass media because a story might endanger national security, defame character or offend public 'decency'.[4] Recent studies suggest that these norms also influence the editorial process within Internet search engines, particularly in the omission of controversial websites from certain search engine directories. Zittrain and Edelman (2005) compared the availability of white supremacist websites on the French and German Google portals, google.fr, and google.de. The study concluded that 113 websites, such as 'Stormfront White Pride World Wide' (www.crusader.net), could not be located on both the French and German versions of Google, despite being listed on google.com (Zittrain and Edelman, 2005). Government legislation forced Google to remove these websites from their French and German portals. The German Supreme Court, the Bundesgerichtshof, ruled in 2000 that German laws against neo-Nazi propaganda would apply to websites maintained by both German citizens and foreign nationals (Bodard, 2003: 266).

There is also some evidence to suggest that political actors may use legal sanctions to remove controversial websites from Internet search engine directories. The Church of Scientology forced Google to remove references to websites that were critical of its religion in 2002. The Scientologists lobbied for the removal of these websites with reference to the US Digital Millennium Copyright Act (1998). They alleged that the sites contained 'copyrighted material' (Zittrain and Edelman, 2005). However, groups that lobby for the removal of online content may be powerless to prohibit its transmission on the Internet, particularly when webmasters are able register their websites in other nation-states. For example, the Chinese Ministry of Information has forced search engines such as Google to remove politically sensitive material from their directories. Thus, if Internet users search for information about Falun Gong on Google's Chinese portal (www.google.cn), they will be directed towards government websites rather than websites that express support for the Falun Gong.[5] However, if Internet users access another Google portal, such as google.co.uk, they will be directed towards websites that are maintained by practitioners of these meditation exercises.[6] This suggests that it may be difficult for nation-states to ensure that all 'harmful' material is removed from the Web.

Yet the norms of the libertarian media model may also be contributing to the predominance of 'more of the same' organisational websites on Internet search engine directories. Advertising revenue and private investment is critical to the longevity of media organisations, particularly in the United States. Internet search engines also maintain their financial self-sufficiency through the sale of advertising space on their respective web portals. Search engines, like Geocities, have even sold 'priority retrieval' to companies, placing their websites first in the results generated by a relevant query. (Noveck, 2000: 24). This is often invisible to Internet users who use these Web portals, as both private companies and search engines are reluctant to disclose this information to the public. Small sub-state actors are likely to be less visible on search engine directories if they are unable to afford priority retrieval.

The filtering of information by search engines has implications for those Internet users who wish to research controversial political issues on the Internet. Some commentators suggest that Internet search engines reward 'more of the same' organisational websites at the expense of less popular content. Gerhart (2004) asserts that 'controversy-revealing' websites are only visible in search engine results through a combination of the right search 'query' and offline experience of the relevant subject (p. 22). Internet users who lack background knowledge of a controversial political issue are increasingly likely to turn to Internet search engines for links to websites of interest. Internet search engines are likely to direct these users towards the websites of extensively linked organisations, many of whom have the capacity to purchase 'priority retrieval.' Therefore, the predominance of 'more of the same' organisations on Internet search engines reduces the 'visibility' of 'controversy-revealing' websites online. If the Internet user is not familiar with the actor behind a controversial website, they are likely to turn to the most 'visible' websites on Internet search engines. These websites are likely to be those of media organisations, which dominate the first page of results generated by their query.

The algorithms of the major commercial search engines arguably perpetuate the suppression of 'controversy-revealing' websites on the Internet. If these websites do not receive a large number of 'hits' from Internet users who lack relevant background knowledge of their subject, they are likely to remain a minority interest online. Consequently, webmasters that publish controversial opinions on their websites are likely to be communicating with people who share their views, as opposed to a potential global audience with no preconception of their particular subject. In sum, Internet search engines filter information with reference to some of the norms of the mass media models. Extensively linked organisations are likely to populate the top 25 results generated by most search queries, often at the expense of 'controversy-revealing' websites. These organisations are more visible on search engines because a higher volume of web traffic passes through their websites, and, in some cases, because they have paid companies like Geocities to ensure a high search-engine ranking.

Northern Irish terrorists and Internet search engines

In this section, the potential online audience for Northern Irish terrorists is analysed with reference to the visibility of their websites on search engines. Internet news consumers and young people might be using the Internet to look up information about Northern Irish terrorists, particularly if they are studying the Northern Irish conflict. This study, conducted in 2004 and 2005, examined whether these Internet users would be directed towards the websites of Northern Irish terrorists if they used Internet search engines to locate this information. The online audience available to Republicans was expected to be much larger than that available to Loyalists, as their websites would be more visible to Internet users on search engine directories. Republican terrorists and their supporters would receive a higher search engine ranking than their Loyalist equivalents, as they provided more links on their website and receive more web traffic, due to their higher international profile (see Chapter 2). In addition, the study tested the hypothesis that 'more of the same' organisational websites would dominate the search results generated by a variety of Loyalist and Republican keyword searches. It was anticipated that websites that expressed support for Northern Irish terrorist organisations, such as those analysed in the previous chapter, would be vastly under-represented in the top 25 results generated by related search queries. Media organisations, with their greater volume of Internet traffic and the ability to purchase priority retrieval from search engines, were expected to feature prominently in the results generated by Loyalist and Republican search queries.

Sample

The sample selected for the study consisted of four leading Internet search engines, namely DMOZ (www.dmoz.org), Google (www.google.co.uk), MSN (www.msn.co.uk) and Yahoo (www.yahoo.co.uk). The British versions of Google, MSN and Yahoo were used for the study, as they included results from their global directories. During the period of data collection they were also the most regularly used Internet search engines around the globe.[7] The three commercial search engines were included to test the rule of 'Googlearchy'. The study was designed to test the hypothesis that extensively linked organisations would populate the top 25 results generated by these search engines at the expense of 'controversy-revealing' websites, such as those that expressed support for Northern Irish terrorists. The DMOZ search engine was also included in the study to reflect the new generation of search engines based entirely upon human editing rather than automated Web crawlers. Consequently, the DMOZ search engine was expected to return more links to websites that could be characterised as either 'pro-Loyalist' or 'pro-Republican' than the other search engines included in the study. Human editors would presumably be less likely to provide links to websites that had nothing to do with the terrorist organisations under analysis.

Research design

A series of keyword searches were conducted using the four Internet search engines in October 2004. The names of the 14 Northern Irish terrorist organisations proscribed under anti-terrorist legislation such as the Prevention of Terrorism Act (1984) were entered into the basic search facility of the four Internet search engines (see Appendix 4).

Two ideological descriptions, 'Ulster Loyalist' and 'Irish Republican', were also entered into the basic search facility of the four search engines. These phrases were selected as they were commonly used to describe the ideological position of Northern Irish terrorist organisations. It was anticipated that webmasters who projected 'pro-Loyalist' or 'pro-Republican' propaganda on the Internet would use these words, or the name of one of the proscribed terrorist organisations, in the meta tag descriptions of their websites. The number of links generated by each individual search query was recorded for further analysis. These statistics provided a rudimentary method of comparing the number of websites whose meta tags resembled Loyalist and Republican keywords.

Searches were conducted using the two ideological descriptions and two terrorist group names, the IRA and the UVF. These groups were selected on the basis that they were two of the most well known terrorist groups in the region. It was anticipated that there would be numerous websites dedicated to these groups on the Web. The search results were then analysed to determine whether the most 'visible' websites belonged to organisations that supported Northern Irish terrorists. The top 25 results of these keyword searches were analysed, as they were considered to be the results that most closely resembled the search terms entered in the respective Internet search engines. The websites that featured in these 25 results were then classified in one of the following eight categories:

1. Official terrorist organisation/ political front
2. Solidarity website
3. Personal web page/blog
4. Research institute/ university
5. External news media
6. Opposition website
7. Government
8. Other

During the period of analysis, none of the 14 proscribed Northern Irish terrorist groups maintained an official web presence under that particular name. Therefore, the category of 'official' website was designed to include the websites of Loyalist and Republican political fronts analysed in this book (see Chapter 2). For example, the Sinn Fein and PUP websites were considered 'official' Republican and Loyalist websites with reference to the First Report of the IMC. The category of 'solidarity' websites referred to those websites that existed solely to provide support for Loyalist or Republican terrorist groups (see Chapter 3). This support could take many forms, including soliciting resources for paramilitary prisoners or issuing propaganda in favour of one of the terrorist groups under analysis.

The other six categories incorporated websites that did not express support for Loyalist or Republican terrorist organisations. Personal web pages and blogs were defined as websites maintained by individual Internet users to express opinions on a variety of issues including terrorism. Although many bloggers expressed opinions on Northern Irish terrorists, personal web pages were not considered to be 'solidarity' websites dedicated to the terrorist groups under analysis. It was anticipated that these websites were set up to record the opinions of their respective authors rather than to issue propaganda in favour of Northern Irish terrorist organisations. It was expected that 'pro-Loyalist' and 'pro-Republican' webmasters would use their websites to criticise the activities of their opponents. This was a period in which both Loyalists and Republicans blamed each other for the impasse over the decommissioning of paramilitary weaponry and the failure of the political parties to agree to restore the power-sharing institutions at Stormont. Therefore it was anticipated that many of these websites might use words relating to their opponents in their meta tag descriptions, thus making their websites visible in results generated by searches conducted using the names of their rivals. Thus, the 'Opposition website' category was created to incorporate 'Republican' websites in the analysis of Loyalist keyword searches, and vice versa.

The next three categories were designed to test the Gerhart hypothesis, namely that 'more of the same' organisational websites dominate search engine results at the expense of less popular websites. The websites of research institutes, external mass media organisations and government agencies were all expected to receive high search-engine ratings, due to the rule of 'Googlearchy'. It was anticipated that research institutes and government agencies that analysed the Northern Irish conflict would also receive a high ranking due to their meta tags. They were expected to use keyword meta tag descriptions on their sites that were similar to the keyword searches used in the study. External news media organisations that report on the activities of Northern Irish terrorists in newspaper, radio and television formats were expected to replicate this coverage on their websites. The category of 'Other' was used to describe websites that did not comment specifically on contemporary Northern Irish terrorist organisations. This category included websites that promoted cultural aspects of Loyalism and Republicanism but offered no overtly political analysis of contemporary Northern Irish terrorist organisations. It also included websites that did not explicitly refer to Northern Ireland, but had meta tags that were similar to the keyword searches used in the study. For example, websites dedicated to the Irish language or Orange flute bands were considered cultural rather than political projections of the two traditions in Northern Ireland.

The data was entered into SPSS for Windows and frequency tables were created to provide a breakdown of the top 25 results by website category. Inferential statistics were not used to analyse the data, due to doubts about the suitability of using Internet search engines for creating data sets. It was anticipated that the stability of results could not be guaranteed, as the behaviour of search engines lacked transparency. As discussed in this chapter, the algorithms behind search engines such as Google are invariably shrouded in secrecy (Thelwall, 2001: 12). The top 25 results could vary from one day to another, due to the updating frequency of each individual search engine, prompted by the high birth and death rates of websites on the Internet. A second phase of data collection in October 2005 was intended to allow a comparison of the descriptive statistics over a period of a year, but these comparisons were illustrative only and no generalisations could be made based upon them.

Results

Descriptive statistics
The study found that more results were generated by searches conducted using 'Irish Republican' than 'Ulster Loyalist' (Table 4.1). As expected, the DMOZ search engine produced the smallest number of search results, although these appeared more stable, as there was minimal deviation between the two phases of data collection, particularly in the 'Irish Republican' keyword search. The other descriptive statistics appeared to illustrate the problem of stability in using search engines to construct data sets. There were some notable differences in the number of search results returned by the other three search engines. For example, the mean score for the number of results generated by the 'Ulster Loyalist' search rose from 32611.8 to 216930.8 between the two phases of data collection.

Searches conducted using terrorist group names also cast doubt over the stability of results generated by search engines. The DMOZ search engine again produced the least number of links in response to searches conducted using the names of Northern Irish terrorist groups. Searches conducted using names such as the Continuity Army Council generated no links on the DMOZ search engine (Table 4.2). Similar to the ideological descriptions, the mean scores across all four search engines for

Table 4.1 Results generated by words 'Irish Republican' and 'Ulster Loyalist'

Group name	DMOZ		Google		MSN		Yahoo		Mean	
	2004	2005	2004	2005	2004	Period	2004	2005	2004	2005
Irish Republican	50	46	404000	3930000	160883	384124	867000	5040000	357983.3	2338542.5
Ulster Loyalist	20	12	34200	290000	13127	59711	83100	518000	32611.9	216930.8

Table 4.2 Results for searches conducted using Republican group names

Group name	DMOZ		Google		MSN		Yahoo		Mean	
	2004	2005	2004	2005	2004	2005	2004	2005	2004	2005
Continuity Army Council	0	0	105000	1780000	25413	188702	144000	751000	68603.25	679925.50
Cumann na mBan	0	0	1860	137	405	3648	383	2180	662.00	1491.25
Fianna na hEireann	0	0	640	9600	570	5434	1690	18900	725.00	6243.50
Irish National Liberation Army	1	1	59200	1430000	25696	136722	146000	807000	57724.25	593430.75
Irish Peoples Liberation Organisation	0	0	12900	724000	8898	111000	51100	35371	18224.50	217592.75
Irish Republican Army	0	16	148000	2300000	66197	214159	366000	2430000	145049.30	1236043.75
Saor Eire	0	0	592	13000	280	4215	507	1510	344.75	4681.25

Republican group names varied greatly between the two phases of data collection. For example, searches conducted using 'Saor Eire' produced mean scores of 344.75 and 4681.25 in phases one and two respectively.

Searches conducted using Loyalist terrorist group names generated a larger number of links than those using Republican names (see Table 4.3). The search conducted using 'Orange Volunteers' received the highest mean score in both phases of data collection. However, searches conducted using Loyalist terrorist group names also showed wide variations between the two periods of data collection. For example, searches conducted using 'Ulster Freedom Fighters' produced mean scores of 8655.25 and 52864.75 in the two phases.

Analysis of search engine results using website categories

Irish Republican

The analysis of the websites types for the links generated by the ideological descriptions suggested that Republican political fronts were more visible on search engines compared to their Loyalist counterparts. For example, while the IRSP featured prominently in the Republican search engines results, the UPRG was conspicuous by its absence from the Loyalist results. Overall, the majority of links generated by the 'Irish Republican' search pointed towards 'pro-Republican' websites (Table 4.4). There was a high degree of convergence between the four search engines in terms of the results generated by this query. For example, all four search engines provided links pointing towards the Ireland's Own website (www.irelandsown.net). Furthermore, the majority of websites generated by this search query could be characterised as either 'pro-Republican' or 'more of the same' organisational websites, all of which provided analysis of Republican terrorist groups. A low percentage of links generated by the four search engines pointed towards websites that offered no political analysis of the Northern Irish conflict. In addition, there were no Loyalist websites visible in the results generated by the 'Irish Republican' query.

Ulster Loyalist

The majority of links generated by the 'Ulster Loyalist' search pointed towards websites that were supportive of Loyalist terrorist organisations (Table 4.5). Loyalist solidarity websites, such as Swansea Loyal (www.swansealoyal.co.uk), featured prominently in the results generated by all four search engines. The study also found that there were no Republican websites visible in the results generated by the 'Ulster Loyalist' search query. In addition, a significant number of links pointed

Table 4.3   Results for searches conducted using Loyalist group names

Group name	DMOZ		Google		MSN		Yahoo		Mean	
	2004	2005	2004	2005	2004	Period	2004	2005	2004	2005
Loyalist Volunteer Force	0	0	13800	148000	5801	29292	33400	195000	13250.25	93073.00
Orange Volunteers	0	4	328000	5010000	154339	816841	857000	4790000	334834.80	2654211.30
Red Hand Commandos	0	1	53100	1790000	22157	130969	158000	732000	58314.25	663242.50
Red Hand Defenders	0	1	130000	1600000	71007	365944	398000	2100000	149741.80	1016486.25
Ulster Defence Association	0	3	48700	423000	9371	53011	58700	307000	29192.75	195753.50
Ulster Freedom Fighters	0	0	7920	92300	3401	17159	23300	102000	8655.25	52864.75
Ulster Volunteer Force	4	1	18200	222000	7711	43526	50800	241000	19178.75	126631.75

Table 4.4 'Irish Republican' search results by website category

Category	DMOZ (%)		Google (%)		MSN (%)		Yahoo (%)	
	2004	2005	2004	2005	2004	2005	2004	2005
Official Republican organisation	32	24	36	20	16	12	52	32
Republican solidarity website	24	32	28	24	24	24	12	44
Personal webpage/ blog	20	16	4	12	20	0	4	0
Research institute/ university	4	8	20	32	8	20	16	16
External news media	12	16	4	8	8	16	0	40
Loyalist	0	0	0	0	0	0	0	0
Government	0	0	0	0	4	8	0	0
Other	8	4	8	4	20	20	16	4
TOTAL	100	100	100	100	100	100	100	100

towards the websites of actors that appeared to have no direct affiliation with Loyalist terrorists. For example, the personal web page of Philip Johnston (www.philipjohnston.com) featured prominently in the study, presumably because of one article he had published on his website that referred to the Northern Irish conflict. Overall, the study suggested that Internet users would be more likely to reach 'pro-Republican' websites than 'pro-Loyalist' websites if they used ideological descriptions as search terms.

Irish Republican Army

Searches conducted using the 'Irish Republican Army' search query generated fewer links to 'pro-Republican' websites than those conducted using the ideological description 'Irish Republican' (Table 4.6). However, the percentage of 'official' terrorist organisation websites generated by the search query was distorted by a very small DMOZ sample. As expected, the DMOZ search engine returned fewer links than the other Internet search engines, the 'Irish Republican Army' search generating a maximum of 16 links in both phases of data collection. Nevertheless, few links generated by the other search engines

Table 4.5 'Ulster Loyalist' search results by website category

Category	DMOZ (%)		Google (%)		MSN (%)		Yahoo (%)	
	2004	2005	2004	2005	2004	2005	2004	2005
Official Loyalist organisation	5	0	0	0	4	0	0	0
Loyalist solidarity website	50	58.3	36	12	48	36	48	36
Personal webpage/ blog	0	0	0	8	0	0	0	0
Research institute/ university	0	0	8	40	8	12	12	16
External news media	0	0	4	8	12	8	16	8
Republican	0	0	0	0	0	0	0	0
Government	0	0	0	0	0	0	0	0
Other	45	41.7	52	32	28	44	24	40
TOTAL	100	100	100	100	100	100	100	100

pointed towards the websites of Republican political fronts such as Sinn Fein (www.sinnfein.ie). For example, the Google search engine sample did not provide any links to official Republican organisations during both phases of data collection.

Republican solidarity websites such as the Irish Republican Movement were slightly more visible in these search results than Republican political fronts. Contrary to the initial hypothesis, the majority of links generated by DMOZ did not point towards websites that were 'pro-Republican'. The DMOZ search engine was more likely to provide links pointing towards the websites of external media organisations, such as the British Broadcasting Corporation (www.bbc.co.uk), than those of 'pro-Republican' actors. Overall, the majority of links within each search engine sample pointed towards the websites of research institutes, or those that offered no political analysis of Northern Irish terrorist groups. For example, the MSN search engine generated links to websites such as Anagram Genius (www.anagramgenius.com) in response to this search. Furthermore, Loyalists received greater representation on the results generated by this search in comparison to the results generated by the 'Irish Republican' search. Both the MSN and

Table 4.6 'Irish Republican Army' search results by website category

Category	DMOZ (%)		Google (%)		MSN (%)		Yahoo (%)	
	2004	2005	2004	2005		2004	2005	2004
Official Republican organisation	0	18.75	0	0	8	4	8	8
Republican solidarity website	0	12.50	12	8	24	12	12	12
Personal webpage/ blog	0	0	4	0	12	0	4	0
Research institute/ university	0	56.25	40	68	12	48	28	60
External news media	0	12.50	0	8	16	8	8	4
Loyalist	0	0	0	0	12	0	0	4
Government	0	0	0	0	0	12	4	0
Other	0	0	44	16	16	16	36	12
TOTAL	N/A	100	100	100	100	100	100	100

Yahoo search engines pointed Internet users seeking information on the IRA towards Loyalist solidarity websites.

Ulster Volunteer Force

Searches conducted using the 'Ulster Volunteer Force' query generated fewer links to the websites of Loyalist political fronts than the 'Ulster Loyalist' search (Table 4.7). Only the DMOZ search engine generated a link that pointed towards an official Loyalist organisation, namely the website of the PUP (www.pup-ni.org.uk). It should be noted that the relatively high percentage of links (25 percent) pointing towards official websites on DMOZ was mainly due to the small number of weblinks (four) generated by this search. However, this search did generate a larger number of links pointing towards Loyalist solidarity websites, as compared to the number of Republican solidarity websites generated by the 'Irish Republican Army' search. Reflecting the wider trend, a large percentage of links generated by this search query pointed towards websites that offered no political analysis of contemporary Northern Irish terrorism, such as the UVF Regimental Band website (www.uvfregimentalband.co.uk). There was some evidence to support

Table 4.7 'Ulster Volunteer Force' search results by website category

Category	DMOZ (%)		Google (%)		MSN (%)		Yahoo (%)	
	2004	2005	2004	2005		2004	2005	2004
Official Loyalist organisation	25	0	0	0	0	0	0	0
Loyalist solidarity website	75	100	16	8	24	24	32	20
Personal webpage/ blog	0	0	0	4	8	4	12	4
Research institute/ university	0	0	28	56	8	24	16	36
External news media	0	0	8	12	12	4	8	4
Republican	0	0	0	0	0	0	0	4
Government	0	0	0	0	4	4	0	0
Other	0	0	48	20	44	40	32	32
TOTAL	100	100	100	100	100	100	100	100

the hypothesis that the DMOZ engine would generate a larger proportion of links to sites that dealt explicitly with Northern Irish terrorism. As expected, the DMOZ search engine generated fewer links than the other search engines under analysis, generating a maximum of four links in response to this query over both periods of data collection. However, the study found that all of the links generated by the DMOZ search engine pointed towards either the websites of Loyalist political fronts, or those maintained by their supporters.

Discussion

Do search engines limit the audience for Northern Irish terrorists online?
The results of the study provided some evidence to support the hypothesis that 'more of the same' organisational websites are more visible on Internet search engines than 'controversy-revealing' websites. Internet search engines direct Internet users towards the websites of media organisations and universities, as opposed to the websites of Loyalist and Republican political fronts. These 'more of the same' organisations appear to be more visible on Internet search engines by virtue of the

amount of web traffic that passes through their websites, and, in some instances, due to their prior purchase of priority retrieval. Furthermore, 'more of the same' organisational websites are more likely to adhere to a set of informal rules that guarantee a high search-engine rating for a website. Companies like Softsteel Solutions recommend that webmasters remove page redirects and place key information about the website towards the top of the page in order to secure a high search-engine ranking (Softsteel Solutions, 2003). The webmasters of 'organisational' websites are likely to possess the resources to hire companies to design their websites in order to maximise their search-engine rating.

The prospect of government sanctions against search engines is likely to lead them to offer priority retrieval to actors who have no tangible link to these terrorist organisations. National governments can also pressure search engines to remove terrorist websites from their directories altogether, citing a perceived threat to national security as their justification for such censorship. There is already some evidence to suggest that nation-states are pressuring search engines to remove 'pro-terrorist' websites from their directories. In March 2005 Google was forced to remove an advertisement placed by the Palestinian terrorist group Hamas from its search engine, following a barrage of criticism from the international media and diplomatic pressure from the US and Israeli governments (Intelligence and Terrorism Information Center, 2005). These factors would appear to militate against official Loyalist and Republican terrorist organisations appearing in the top 25 results of Internet search engine results, particularly in response to searches conducted using the names of proscribed terrorist groups. The audience for these groups may therefore be limited to those who already were familiar with the URLs of their official websites.

Yet the evidence presented in this book so far suggests that it may be impossible for nation-states to remove all pro-terrorist content from the Web. Soft power relies upon 'the appeal of one's ideas or culture', as opposed to the activities of one particular actor (Keohane and Nye, 1998: 86). Diverse groups such as political parties and private individuals may project the ideology of the terrorist actor. As we have seen in this research, the websites of solidarity actors may be used to generate soft power on behalf of a terrorist organisation. These websites comply with the norms of acceptable behaviour online, as their webmasters do not encourage acts of terrorism nor provide material support for pro-scribed paramilitary organisations. In theory, these are all sources of soft power for Loyalist and Republican terrorists that have only limited access to the conventional media. However, the extent of terrorist soft power still depends upon the attractiveness of their political ideologies, and the accessibility of websites that transmit propaganda in their favour. The analysis presented in this chapter suggests that these actors are likely to be 'preaching to the converted' on the Web. Only Internet users who are familiar with these actors in the offline world will use the correct search terms that reveal the location of their websites on Internet search engines. Those users who do not know the correct search terms are likely to be directed towards the websites of media organisations and research institutes.

Have Internet users lost interest in Northern Irish terrorists?
Loyalist and Republican websites may lack visibility on search engines because they receive fewer visitors than the websites of media organisations. The volume of traffic that goes through a website is one of the factors that determine its ranking on search engines. Terrorist atrocities often lead to increased web traffic, as people search for information about the perpetrators online. For example, an estimated 36 million Internet users in the United States went online looking for news in the first two days after the attacks on New York and Washington on 11 September 2001 (Pew Internet and American Life Project, 2001: 3). This temporarily increased the online audience for radical Islamists online, as people used search engines to look for information on what had motivated the perpetrators.

Contextual factors might also explain why people are less inclined to search for information on Northern Irish terrorists online. The political process in Northern Ireland had stagnated during the period of data collection, as the British and Irish governments sought to restore devolution to the province. Nevertheless, paramilitaries on both sides continued to declare publicly their support for the peace process and did not renew their 'armed struggle' to achieve their objectives. It could be argued that these groups were not as newsworthy as other 'active' international terrorist organisations, such as Al Qaida, during the period of the study. It is also reasonable to speculate that the number of people using search engines to follow news stories involving Loyalists and Republicans declined during this period. As such, the volume of traffic through Loyalist and Republican websites would decrease, leading to a lower profile on search engines in comparison to more popular media websites. This suggests that global search patterns, as well as the number of links available on their websites, may limit the audience for these groups. Future research should consider how global search patterns influence the visibility of websites on Internet search engines. This research might use innovative research tools that were not available during the study, such as Google Trends (www.google.com/intl/

en/trends). Google Trends enables Internet users to view the fastest-growing search queries around the globe. This would enable researchers to determine whether terrorist atrocities lead to a rapid increase in the number of search queries about their perpetrators.

Terrorist framing and search engine visibility
Loyalists and Republicans may not wish to appear visible on search engines when Internet users look for information on their respective terrorist organisations. Many of these groups have pursued their political objectives through their political representatives since the Belfast Agreement (1998). Parties such as Sinn Fein use their websites to differentiate themselves from their terrorist sponsors. The content of political front websites is virtually indistinguishable from the content posted on the websites of constitutional political parties (see Chapter 2). Therefore, some Loyalist and Republican organisations are unlikely to maintain a website under the guise of their military organisation, as this would cast doubt upon their long-term commitment to the peace process. These groups might not wish to attract an online audience that is looking for information on their military activities.

Yet, low search-engine visibility does not guarantee that Internet users will differentiate political fronts from terrorist organisations. People who look for information on the Troubles include not just those who rely upon search engines to direct them towards relevant websites but also those who are familiar with the actors involved in the Northern Irish conflict. Internet users with prior knowledge of Northern Irish terrorist groups will be able to locate their official websites by altering the search terms they use on search engines. Knowledge of the link between political front and terrorist organisation will lead many Internet users to use different search terms than those employed in the study. Conversely, people who rely upon search engines will be directed towards the most visible websites, such as those of media organisations and universities. These Internet users are still likely to be made aware of the links between political fronts and terrorist organisations. The websites of media organisations are likely to provide information on the links between political fronts and their terrorist sponsors, as well as providing links to their websites. This suggests that the online framing of Loyalists and Republicans may have limited effect upon people who use search engines as research tools. Irrespective of their background knowledge, people who use search engines to research the Northern Irish conflict will be able to view the links between political fronts and their respective terrorist organisations.

Dissident terrorists may not wish people to visit their websites if they have no link to their respective organisations. A higher profile on Internet search engines will inevitably lead to increased scrutiny of the group's covert activities by intelligence agencies and the potential closure of the site by national governments. Weimann (2004) suggests that terrorists might use the Web for a number of covert purposes, like data mining and providing tutorials on sabotaging computer networks (p. 7). Consequently, dissidents on both sides might seek to avoid a higher degree of exposure on Internet search engines. Many of these groups have continued to perpetrate acts of political violence since the signing of the Good Friday Agreement in April 1998. Dissident Republican groups, such as the 32CSM, use their websites to justify political violence and to make thinly veiled threats against supporters of the Belfast Agreement (see Chapter 2). In addition, most of the Loyalist terrorist organisations that initially supported the Good Friday Agreement have been 'specified' as 'active' terrorist organisations at one point or another since 1998. There is already some evidence to suggest that these groups use ICTs to plan and perpetrate atrocities in the 'offline' world. Groups such as the UFF have used the websites of solidarity actors to select potential targets.[8] For groups who use the web covertly to support their military operations, a high degree of visibility on search engines might prove a hindrance.

Conclusion

The online audience for Loyalists and Republicans consists primarily of Internet users who use the web for political research and supporters of these groups. While there is some evidence to suggest that the digital divide is narrowing, this audience is still likely to be male, middle class, well educated and situated in Europe or North America. People without links to Northern Irish terrorists may use search engines to locate information about the Northern Irish conflict online. The analysis presented in this chapter suggests that search engines can also be characterised as 'gatekeepers', albeit without the ability to shape the content of websites before it reaches Internet users. Internet search engines direct this audience towards 'more of the same' organisational websites rather than 'pro-Loyalist' or 'pro-Republican' websites. The rule of Googlearchy and the sale of priority retrieval militate against a high search-engine ranking for websites that express support for these terrorists. However, this might actually benefit groups who wish audiences to differentiate their political fronts from the atrocities of their military wings. Internet users with limited knowledge about the Northern Irish conflict may accept the framing of pro-Agreement groups such as Sinn Fein if their websites are not visible on these search results. However, media organisations – often the most visible websites on search engine results – may still direct people with limited knowledge about the Northern Irish conflict towards the websites of Loyalist and Republican political fronts. Thus, search engines enable a 'mediated interaction' between terrorist-linked groups and a potential global audience online. This may not be to the detriment of a dissident terrorist organisation. Low visibility on search engines may prove beneficial to dissident Republicans who are still engaged in 'armed struggle', such as the 32CSM. These groups may not wish to attract a large audience online for fear of compromising future military operations and the security of their members. Overall, the analysis suggests that the online audience for Northern Irish terrorists may fluctuate in response to events in the offline world. As these political fronts have committed to the peace process, they have arguably become less newsworthy. Internet users are more likely to use the Web to follow breaking news stories than to look up information on Northern Irish terrorists, many of whom have declared a cessation to their military activities.

Notes

1 Dutton, W.H., Helsper, E.J. and Gerber, M.M. 2009. *The Internet in Britain 2009*. Oxford: Oxford Internet Institute.
2 The relationship between social capital and ICTs will be discussed in greater detail in the next chapter.
3 Lasar, M. 2009. 'The Internet has not transformed civic engagement . . . yet'.
4 See Siebert, F.S., Peterson, T. and Schramm, W. 1963. *Four Theories of the Press*. Chicago: University of Illinois Press.
5 Falun Gong, a movement dedicated to a series of meditation exercises, was banned in July 1999 in the People's Republic of China. An estimated 70 million people in the country are thought to engage in these exercises. The censorship of the movement has been criticised by Western NGOs such as Amnesty International.
6 In February 2007, searches were conducted for information about Falun Gong using Google portals.
7 Sullivan, D. 2005. 'Share of Searches: July 2005'. www.searchenginewatch.com/reports/article.php/2156451 (accessed 20 October 2005).
8 *Belfast Telegraph*. 2001. 'New Internet Terror Fear: Loyalists are Using Web to Pick Targets'. (15 March).

5

Competing victimhoods? The websites of Northern Irish residents' groups

Introduction

Chadwick (2006) asserts that the Internet may help to bridge political divides between 'areas of a city informally segregated along ethnic or religious lines' (p. 107). This chapter will assess the 'dialogic' potential of ICTs through the lens of residents' groups in Northern Ireland. Authors as far back as Giddens (1995) have argued that an independent arena is necessary in order to facilitate a 'positive spiral of communication' between interface communities in Northern Ireland (p. 16). Cyber enthusiasts argue that the Internet has the potential to create a Habermasian public sphere that 'liberates' people from their real-world identities and locations. This chapter will focus on whether the Internet is being used by residents' groups to foster better community relations across sectarian interfaces. An interface is defined here as a 'conjunction or intersection of two or more territories or social spaces which are dominated, contested, or claimed by some or all members of the differing ethno-national groups' (Jarman, 2004: 8). Interface areas have suffered disproportionate levels of political violence since the outbreak of the Troubles in the late 1960s. Website functionality and online framing will be examined in order to test Chadwick's hypothesis that the Internet may generate bridging social capital between rival interface communities. In doing so, the analysis will provide further insight into the potential of the Internet as a tool to integrate marginal groups within ethnically divided societies. The chapter will conclude by considering whether community activists themselves believe that the Internet can help to manage relationships between rival interface communities. The analysis suggests that residents' groups on both sides use their websites to further their 'competition' of victimhoods. There is no evidence on the websites of residents' groups to suggest they are using their websites to promote better community relations in interface areas. However, these websites might be better understood as a manifestation of the sectarian violence that blighted these interface communities between 1996 and 2003.

Community relations in Northern Ireland: benign apartheid?

In order to analyse how ICTs may be used to help manage interface relationships, one must first develop an understanding of the nature of inter-community relations in and around sectarian interfaces today. Community activists assert that the term 'community relations' is better understood as 'cross-community' relations in the context of Northern Ireland (Hall, 2001: 5). In Northern Ireland, the majority of people choose to live in politically and religiously homogeneous areas that do not include members of the 'other' community. In the words of a resident of the Fountain enclave in Londonderry, people feel 'safe and secure within the [interface] area especially with the walls and barricades' (Templegrove Action Research Ltd, 1996: 29). A form of 'benign apartheid' has developed in Northern Ireland since the mid-1990s (O'Connor, 1993: 195). The Good Friday Agreement promoted multiple layers of identity and representation, allowing Catholics to identify themselves as Irish while their Protestant neighbours could identify themselves as British (Williams and Jesse, 2001: 571). Societal cleavages were to be recognised, and even encouraged, through the 'single identity' community development projects that followed the Belfast Agreement. This has entrenched divisions between Northern Ireland's two communities, with some commentators claiming that the province can now be divided into two separate Unionist and Nationalist polities (Farry, 2004).

This 'benign apartheid' is evident in the attitudes held by Protestant and Catholics towards each other. The early 1990s had seen increasing numbers of people from both communities express a preference for mixing with members of the 'other' community. The early indications are that the Good Friday Agreement has reversed this trend. Evidence from the Northern Ireland Life and Times Survey (ARK, 2004) suggests that the two communities have become more 'isolationist' since 1998. For example, the total number of respondents wishing to live in mixed-religion neighbourhoods fell from 82 percent in 1996 to 73 percent in 1999. The Protestant community has seen the biggest shift in attitudes towards the 'other' community. A higher proportion of Protestants (26 percent) than Catholics (18 percent) said that they would prefer to live in neighbourhoods with only their own religion (Hughes and Donnelly, 2001). This reflects the widely held perception amongst the Protestant community that the Catholic community has been the prime beneficiary of the Good Friday Agreement (Hughes and Donnelly, 2004: 573). Hayes and McAllister (2009) found that Northern Ireland has become increasingly divided along religious lines since 1998, particularly amongst young people. However, a recent study has suggested that the social identities adopted by the two communities in Northern Ireland may be more permeable now than at any time during the Troubles (Muldoon et al, 2008). The study found that 23 percent of Catholics and 26 percent of Protestants identified themselves as Northern Irish, over other options that included British and Irish, representing an increase over previous studies.

The erection of physical barriers appears to have amplified the siege mentality of many interface communities. Shirlow (2003) asserts that these 'peacelines' appoint the 'opposing community as a menacing spatial formation' (p. 81). Common interests do not transcend ethno-political identities of communities situated in or around sectarian interfaces. A survey of adults in the Ardoyne and Glenbryn districts of North Belfast illustrates the low levels of cross-community interaction across these 'peacelines'.[1] Only 20 percent of the Glenbryn residents surveyed used shopping facilities situated in the Ardoyne, while 18 percent of the Ardoyne residents used the nearest sports complex, situated in the Glenbryn district (Shirlow, 2003: 81). Both Catholic and Protestant residents cited the fear of attack as the primary reason for their low level of interaction with the 'other' community (p. 85). Protestant residents believe that an 'expansionist' Catholic community is trying to force them out of areas like North Belfast. The Protestant community perceives that its areas are turning 'green', as a young Catholic community displaces an ageing, declining Protestant community (Jarman, 2002: 16). The murals in Loyalist interface areas illustrate this 'siege mentality'. Loyalist interface communities are demarcated via red, white and blue kerbstones, the flying of Union Jacks and murals that celebrate Loyalist terrorist groups such as the UVF (Figure 5.1). These 'militaristic' murals invariably depict men in balaclavas brandishing AK47s, alongside provocative political statements such as 'No Surrender'.[2] Loyalist residents invariably resist efforts by the Northern Ireland Housing Executive to allocate houses in their areas to members of the Catholic community. The decision to leave these houses vacant was presumably influenced by the objections of local residents, and the potential conflict that might arise from Protestants and Catholics living in the same district.

There tend to be fewer militaristic murals on the other side of the peace walls. Over the past decade Republican murals have been removed from gable walls situated close to interfaces. Some Republican murals have been left in a state of disrepair (Figure 5.2). However, suspicion still remains about the motivations of their Protestant neighbours. The Protestant community is frequently accused of 'ethnic cleansing' in contested areas like North Belfast. This negative stereotyping is

Figure 5.1 Cluan Place/Short Strand interface, taken from Cluan Place perspective

Figure 5.2 Anti-Orange Order mural situated off Lower Ormeau Road, Belfast

often influenced by people's memories of living under Unionist rule in the 1960s. Many of the Catholic residents in interface areas have vivid memories of being driven out of their homes in the late 1960s, primarily due to the violence of their Protestant neighbours (O'Connor, 1993: 160). Furthermore, the Catholic community also faced discrimination in terms of public housing provision in the late 1960s, as highlighted during the Caledon protest in June 1968.[3] It would be fair to say that a positive cycle of communication in a neutral environment might help to build greater understanding of the common interests that unite rival interface communities in Northern Ireland.

Community relations and new technologies

Increased opportunity for participation
New media technologies might provide an arena in which rival interface communities could simultaneously reduce conflict in and around 'peacelines' and promote better community relations. Recent studies suggest that people who live in and around interfaces feel that nobody represents their interests. For example, one survey found that 59 percent of Protestants who lived in East Belfast felt that they had no say in what happened within their own community (Lewis et al 2008: 5). Both Loyalist and Republican residents' groups often claim that they have no real voice in the conventional mass media. When one considers the lack of inter-community contact across sectarian interfaces, this gap between political representatives and their constituents may make it even more difficult to generate a positive spiral of communication between rival interface communities. While political leaders on both sides of the sectarian divide may be able to discuss common interests that affect their areas, they may not be speaking for the vast majority of their respective communities. Authors such as Bennett (2003) and Chadwick (2006) suggest that the Internet may help to narrow the gap between established political institutions and interface residents who perceive that they lack political representation.

According to authors such as Spears and Lea (1994) and Norris (2000), the Internet has the potential to increase opportunities for political participation amongst groups and individuals who feel they lack political representation, such as people who live in close proximity to interfaces. It lowers the threshold for individuals and groups to participate in politics, allowing for a new form of issue-led mobilisation. Agre (2002) suggests that ICTs have the potential to both accelerate and amplify many of the information flows that circulate round the political process (p. 317). While the 'peacelines' might appoint the other community as a menacing spatial formation in the offline world, the Internet might enable rapid low-cost communication between rival residents' groups. Residents' groups would be able to choose their own frames, free from the ideological refraction of the mass media. This would allow community activists on both sides to direct members of their community away from potential flashpoints across the sectarian interface. While it would be too simplistic to argue that increased information flows will alleviate tensions around sectarian interfaces, 'digital' empowerment might help to generate the inter-community contact necessary to reduce tensions between the Loyalist and Republican interface communities. Grass-roots community organisations on both sides might be better placed to engage in a positive cycle of communication with one another than their elected political representatives. This was evident in a recent study of residents in North Belfast, which found that just under half of the respondents felt that they should be left alone to improve things in their own areas (Lewis et al, 2008: 17).

The public sphere and rational discourse
Cyberoptimists also argue that the Internet has the potential to enrich the democratic process through the creation of a public sphere of rational-critical citizen discourse (Dahlberg, 2001: 616). They argue that the Internet provides communicative spaces that permit not only the circulation of information and ideas, but also the formation of political will amongst subcultures (Dahlgren, 2005: 148). In this public sphere people would be encouraged to listen to other views and critically reflect upon their own opinions on a variety of issues (see Froomkin, 2003). Authors such as Giddens (1995) believe that a Habermasian public sphere might provide a context in which residents' groups in Northern Ireland could address the causes of inter-communal violence. However, there are a number of caveats that must be applied to the cyberoptimist conception of the Internet as a public sphere. Firstly, despite its inherent potential for democratising the publication of opinions, power relations are built into communicative situations online (Dahlgren, 2005: 154). People are still likely to turn to the most popular websites when looking for information online, leading to discourse being dominated by certain groups. Secondly, the Internet cannot create a community if there are no pre-existing common interests in the offline world (Baker and Ward, 2002: 211). People are only motivated to join virtual communities if they reflect their own private interests. This may militate against minority groups who seek to engage larger audiences via their websites. Thirdly, there is little evidence to support the notion that reflectivity is common in online discussions.

People do not tend to listen respectfully to the opinions of others on the Internet. Brandenburg (2006) suggests that the Internet promotes 'selectiveness, escapism, insulation and rational ignorance' rather than the rational discourse envisaged in the Habermasian public sphere (p. 218). Moreover, authors such as Sunstein (2007) and Dahlberg (2001) argue that the Internet promotes only very weak forms of participation, due to the exclusive nature of virtual communities. Thus, the Internet may facilitate the creation of 'islands of political communication' rather than the egalitarian public sphere envisaged in the cyberoptimist model (Dahlgren, 2005: 152).

Social capital and community formation
Cyberoptimists also suggest that the Internet can fill the gap left by the decline in real-world communities (see Wellman et al, 2003). They believe that the Internet undermines the effects of distance on community formation and lowers the threshold for people to participate in collective action (see Rheingold, 1993; Bimber, 1998; Postmes and Brunsting, 2002). The Internet is considered to be a potential agent of social capital within divided societies such as Northern Ireland. Social capital refers to the 'institutions, relationships, and norms that shape the quality and quantity of a society's social interactions' (Griffiths, 2004: 4). People learn the skills necessary to practise democracy through their participation in civic associations such as local residents' groups. This may take the form of bonding and bridging social capital. Bonding (or network) social capital can be characterised as a form of 'sociological superglue that creates strong in-group loyalty and occasionally strong out-group antagonism' (Putnam, 2000: 23). Both Catholic and Protestant communities in Northern Ireland traditionally demonstrate high levels of bonding social capital, as demonstrated by recent attitudinal studies conducted in interface areas (see Lewis et al, 2008). Conceivably, civil society organisations might use websites to reinforce bonding social capital within their own communities. This would involve using websites to highlight the common interests that bind these communities together.

Perhaps of greater significance to this chapter is the nexus between bridging social capital and ICTs. Bridging social capital refers to the creation of linkages across societal cleavages such as class and ethnicity (see Putnam, 2000). Cyberoptimists contend that the Internet allows people to accentuate common identity in an otherwise heterogeneous group (Postmes and Brunsting, 2002: 295). The lack of bridging social capital between Loyalist and Republican residents' groups makes it more difficult to promote better community relations in and around sectarian interfaces. Cyber enthusiasts believe that the Internet reduces social context 'in or around a message transmitted from sender to receiver' (Spears and Lea, 1994: 431). People who live near sectarian interfaces might feel more empowered to speak up in an online environment rather than risk their personal safety and get involved in a residents' group. However, ICTs might not lead to greater bridging social capital between rival interface communities. As Shah et al (2001) suggest, the relationship between new media and social capital may be 'dynamic and highly contextual' (p. 154). The relative anonymity offered by online communications may actually lead to fragmentation of the public sphere rather than the collective action envisaged by cyberoptimists. This chapter will analyse the relationship between social capital and ICT use through the lens of rival residents' groups in Northern Ireland. It will provide further insight into whether the Internet is capable of fostering a public sphere in which rival residents' groups can both consolidate and deepen inter-community relationships.

Mobile phone networking: an antecedent for wired community relations?
The success of the mobile phone network suggests that computer-mediated communication could help to manage inter-community relationships in interface areas. In the summer of 1997, the Community Development Centre (CDC) piloted a mobile phone network to try to reduce the inter-communal tensions generated by the contentious 'Tour of the North' march in North Belfast. Mobile telephones were distributed to nominated individuals within both Loyalist and Republican communities in North Belfast, including a number of ex-paramilitaries who resided in the area. The phones enabled these individuals to inform their opposite numbers of potential 'flashpoints' when crowds gathered on either side of the interface (Jarman, 2002: 43). Crucially, the CDC acted as an intermediary in the network, allowing communication between groups that refused to speak to one another in the offline world. By 2000, there were similar mobile phone networks in 25 interface areas across Belfast. While the network may have had limited utility in relieving the siege mentality of both communities, it did help to facilitate dialogue between Republican and Loyalist interface communities, many of whom had previously refused to talk to one another. According to Jarman (2005), the CDC mobile phone network demonstrated the potential of using low-cost technology to manage conflict between interface communities in Northern Ireland. There are already some indications that community groups themselves believe that ICTs might help to promote better community relations in interface areas. In its annual report, the North Belfast Community Action Group

(2002) suggested that an extension of broadband cabling networks could provide a means for developing intra- and inter-community dialogue (p. 80). This chapter will provide further insight into the dialogic potential of ICTs through an analysis of the websites of Loyalist and Republican residents' groups.

Interface communities and the Internet

Sample

O'Dochartaigh (2007) found that online discussion forums provided an arena in which Loyalist and Nationalist youths used sectarian language to reproduce the segregated spaces of interface communities in cyberspace. This chapter presents an analysis of the websites of rival residents' groups in February 2005 in order to determine whether they are also being used to reinforce divisions between interface communities. Loyalist and Republican residents' groups were selected with reference to the conclusions of the Belfast Interface Project publication 'A Policy Agenda for the Interface' (O'Halloran, Shirlow and Murtagh, 2004). The names of residents' groups were entered into the British versions of two search engines, Google (www.google.co.uk) and Yahoo (www.yahoo.co.uk), to locate their official websites. The sample (three Loyalist and three Republican) represented the total population of Northern Irish residents' groups available during the period of the study (Table 5.1). It should be noted that the White City and Short Strand websites appeared to be maintained by private individuals who lived in close proximity to these two sectarian interfaces. At the time of writing, there was no evidence to suggest that the people of the Short Strand and White City districts had formed a residents' group in the offline world. While these webmasters may not have constituted a community group as such, their websites were included in the study as they were used to frame the inter-communal problems that blighted their respective interfaces. The study refers to these groups as either Loyalist or Republican, with reference to the rhetoric used on their websites. The

Table 5.1 Loyalist and Republican residents' groups

Loyalist	Republican
Cluan Place	Garvaghy Road Residents' Coalition
Greater Glenbryn Community Initiative	Lower Ormeau Concerned Community
White City Under Attack	Short Strand Under Siege

framing and function of websites maintained by residents' groups was analysed during the study. Interviews with six community workers were also held in April 2009 to analyse whether community groups were using the Internet to foster better community relations in these areas. The interviewees represented a number of umbrella community groups that were affiliated with approximately 100 interface residents' associations across Northern Ireland. The original research design had included interviews with some of the webmasters responsible for the websites. However, these interviews did not take place during the period of data collection, as no response was received from any of the webmasters of the websites under analysis.[4]

Website registration data
Only three of the websites under analysis provided registration details on Nominet.co.uk or Whois.net (see Appendix 3, Table 4). Cluan Place was the only residents' group to register its website with a British company. In a similar vein to Republican solidarity actors, the Garvaghy Road Residents' Coalition registered its website in the United States, with a company called Go Daddy. Meanwhile, the Greater Glenbryn Community Initiative website was registered to Schlund, the German host of Loyalist websites such as the British Ulster Alliance. In contrast to Loyalist and Republican solidarity websites, these webmasters did tend to reveal their identities on the Whois and Nominet websites. For example, the webmaster responsible for the Cluan Place website provided both his name and a full postal address for Internet users to contact the organisation. Meanwhile, a contact was given for the Garvaghy Road Residents' Coalition on its Whois entry. As these websites were registered in Europe or North America, it was anticipated that their webmasters would self-regulate to comply with the norms of acceptable behaviour online. It should be noted that the Short Strand Under Siege website was the only one that was still accessible in November 2009. A Cluan Place Bebo profile was available, although there was no evidence to suggest that it had been created by the webmaster responsible for the original website.

Research design: online framing
The study was designed to test whether Loyalist and Republican residents' groups would use their respective websites to communicate more effectively with their counterparts on the other side of the 'peaceline'. Online framing was analysed by examining the discourse and images used by these groups on their websites. Despite having many common problems such as high levels social deprivation, rival residents' groups

tend to blame one another for inter-communal tensions at sectarian interfaces. The study was designed to determine whether these actors used language on their websites that perpetuated this zero-sum perception of Northern Irish politics. The analysis provided further insight into the debate over whether the Internet has extended the public sphere in Northern Ireland. Cyber enthusiasts suggest that liberating people from their locations might enable a form of rational-critical citizen discourse between rival ethnic groups. Interface communities typically exhibit a strong sense of bonding social capital, due to their shared experience living in a particular area, with little capacity for bridging social capital with their counterparts on the other side of the 'peaceline'. The analysis focused on whether the Internet was a suitable arena for managing relations between rival interface communities in the absence of bridging social capital in these areas.

The widely held perception amongst interface residents that they are unable to influence policy in their own areas has contributed towards the siege mentality of both communities. While it may be unrealistic to expect that rival residents' groups would use the Web to assert their common interests, their websites could help to manage relations between rival interface communities. As was seen with the mobile phone network, the transmission of accurate information between community representatives could help to reduce the level of violence in and around sectarian interfaces. These websites might also facilitate a form of 'megaphone diplomacy' between Loyalist and Republican interface communities. In the absence of open channels of communication between rival interface communities, it is feasible that residents' groups might use their websites to present information to the media in newsworthy formats. This would facilitate communication with community representatives who lived on the other side of the 'peaceline', in a similar vein to the interaction between Sinn Fein and the UK government during the mid-1990s.

Website function
The study also assessed the extent to which Loyalist and Republican residents' groups were realising the potential of the Internet as a vehicle for their group objectives. It tested the hypothesis that residents' groups would use their websites to foster bonding social capital rather than promote better community relations with members of the 'other community'. While cyber enthusiasts argue that the Internet has the capacity to generate bridging social capital in divided societies, it was considered highly unlikely that interface communities who felt that they had not benefited from the peace process would adopt a

conciliatory tone on their websites towards their counterparts situated across the 'peaceline'. In order to analyse what function these websites fulfilled for their respective organisations, each website was scored with reference to the coding scheme developed earlier in this book (see Chapter 1). This allowed a direct comparison between the websites of residents' groups and those maintained by other Northern Irish societal groups, such as solidarity actors and political parties. A point was given to a website if it included one of the features identified in the coding scheme. These points were then compiled to give an overall score in two categories that measured website function, namely interactivity, and organisational linkage. It was anticipated that the Loyalist websites analysed in the study would reciprocate links with one another, as all three groups were based in Belfast. Loyalist residents in Glenbryn and White City, separated by just a few streets, would presumably have common interests and regular contact with each other in the offline world. Republican residents' groups were also expected to reciprocate links with each other online. In contrast to their Loyalist counterparts, Republicans were expected to provide links to a range of other websites. It was anticipated that these groups would direct Internet users towards the websites of groups that opposed Orange Order demonstrations. This reflected the primary focus of groups such as the Lower Ormeau Concerned Community, namely to oppose contentious Orange Order demonstrations that passed through Republican areas.

Results

Online framing

Victimhood

Roe, Pegg, Hodges and Trimm (1999) assert that there are 'competing psychologies of victimhood' between Northern Ireland's Protestant and Catholic communities (p. 125). This is particularly evident amongst inter-face communities that have suffered disproportionate levels of violence during the Northern Irish conflict. Both sides claim that the media favour the other community over their own interests. The study suggested that the Internet perpetuates this competition rather than promoting better community relations. In a similar vein to the O'Dochartaigh (2007) study of three websites associated with the Whitewell area in Belfast, these residents' groups used their websites to suggest that they had suffered at the hands of the 'other' community. Consequently, the term 'ethnic cleansing' featured on all of the websites under analysis. For example, the Short Strand Under Siege website featured a 'diary of attacks', which alleged that Loyalists from nearby Cluan Place were attacking residents on a daily basis between May and June 1998.[5] The website repeated the threats that were posted on the walls of nearby Loyalist areas, such as 'Short Strand taigs enter at your own risk.'[6] The websites of the Lower Ormeau Concerned Community and the Garvaghy Road Residents' Coalition focused upon contentious Orange Order demonstrations in their districts, highlighting alleged human rights abuses against their communities. These residents' groups also portrayed Catholics as second-class citizens on their websites. Invariably, they alleged that the Orange Order, the Police Service of Northern Ireland (PSNI) and the institutions of the 'Orange' state suppressed their rights. For example, the Garvaghy Road Residents' Coalition declared on its homepage 'the residents continue to stand strong and struggle for their right to equality, freedom from sectarian discrimination and harassment'.[7] This resonated with the material posted on the website of the Lower Ormeau Concerned Community. The Lower Ormeau Concerned Community webmaster discussed the problems caused by 'sectarian' parades in the area, including 'curfews for up to 25 hours, plastic bullets and beatings'.[8]

Loyalist residents' groups also used their websites to focus upon alleged 'ethnic cleansing' within their areas. Republicans were accused of intimidating local residents within Loyalist interface areas. For example, the Cluan Place residents' group declared on its website, 'Republicans are trying to ethnically cleanse the area. THEY WILL NOT SUCCEED!'[9] This website also featured an article written by the local MP, Peter Robinson, which described the 'daily nightmare of living with orchestrated Sinn Fein/PIRA violence'.[10] This article dismissed the material posted on the Short Strand Under Siege website as Republican 'spin'. The other websites featured accounts of alleged Republican intimidation against members of the local community. The White City Under Attack webmaster claimed that Republicans were responsible for graffiti sprayed on derelict houses in the area, questioning why the offenders had not been caught on CCTV situated nearby.[11] In a similar vein to the Short Strand website, the website provided a chronology of alleged Republican attacks in the area. The Greater Glenbryn Community Initiative also highlighted vandalism on its website. The webmaster responsible for this website was scathing in his criticism of the PSNI, claiming 'thugs are perfectly free to enter Glenbryn at will, do whatever damage they please, with absolutely no response from the muppets in the PSNI'.[12] Overall, these websites did not appear to facilitate a form of megaphone diplomacy between rival interface communities. Both Loyalists and Republicans used their websites to suggest they were victims of ethnic cleansing at sectarian interfaces.

Images

The theme of victimhood was also evident in the images used on the websites of these residents' groups. All of the Republican residents' groups used their websites to publish pictures of local residents who had allegedly been 'brutalised' by either Loyalists or the PSNI. For example, the Lower Ormeau Concerned Community website featured images of armoured British Army Saracen vehicles 'hemming in' members of the Catholic community as an Orange Order parade passed through the area.[13] Similar images featured on the website of the Garvaghy Road Residents Coalition. The first page of the Garvaghy Road Residents Coalition website featured an image of a woman comforting a man with an open head wound. As if to confirm that Northern Irish Catholics are an oppressed minority, the man in the picture is wearing a Glasgow Celtic football jersey.[14] The Short Strand Under Siege website also alleged that the PSNI had 'brutalised' the Catholic community. This website featured images of local residents displaying injuries attributed to PSNI attacks on a peace rally in the Short Strand. A 14-year-old boy appeared in one of these images displaying a scar (the site alleges was) caused by a PSNI plastic baton round.[15]

Each of the Loyalist websites under analysis contained pictures of property allegedly vandalised by 'Republican thugs'. For example, a picture of a row of vandalised derelict houses welcomed visitors to the White City Under Attack website. The slogan beneath these stark images read, 'Who lives in houses like these? NOBODY!'[16] The homepage of the Greater Glenbryn Community Initiative also drew attention to Republican attacks on Loyalist residents. The menu at the top of the screen featured images of boarded-up houses, PSNI armoured vehicles, and members of the Loyalist community displaying injuries, presumably caused by Republicans.[17] This website was notable as it published photographs of Republicans, who the webmaster alleged were involved in a campaign of intimidation against Loyalist residents in North Belfast.[18] In a similar vein to the solidarity actors, the Cluan Place residents used pictures of murals and 'peacelines' on their website. The central image on this homepage was a mural painted on a gable wall at the interface between Cluan Place and Short Strand. This mural contained a Union Jack and the sentence 'Cluan Place – 20 families intimidated by Sinn Fein/IRA'.[19]

Overall, the study provided some evidence to support the notion that there is a competition of victimhood between Loyalist and Republican communities situated at sectarian interfaces. These groups used images and language on their websites that suggested the community situated on the other side of the 'peaceline' was besieging them. The online framing of these groups appeared more likely to strengthen the bonding social capital of their communities, as opposed to generate bridging social capital between rival residents' groups. However, this observation was congruent with previous analyses of social capital. Putnam (2000) suggested that bonding social capital was good for mobilising solidarity in ethnic enclaves, as it provided 'social and psychological support for less fortunate members of the community' (p. 22). While it may not be possible to attribute the high levels of bonding social capital in these areas to these websites, the online strategy of these actors did appear to emphasise the shared victimhood of people who lived in their areas. The study suggested that the online frames adopted by these actors were unlikely to foster better community relations in Northern Ireland.

Self-identification

One of the most notable research findings was that residents' groups did not identify their leadership on their websites. For example, the Garvaghy Road Residents' Coalition described itself as an 'umbrella group set up by the residents of the Catholic/Nationalist Garvaghy Road area of the town of Portadown'.[20] The name of its leader, Brendan MacCionnaith, was conspicuous by its absence from this website. The Lower Ormeau Concerned Community also defined itself as a community group, asserting on its website, 'It was set up solely to campaign for civil rights for our community.'[21] A similar pattern emerged during the analysis of the three Loyalist websites. For example, the Greater Glenbryn Community Initiative issued a disclaimer on its website, in which the webmaster declared that 'no part of this website has been supported either financially or otherwise by ANY companies, funding agencies whether government or private or by any individuals'.[22] In the case of the White City Under Attack website, the civil society credentials of the webmaster were less clear. The homepage merely described itself as the 'official website for White City under attack online'.[23] Yet, irrespective of how they defined themselves, both Loyalist and Republican residents' groups chose not to name their respective leaders on their websites.

Website function

Organisational linkage

Loyalist residents' groups demonstrated a greater range of organisational linkages on their websites than Republican residents' groups. The Cluan Place and Greater Glenbryn Community Initiative achieved

153

Table 5.2 Organisational linkages visible on Loyalist residents' group websites

Website	Solidarity links	International terrorist links	Educational links	Commercial/ non-political links	Number of links >15	Score (/5)
Cluan Place	1	0	1	1	0	3
Greater Glenbryn Community Initiative	1	0	1	1	1	4
White City Under Attack	1	0	0	0	0	1
Mean	1	0	0.67	0.67	0.33	2.33

the highest score in this category of the coding scheme (Table 5.2). These websites tended to provide links pointing towards the websites of external news media organisations, Loyalist solidarity organisations and Northern Irish political parties. For example, the Greater Glenbryn Community Initiative website provided links to such diverse groups as Disability Action, NHS Direct and the Ulster Protestant Movement for Justice.[24] This website was also noteworthy as it was the only one to provide links to the websites of the other Loyalist residents' groups under analysis. The Cluan Place website also provided links pointing towards the websites of external agencies, media organisations such as the *Belfast Telegraph* and the University of Ulster's CAIN.[25] However, there was limited evidence to suggest that these groups were using the Web to mobilise support from groups based outside the United Kingdom. As such, none of the Loyalist websites received a point in the 'International terrorist link' section.

Republicans achieved a lower average score in this category than did their Loyalist counterparts. In contrast to Republican amateurs and political fronts, these groups did not provide a broad range of links on their websites. The links provided by Republican residents' groups tended to reflect the 'single issue' around which these groups formed, namely to oppose Orange Order demonstrations that passed through Republican areas. The Garvaghy Road Residents Coalition shared the highest score in this category (Table 5.3). It provided links to websites maintained by groups involved in the debate over 'sectarian' marches, including the Irish Parades Emergency Committee and Orange Watch.[26]

Table 5.3 Organisational linkages visible on Republican residents' group websites

Website	Solidarity links	International terrorist links	Educational links	Commercial/ non-political links	Number of links >15	Score (/5)
Garvaghy Road Residents Coalition	1	0	0	1	1	3
Lower Ormeau Concerned Community	1	0	0	0	0	1
Short Strand	0	0	0	0	0	0
Mean	0.67	0	0	0.33	0.33	1.33

The Lower Ormeau Concerned Community also used its Web presence to direct Internet users towards websites that addressed the marching issue, such as the Parades Commission for Northern Ireland.[27] Short Strand was the only group under analysis to receive no score in this section, as it provided no links on its website. Overall, the links pages of these websites reflected the single issue around which these groups formed. In a similar vein to the analysis of political fronts and amateur terrorists, there was limited evidence here to suggest that residents' groups were experiencing a critical multiplier effect in terms of organisational linkage.

Interactivity

Republican residents' groups achieved a higher score in this category than did their Loyalist counterparts. The websites of the Lower Ormeau Concerned Community and the Garvaghy Road Residents Coalition contained the largest number of interactive features in the study (Table 5.4). The Lower Ormeau Concerned Community solicited donations from Internet users on its website, providing bank details and a postal address.[28] The Garvaghy Road Residents Coalition provided a similar 'donation' facility on its website. The Friends of Garvaghy Road USA encouraged people living in North America to provide material support for the Garvaghy Road community group.[29] In addition, both these residents' groups provided postal addresses and telephone numbers for

Table 5.4 Interactive features available on Republican residents' group websites

Website	Email newsletter	Bulletin board	Postal address	Telephone/ fax number	Email webmaster	Email individual members	Resource solicitation	Score (/7)
Garvaghy Road Residents Coalition	0	0	1	1	1	0	1	4
Lower Ormeau Concerned Community	0	0	1	1	1	0	1	4
Short Strand	0	0	0	0	1	0	0	1
Mean	0	0	0.67	0.67	1	0	0.67	3

Internet users who wished to contact their respective organisations for further information. However, despite these websites promoting interaction between Internet users and their respective organisations, none of the Republican groups provided details about their leadership online. The Short Strand Under Siege website received the lowest score in this category. It limited interactivity on its website to an 'Email webmaster' facility, and did not provide a postal address for written correspondence.[30]

Loyalist residents' groups provided limited interactivity on their websites (Table 5.5). The White City Under Attack website proved the most interactive of the Loyalist websites analysed in the study, providing an 'Email webmaster' facility and a bulletin board.[31] The other Loyalist residents' groups limited interactivity on their websites to an 'Email webmaster' facility. None of the groups under analysis used their websites to solicit resources from sympathisers. Overall, both Loyalist and Republican residents' groups provided limited opportunity for Internet users to contact their organisations online.

Online recruitment resources

Both Loyalist and Republican residents' groups achieved low scores in this category of the coding scheme. The analysis suggested that Loyalist residents' groups did not use their official web presence to recruit new members (Table 5.6). None of the websites under review included a 'Members only' section. This was perhaps to be expected, given that none of the Loyalist residents' groups under analysis referred to their membership on their website. Both the Cluan Place and White City Under Attack websites did enable Internet users to download propaganda onto their desktops. The Cluan Place website enabled Internet users to download a Cluan Place booklet, which told the 'tale of the trouble' at the sectarian interface.[32] The White City Under Attack website also provided a series of posters for Internet users to display, including one drawing attention to the murder of a local resident.[33]

There was little to differentiate between Loyalists and Republicans in terms of online recruitment resources. Republican residents' groups also received low scores in this category (Table 5.7). None of these groups used online recruitment strategies or provided a 'Members only' section. Yet Republican residents' groups did enable Internet users to download material from their websites in an alternative format. For example, the Garvaghy Road Residents' Coalition website provided a downloadable map of the contentious Orange Order parade, along with a Peace Watch report containing statements from local residents.[34] Overall, residents' groups did not appear to use their official Web presence to draw Internet users into their respective organisations.

Table 5.5 Interactive features available on Loyalist residents' group websites

Website	Email newsletter	Bulletin board	Postal address	Telephone/ fax number	Email webmaster	Email individual members	Resource solicitation	Score (/7)
Cluan Place	0	0	0	0	1	0	0	1
Greater Glenbryn Community Initiative	0	0	0	0	1	0	0	1
White City Under Attack	0	1	0	0	1	0	0	2
Mean	0	0.33	0	0	1	0	0	1.33

Table 5.6 Online recruitment resources of Loyalist residents' group websites

Website	Members only section	Full member- ship advertised	Full member- ship available via online application	Download- able public relations material	Score (/4)
Cluan Place	0	0	0	1	1
Greater Glenbryn Community Initiative	0	0	0	0	0
White City Under Attack	0	0	0	1	1
Mean	0	0	0	0.67	0.67

Table 5.7 Online recruitment resources of Republican residents' group websites

Website	Members only section	Full member- ship advertised	Full member- ship available via online application	Download- able public relations material	Score (/4)
Garvaghy Road Residents Coalition	0	0	0	1	1
Lower Ormeau Concerned Community	0	0	0	0	0
Short Strand	0	0	0	1	1
Mean	0	0	0	0.67	0.67

However, this probably reflected the fact that their membership was limited to people who lived in their respective neighbourhoods.

Presentation

Overall, residents' groups provided little innovation in terms of information delivery online, receiving lower scores than both political parties and solidarity actors in this category. Loyalist residents' group websites achieved a higher score in this category than did their Republican

Table 5.8 Presentation and delivery of Loyalist residents' group websites

Website	Graphics	Frames	Sound	Video streaming	Pages in alternative format e.g. PDF	Score (/5)
Cluan Place	1	0	0	0	0	1
Greater Glenbryn Community Initiative	1	1	1	1	0	4
White City Under Attack	1	0	1	1	0	3
Mean	1	0.33	0.67	0.67	0	2.67

counterparts. The Greater Glenbryn Community Initiative website received the highest score in this section of the coding scheme (Table 5.8). This website contained a section entitled 'Media files', which included a recorded video statement by local DUP MP Nigel Dodds. The website also provided video footage of nationalist 'thugs' attacking young [Protestant] children as they waited to board a school bus.[35] The White City Under Attack also provided video streaming on its website. The documentary film *Victims of Sinn Fein/IRA*, produced by the Ulster Protestant Movement for Justice, was available for free download on its website. In contrast, the Cluan Place website was devoid of multimedia facilities and received a low score in this category.

Republican residents' groups also received low scores in this category (Table 5.9). These groups relied upon text and scanned pictures for information delivery on their websites. As discussed earlier, the Lower Ormeau Concerned Community website contained pictures of local residents who had allegedly been attacked by the PSNI. This resonated with the images used on the websites of the other Republican residents' groups under analysis. For example, pictures of local residents protesting against an Orange Order demonstration dominated the Garvaghy Road Residents' Coalition website.[36] Overall, the study suggested that residents' groups provide 'basic' websites, devoid of technological innovations such as live video streaming.

Frequency of updates

The frequency of updates on these websites suggested that these residents' groups have yet to realise the potential of the Internet as

Table 5.9 Presentation and delivery of Republican residents' group websites

Website	Graphics	Frames	Sound	Video streaming	Pages in alternative format e.g. PDF	Score (/5)
Garvaghy Road Residents Coalition	1	0	0	0	0	1
Lower Ormeau Concerned Community	1	0	0	0	0	1
Short Strand	1	0	0	0	0	1
Mean	1	0	0	0	0	1

a tool for political communication. The study found that there had been no updates on each of the Republican websites for several years. The Greater Glenbryn Community Initiative website was the most recently updated, with an article on a Loyalist rally uploaded in March 2003.[37] The Lower Ormeau Concerned Community could be characterised as an archive, with the last update recorded on 9 July 1998.[38] This was also evident in the chronology of events provided on these websites. The Lower Ormeau Concerned Community and Garvaghy Road Residents' Coalition websites focused upon the Orange Order 'marching seasons' of 1995–97, a few months before the Good Friday Agreement (1998) and the political reforms that accompanied it. In addition, these websites frequently referred to the police as the Royal Ulster Constabulary (RUC), rather than the PSNI that was established in its place in 2001. The Short Strand Under Siege website was the only Republican site to have been updated since 2003. The most recent entry on this website referred to Loyalist attacks on the area that took place in July 2003.[39] None of the Loyalist websites had been updated in the 12 months prior to the study, as illustrated by the Cluan Place website, which had last been updated in January 2003.[40] The lack of regular updates suggests that residents' groups prefer to use the conventional mass media as a tool of political communication rather than the Internet.

Interviews with community workers

The Internet may have a negative impact upon community relations
The interviews with community workers revealed that these websites might not aid the cultivation of better community relations in and around sectarian interfaces. One community worker went as far as suggest that the Internet 'defeats the purpose of the work we do'. The hacking of two residents' group websites was cited as one reason why interface communities themselves did not trust the Internet. There was a consensus amongst these community workers that they had 'turned their back' on computer-mediated communication as they felt their views could be misrepresented to a potential global audience. All of the interviewees confirmed that the Internet had been used to orchestrate so-called 'recreational rioting' in interface areas. Social networking websites in particular were identified as source of conflict between interface communities. For example, one community worker stated that the fighting in Belfast city centre in December 2008 had been organised on Bebo. Young people were said to be using language and symbols associated with the Troubles on their social networking profiles in order to cause trouble with their counterparts on the other side of the interface. According to one interface worker, young people in his area frequently brag about how they use both Bebo and mobile phone messaging to coordinate rioting in close proximity to the 'peaceline'. It should be noted that all of the interviewees stated that the PSNI was monitoring these websites to identify potential flashpoints between interface communities.

Face-to-face meetings are essential to build trust between interface communities
All of the community activists believed that the Internet was not a suitable arena in which interface communities could foster better inter-community relationships. None of the interviewees knew of a shared space online in which interface communities regularly discussed inter-communal issues. One interface worker stated that email was the least desirable method of communication between rival residents' groups, as the recipient of the message might misinterpret its tone or content. In the words of one community worker, 'one word in Belfast can have two very different meanings'. Community workers believed that this lack of trust in computer-mediated communication was probably one of the reasons why these actors had not realised the full potential of the Internet to date. Instead, the consensus amongst the interviewees was that face-to-face meetings were essential to build trust between

interface communities. For example, one community organisation encouraged all of its affiliated interface groups to follow up every telephone call made to another organisation with a face-to-face meeting, to be conducted no more than a day after the original conversation. The interviews also suggested that there had been a shift in interface relationships over the past five years. All of the interviewees confirmed that there were now regular meetings held between Loyalist and Republican community activists in interface areas, something that was less common during the Mobile Phone Network pilot in the mid-1990s. While the content analysis suggests that these groups are still engaged in a competition of victimhoods, the evidence from community workers suggests that these groups are engaging in dialogue in the offline world.

Residents' group websites may not reflect current state of community relations

Community workers expressed concern at how interface relationships might be misrepresented by the websites analysed in this chapter. In areas such as the Short Strand/Cluan Place interface, there had been a dramatic reduction in the number of violent incidents between the two communities over the past five years. Loyalist and Republican residents' groups talk on a more regular basis through organisations such as the Belfast Conflict Resolution Consortium. Yet the websites appeared to provide only a snapshot of the sectarian violence that blighted these interface communities between 1996 and 2003. One community worker was concerned that people who visited these websites might believe that this level of violence persisted in interface areas. There was more concern amongst the interviewees about the organisation of recreational rioting on social networking websites.[41] Two of the community workers referred to a 'new brand of sectarianism' that was forming on sites such as Bebo. This took the form of young people posting messages and symbols associated with the Troubles in order to generate conflict with the 'other' community. Although the scale of such activity was hard to establish, the consensus was that it was probably the work of a 'small but vocal minority'. Overall, the community workers believed that the websites of residents' groups misrepresented the state of community relations in and around sectarian interfaces. Community relations in interface areas had improved since the period of unrest that was the subject of the websites of these residents' groups. While by the nature of their work community activists might be expected to favour face-to-face meetings to build relationships between interface groups, this was a consistent and persuasive theme throughout all of the interviews and is congruent with literature in the field.

Discussion

Has the Internet liberated these groups from their social context?
The absence of information about the leadership of these residents' groups online militates against the cyberoptimist notion that the Internet liberates people from their offline context. There are several reasons why Loyalist and Republican residents' groups might have omitted leadership details from their websites when they were last updated in 2003. The fear of being 'exposed' as a community activist, and subject to attack by the 'other' community has been identified as a key factor inhibiting community relations projects in interface communities (Jarman, 1997: 102). Therefore, members of local residents' groups might prefer to remain anonymous in order to avoid any violent repercussions for themselves or their families. Yet the appearance of Republican residents' leaders on television, particularly during periods of civil unrest, suggests that fear of personal attack does not explain the omission of leadership details from their websites.

Anecdotal evidence, which is rarely reported in the conventional mass media, suggests that these residents' groups are often manipulated by paramilitary organisations.[42] Conceivably, international audiences might look less favourably upon these residents' groups if their links to paramilitary organisations were publicised on their websites. Political violence is now considered less permissible in the region, even amongst the Irish-American groups that provided logistical support to the Republican movement during the Troubles. Irish-American support groups have lobbied in favour of the Republican movement for over three decades, acheiving some degree of influence over US policy vis-à-vis Northern Ireland. Opposition towards dissident Republicans stirred after the Omagh bombing (August 1998), which has been condemned by groups such as the Irish American Unity Conference on their websites.[43] Consequently, residents' groups are unlikely to reveal on their websites that their membership includes former paramilitary prisoners, such as Brendan MacCionnaith. If they were to reveal terrorist linkages, whether historic or contemporary, they might lose support from influential diasporas. The importance of the Irish-American lobby was particularly apparent on the Garvaghy Road Residents' Coalition website, which included a section for Irish-American supporters to donate funds to their campaign. In sum, residents' groups are less transparent on their websites than they appear to be in the conventional mass media. The websites analysed in the study cast little light upon the membership of Loyalist and Republican residents' groups. The evidence presented here suggests that the Internet has not yet liberated these residents' groups from their offline identities. Although concerns for the personal safety of members might be relevant, these groups may omit references to terrorism from their websites in order to demonstrate their civil society credentials.

The Internet and residents' groups: narrowcasting?
Authors such as Chadwick (2006) and Jarman (2005) suggest that new media technologies have the potential to help community groups reduce inter-communal tensions in ethnically divided societies such as Northern Ireland. The study suggested that the Internet is more likely to help these groups with the 'targeting of specific niche audiences', otherwise known as narrowcasting (Smith-Shomade, 2004: 70). There was limited evidence to suggest that rival residents' groups were using their websites to enable a form of megaphone diplomacy across sectarian interfaces. Rather than promote a public sphere of rational critical discourse, ICTs enabled these actors to establish their own 'islands of political communication'. The barriers between these groups in the offline world appeared to be replicated in an online context. Thus, Loyalist and Republican residents' groups use their websites to highlight the social and economic deprivation that blights their communities, invariably suggesting that the community situated on the other side of the 'peaceline' is trying to ethnically cleanse their areas. Common interests such as the need for economic regeneration in interface areas are only identified in the context of their own respective communities. It is reasonable to assume that the audience for these websites is likely to consist of people who have similar experiences of living in close proximity to interfaces, or those who are sympathetic to the plight of these communities. These actors cannot assume that their websites will find an audience beyond their own constituencies if their websites lack visibility on Internet search engines (see Chapter 4). Therefore, the study suggested that there was no evidence to support the cyberoptimist notion that the Internet will undermine unequal power relations in ethnically divided societies such as Northern Ireland. Moreover, the underlying causes of interface violence, from social deprivation to the perceived lack of political representation, are unlikely to be remedied through increased use of ICTs by interface communities.

Creating social capital in divided societies: is the Internet a substitute for face-to-face meetings?
This research analysed whether the Internet was an effective channel of communication between rival interface communities in Northern Ireland. In doing so, it provided an insight into the potential of the

Internet as a tool for generating bridging social capital in divided societies. The study found that these websites were likely to generate only bonding social capital in divided societies. Internet use appeared to support the two-community model in Northern Ireland rather than provide opportunities for the cultivation of broader identities that encompassed Loyalist and Republican interface communities. This finding was consonant with the Leonard (2008) study of social capital amongst young people in Northern Ireland. She argued that the 'norms and networks generated by social capital may be community specific and reproduce the religious divide' between the two communities (p. 10). The evidence presented in this chapter shows that both Loyalist and Republican residents' groups use ICTs to create their own Internet subcultures, exchanging links with like-minded actors rather than with representatives of the 'other' community. They make constant references to victimhood on their websites rather than engaging in the rational critical discourse prescribed by Habermas in his public sphere. As Dahlberg (2001) suggests, there is no 'reasonable level of respectful listening' evident on the websites of these groups. Overall, the study suggested that the Internet was a communicative space best suited towards the production of bonding social capital in ethnically divided societies such as Northern Ireland.

Chadwick (2006) suggests that social capital is the product of civic associations that bring people together (p. 87). People learn the skills necessary to participate in democratic structures in these associations, such as negotiation, tolerance and problem solving. The evidence presented here suggested that Northern Irish interface communities chose not to engage with one another in an online context. The interviews with community workers suggested that better community relations could only be fostered through face-to-face meetings between representatives of rival interface communities. They cited the fear of having their views misrepresented as one of the reasons why residents' groups favoured face-to-face meetings over computer-mediated communication. This has implications for the cyber enthusiast notion that the Internet might facilitate bridging social capital in divided societies such as Northern Ireland. It suggests that online interactions alone are unlikely to yield bridging social capital in ethnically divided societies. People can never be completely liberated from their offline location or identities. Common interests that do not transcend ethno-political identities in the offline world are unlikely to unite rival ethnic groups in cyberspace. Moreover, face-to-face meetings may be the only way to generate trust and mutual understanding between groups that demonstrate high levels of bonding social capital. The establishment of sustainable inter-community relationships in the offline world is a necessary precondition for the development of bridging social capital in Northern Ireland.

Conclusion

This chapter suggests that the prospects for better community relations in Northern Ireland are not enhanced via the websites of rival residents' groups. The study found little evidence to support the notion that the Internet was an arena in which these actors were engaging in rational critical discourse about their common interests. While the early literature on the Internet suggested that it could liberate people from offline identities, this research suggested that ICTs are more likely to supplement communities. Both Loyalist and Republican residents' groups use their websites to strengthen in-group identities, which are based around a perception of victimhood at the expense of the 'other' community. However, these websites might be better understood as a manifestation of interface conflict between 1996 and 2003. They did not reflect the current state of community relations, as they had not been updated for several years. Both Loyalist and Republican residents' groups appear wary of using ICTs to communicate with one another. Community activists suggest that rival residents' groups prefer face-to-face meetings as their intended recipients may misinterpret online communications. There was also evidence to suggest that ICTs were being used to orchestrate violence between rival factions in and around sectarian interfaces. The study suggested that regular face-to-face meetings are a prerequisite for the creation of bridging social capital in divided societies. Online interactions alone are unlikely to generate greater trust and understanding between communities that perceive that politics is a zero-sum game.

Notes

1 These districts are divided by a number of peacelines. The Ardoyne is an area predominantly populated by the Catholic community, while Glenbryn is predominantly a Protestant area.
2 See Appendix 3 for examples of Loyalist murals. Additional pictures of Loyalist and Republican murals are available on a disc. This can be obtained directly from the author.
3 On 20 June 1968, a number of squatters, including MP Austin Currie, were evicted from a house in Caledon, County Tyrone. The protest was designed to highlight the discrimination against the Catholic community in public

housing provision. The house had been allocated to the secretary of a Unionist politician. (See Bew and Gillespie, 1993: 2).

4 An email was sent to each webmaster informing them that their website was to be analysed in this study. No responses were received from the webmasters responsible for the websites of residents' groups.

5 Short Strand Under Siege. www.geocities.com/shortstrandsiege/home. html (accessed 12 February 2005)

6 Short Strand Under Siege. www.geocities.com/shortstrandsiege/home. html (accessed 12 February 2005). Taig is a derogatory term used by Loyalists to describe members of the Catholic community in Northern Ireland. For further information see CAIN. 2007. 'Glossary of Terms on Northern Irish Conflict'. http://cain.ulst.ac.uk/othelem/glossary.htm#T (accessed 10 August 2007).

7 Garvaghy Road Residents Coalition. www.garvaghyroad.org/ (accessed 13 February 2005).

8 Lower Ormeau Concerned Community. www.saqnet.co.uk/users/locc (accessed 10 February 2005).

9 Cluan Place. www.cluanplace.co.uk (accessed 10 February 2005).

10 Cluan Place. www.cluanplace.co.uk (accessed 10 February 2005).

11 White City Under Attack. www.wcua.2ya.com (accessed 10 February 2005).

12 Greater Glenbryn Community Initiative. www.ggci.co.uk (accessed 10 February 2005).

13 Lower Ormeau Concerned Community. www.saqnet.co.uk/users/locc (accessed 15 February 2005).

14 Garvaghy Road Residents Coalition. www.garvaghyroad.org/ (accessed 13 February 2005). Glasgow Celtic FC is a Scottish football club with a strong Irish heritage, who enjoy widespread patronage among Northern Ireland's Catholic community.

15 Short Strand Under Siege. www.geocities.com/shortstrandsiege/home. html (accessed 12 February 2005).

16 White City Under Attack. www.wcua.2ya.com (accessed 10 February 2005).

17 Greater Glenbryn Community Initiative www.ggci.co.uk (accessed 10 February 2005).

18 Greater Glenbryn Community Initiative. www.ggci.co.uk (accessed 10 February 2005).

19 Cluan Place. www.cluanplace.co.uk (accessed 10 February 2005).

20 Garvaghy Road Residents Coalition. www.garvaghyroad.org/ (accessed 10 February 2005).

21 Lower Ormeau Concerned Community. www.saqnet.co.uk/users/locc (accessed 10 February 2005).

22 Greater Glenbryn Community Initiative. www.ggci.co.uk (accessed 10 February 2005).

23 White City Under Attack. www.wcua.2ya.com (accessed 10 February 2005).

24 Greater Glenbryn Community Initiative. www.ggci.co.uk (accessed 10 February 2005).
25 Cluan Place. www.cluanplace.co.uk (accessed 10 February 2005).
26 Garvaghy Road Residents Coalition. www.garvaghyroad.org/ (accessed 13 February 2005).
27 Lower Ormeau Concerned Community. www.saqnet.co.uk/users/locc (accessed 10 February 2005).
28 Lower Ormeau Concerned Community. www.saqnet.co.uk/users/locc (accessed 10 February 2005).
29 Garvaghy Road Residents Coalition. www.garvaghyroad.org/ (accessed 10 February 2005).
30 Short Strand Under Siege. www.geocities.com/shortstrandsiege/home. html (accessed 12 February 2005).
31 White City Under Attack. www.wcua.2ya.com (accessed 10 February 2005). At the time of survey the bulletin Board was suspended.
32 Cluan Place. www.cluanplace.co.uk (accessed 10 February 2005).
33 White City Under Attack. www.wcua.2ya.com (accessed 10 February 2005). The murder of Thomas McDonald was highlighted in this poster. The poster highlighted the lenient sentence given to the perpetrator.
34 Garvaghy Road Residents Coalition. www.garvaghyroad.org/ (accessed 13 February 2005).
35 Greater Glenbryn Community Initiative. www.ggci.co.uk (accessed 10 February 2005).
36 Garvaghy Road Residents Coalition. www.garvaghyroad.org/ (accessed 13 February 2005).
37 Greater Glenbryn Community Initiative. www.ggci.co.uk (accessed 10 February 2005).
38 Lower Ormeau Concerned Community. www.saqnet.co.uk/users/locc (accessed 10 February 2005).
39 Short Strand Under Siege. www.geocities.com/shortstrandsiege/home. html (accessed 12 February 2005).
40 Cluan Place. www.cluanplace.co.uk (accessed 10 February 2005).
41 The term 'recreational rioting' refers to clashes between young people living on both sides of a sectarian interface. For more detail see Jarman, N. 2002. *Managing Disorder: Responding to Interface Violence in North Belfast*. Belfast: Office of First Minister and Deputy First Minister Research Branch.
42 Local journalist Malachi O'Doherty, attending a meeting of the Lower Ormeau Concerned Community in July 1995, commented, 'the people who had gone to call for an end to the protests might as well not have gone at all' (O'Doherty, 1998: 130). In the meeting, approximately one third of the attendees declared themselves to be against further street protests against an impending Orange Order parade in the area. Gerard Rice, spokesperson for the residents' group, passed the motion without a vote, later declaring that there was a unanimous consensus against the parade. See O'Doherty,

M. 1998. *The Trouble with Guns: Republican Strategy and the Provisional IRA*. Belfast: Blackstaff.
43 The Omagh bombing in August 1998 drew international condemnation for its perpetrators, the Real IRA. The atrocity saw 29 people lose their lives, one of the most lethal attacks perpetrated in Northern Ireland since the late 1960s.

Conclusion

The analysis presented in this book suggests that both civil and uncivil actors in Northern Ireland have yet to realise the potential of the Internet as a tool for political communication. Many of these groups appear to use the Internet to supplement their existing relationships with the mass media, rather than to stimulate innovative forms of political activism like social netwar. The study suggested that all Northern Irish political parties use their websites to verify their democratic credentials. There was little to differentiate between the websites of terrorist-linked groups, such as Sinn Fein, and the websites of constitutional parties, such as the SDLP. Groups such as Sinn Fein and the PUP did not justify contemporary political violence on their websites, nor raise funds on behalf of their respective terrorist organisations. Themes such as equality and shared responsiblity permeated all of the party websites analysed in this book. Nevertheless, the online framing of political parties reflected their position vis-à-vis the Good Friday Agreement. Pro-Agreement parties used their official web presence to offer support for the power-sharing institutions. In this respect, the online framing of these groups had an antecedent in the peace frame projected by the mass media in the mid-1990s. However, a clear majority of actors under analysis used their websites to criticise the Belfast Agreement and its supporters. Anti-Agreement Unionists such as the DUP criticised the UUP for sharing power with Sinn Fein. In the opinion of these groups, Sinn Fein had yet to demonstrate that it was committed to the use of exclusively democratic means to achieve its objectives. Dissident Republicans were also critical of the peace process, albeit for a different reason. Groups such as the 32CSM believed that Sinn Fein had abandoned core Republican principles, leaving the Catholic community at greater risk of attack from Loyalist paramilitaries.

Although the Internet does provide a communicative space for dissidents that is not available to them in the conventional mass media, this research suggests that it does not provide a critical mutiplier effect for these groups in terms of political mobilisation. Indeed, Loyalist and Republican fan communities appeared to use their websites to reproduce the political messages of their most favoured terrorist organisations rather than to spur collective action in the real world. These groups need to attract a large audience to their websites if their online framing is to influence public opinion at an aggregate level. The online audience for Loyalist and Republican websites is likely to be limited to Internet users who use the Web for political research and supporters of Northern Irish terrorist groups. Furthermore, the analysis of Internet usage patterns suggests that these Internet users are likely to be male, middle class, well educated and situated in Europe or North America. People with no prior knowledge of Northern Irish terrorism may turn to Internet search engines to locate information on these organisations online. These search engines faciltiate a form of mediated interaction between webmasters and Internet users. They will direct Internet users towards 'more of the same' organisational websites, rather than the websites of Loyalist and Republican political fronts. The sale of priority retrieval and the rule of Googlearchy are just two reasons why terrorists may not be visible on search engine directories. However, low visibility on search engines may be to the advantage of terrorist organisations who remain engaged in armed struggle. These groups may not wish to attract a large online audience, for fear of compromising future military operations.

Terrorists, ICTs and soft power: is there a cyber-optimist solution for terrorism?

Cyberoptimists believe that the bridging of the 'digital divide', the gap between those who are able to benefit from information technology and those who are not, is a precondition for resolving terrorism.[1] The cyberoptimist model implies that terrorists might be able to use their websites to generate soft power, to persuade 'others to want the same outcomes' (Nye, 2004: 5). This would presumably reduce the need for terrorists to perpetrate atrocities in order to generate publicity for their cause. The cyberoptimist model works on the assumption that terrorists will be able to attract an audience to their websites, thus reducing their need to perpetrate political violence in order to secure publicity. As we have seen in this research, soft power has become integral to the current strategy of the Republican movement. Due to its unprecedented electoral success in recent years, Sinn Fein is likely to attract a large number of visitors to its official website. While this could be interpreted as evidence of Sinn Fein's transition from political front to constitutional political party, this does not necessarily mean that the Provisional IRA has become irrelevant to the Republican campaign. Indeed, one interpretation of the Republican movement's reluctance to announce a permanent cessation to hostilities during the late 1990s might be that it was keeping its options open as to how it would pursue a united Ireland.

Dissident Loyalists and Republicans would appear to have limited international appeal in comparison to pro-Agreement groups such as Sinn Fein. While Sinn Fein has been given regular media coverage, due to its support for the peace process, these groups and their political affiliates remain committed to armed struggle and outside the triangle of political communication. The online audience available to these actors is likely to consist of Internet users who use the Web for political research and their supporters in the offline world. One interpretation of the evidence presented in this book would be that Northern Irish terrorists might have to abandon political violence in order to gain soft power beyond their own narrow constituencies. There is no longer an appetite for armed struggle in the region amongst groups that provided support for Loyalists and Republicans during the Troubles. However, an alternative interpretation would be that acts of terrorism are likely to temporarily increase the amount of traffic through the websites of dissident terrorists. People are more likely to search for information about these terrorist groups if they have been responsible for a high-profile atrocity that has received extensive media coverage. While the increase in traffic through a 'pro-terrorist' website might only last for a short period, it still represents an opportunity for the terrorist organisation to obtain publicity for its objectives. However, it is highly doubtful that this audience will be receptive to the cues of dissident Loyalists and Republicans unless they are already sympathetic to their cause.

The analysis presented in this book suggested that the websites under study presented the 'public face' of Northern Irish terrorist organisations. Loyalists and Republicans choose to maintain websites under the guise of their political fronts rather than of their military wings. The online framing of these groups suggests that they have no links to Loyalist and Republican paramilitaries, despite compelling evidence to the contrary in the mass media. While these political fronts framed themselves as legitimate political parties on their websites, their respective terrorist groups remained involved in paramilitarism during the period of data collection. For example, between 1 March 2003 and 31 August 2005 there were 17 murders committed by paramilitary organisations within Northern Ireland.[2] Therefore, it is perhaps no surprise that these political fronts omitted references to their terrorist sponsors from their websites. Revelations about ongoing terrorist activity might further damage relations between dissident Republicans and Irish-American diasporas, many of whom remain staunch supporters of the peace process. However, this research suggests that efforts by political fronts to establish their democratic credentials may be in vain. Internet users who rely on search engines to locate information about the Troubles are still likely to be made aware of the links between political fronts and terrorist organisations. The most visible websites on search engines are likely to belong to media organisations and research institutes that disclose the terrorist linkages of groups such as the PUP and Sinn Fein.

The Northern Irish case study suggests that bridging the digital divide is unlikely to help resolve the grievances that inspire terrorism. Yet, it could be argued that Castells' (2001) prescription for resolving terrorism assumes that its practitioners are motivated by the pursuit of publicity. It neglects the fact that terrorists perpetrate violence to subject a target audience to their ideologies rather than to gain their approval. Publicity is arguably less important to state-sponsored and holy terrorism, as these strands of political violence fulfil a range of different objectives for their perpetrators. Therefore, the availability of ICTs will not lead to a change in strategy for these terrorist actors. The Internet is more likely to be used to supplement existing relationships between terrorist-linked groups and the media. In sum, ICTs should be considered an additional mode of communication, to be added to traditional forms of terrorist manipulation of the conventional mass media. In any particular situation, terrorist organisations may choose their strategies from this range of options according to the expected utility of each in that context. Terrorists will only abandon their military campaigns if they perceive that they can achieve their political objectives through the political process, as demonstrated by Sinn Fein's integration into the political establishment in Northern Ireland.

The Internet may not facilitate better community relations in divided societies

Cyberoptimists suggest that the Internet has the potential to extend the public sphere in ethnically divided societies such as Northern Ireland. Authors such as Giddens (1995) have suggested that the Web might liberate interface communities from their offline identities and facilitate a positive spiral of communication between rival residents' groups. Yet the evidence presented in this book suggests that the websites of residents' groups represented 'islands of political communication' in cyberspace. Consonant with O'Dochartaigh's (2007) study of online discussion forums, the Internet appeared to further the competition of victimhoods between Loyalist and Republican interface communities. Rival residents' groups upload their grievances into cyberspace, using their websites to highlight the social and economic deprivation that blights their communities. These groups invariably claim that inter-communal violence is solely the responsibility of the 'other' community. The analysis presented in this book suggested that these websites were likely to reinforce bonding social capital amongst Loyalist and Republican interface communities. The audience for these websites was likely to consist of people who have similar experiences of living in interface communities, or those who are sympathetic to their plight. There was no evidence to suggest that these actors were using their websites to facilitate a form of megaphone diplomacy with their counterparts situated across the interface. These websites appeared to be a manifestation of the 'benign apartheid' that has emerged in Northern Ireland since the Belfast Agreement.

Community activists argued that these websites were a virtual representation of the sectarian violence that blighted these interface communities between 1996 and 2003. These websites had not been updated for several years before the period of data collection and often referred to actors that no longer existed, such as the RUC.[3] The interviews with community workers also revealed that many interface communities had 'turned their back' on computer-mediated communication as they felt their views could be misrepresented to a potential global audience. They believed that this lack of trust in computer-mediated communication was probably one of the reasons why these actors had not realised the full potential of the Internet to date. Moreover, all of the community activists believed that the Internet was not a suitable arena in which interface communities could foster better inter-community relationships. None of the interviewees knew of a shared space online in which interface communities regularly discussed inter-communal issues. Furthermore, the interviews revealed that there are now regular meetings held between Loyalist and Republican community activists in interface areas, something that was less common during the Mobile Phone Network pilot in the mid-1990s. Face-to-face meetings are now considered to be the most effective method of building trust between representatives of rival residents' groups. Overall, the evidence presented in this book suggested that the Internet might not facilitate a positive cycle of communication in ethnically divided societies such as Northern Ireland. However, these groups may be using less public forms of computer-mediated communication, such as email, to arrange the face-to-face meetings that are required to promote better community relations.

Future research should consider the impact of Web 2.0, the section of the Internet that provides a platform for user-generated content, upon community relations in Northern Ireland.[4] The use of Twitter to organise protests against alleged voter fraud in the 2009 Iranian elections suggests that Web 2.0 might have greater potential than Web 1.0 as an agent of political mobilisation.[5] The proposed research would provide empirical evidence to inform the current debate over the transformative potential of Web 2.0. O'Reilly (2005) characterises Web 2.0 as a Habermasian public sphere in which 'bottom-up' communication is facilitated by both blogs and social networking websites. Drezner and Farrell (2004) argue that the network structure of the blogosphere allows interesting ideas to 'bubble up' to focal-point blogs. Conversely, authors such as Froomkin (2003) and Sunstein (2007) suggest that blogs may accelerate existing trends of cyberbalkanisation, with bloggers likely to read the opinions of like-minded activists and little else. There is already some evidence to suggest that Northern Irish political parties are trying to mobilise supporters by using social networking websites. All of the parties that featured in this book have set up Facebook and Twitter pages since 2007. While the evidence presented in this book suggests that Northern Irish parties have been slow to adopt new communication technologies, the development of Web 2.0 might herald a new era in political mobilisation in the Province.

The interviews conducted with community workers in this book suggested that social networking websites were a source of conflict between rival interface communities in Northern Ireland. Recent studies have suggested that online interactions between rival interface communities on Web 2.0 may be undermining efforts to foster better inter-community relationships. A report from the Centre for Young Men's Studies (2009) suggested that young men aged between 13 and 16 were using Bebo and MSN Messenger to threaten members of the 'other community' and to coordinate fighting in interface areas. There have also been a number of widely reported incidents of so-called recreational rioting between rival groups that have been linked to social networking websites. The PSNI reported in April 2008 that a riot in the Rosemount area of Londonderry had been organised on Bebo.[6] An estimated 100 youths were alleged to have been involved in the rioting, many of whom were identified by the police as having come from the local area. More recently, videos have appeared on YouTube showing young people in the Ardoyne district of North Belfast throwing missiles at the PSNI during disturbances that surrounded a controversial

Orange Order march in the area in July 2009. A preliminary analysis of these videos showed that much of the footage had in fact been taken from the television coverage of the event provided by Sky News.[7] Only one of these videos appeared to have been shot by a member of the local community, apparently from a bedroom window in a house situated across the road from where the police were coming under attack.

A preliminary analysis of 10 Bebo profiles in April 2009 suggested that there was a high degree of inter-community interaction on this social networking platform, albeit that it was often similar in character to the online intimidation reported by young people in the Centre for Young Men's Studies report (2009). All of the individuals who had set up these social networking profiles received negative and often sectarian comments from visitors to the site. Another persuasive theme throughout all of the sites was the use of language and imagery that were associated with the Troubles. Thus, many of the Loyalist Bebo pages contained paramilitary insignias from proscribed organisations such as the UVF, with one site reproducing a picture of a Loyalist mural situated close to the Cluan Place interface in East Belfast. While Republican Bebo pages contained fewer paramilitary references, nevertheless they also used some violent images, such as a video showing Republican youths rioting in an interface area. Future research should consider what impact, if any, this form of web activism is having upon community relations in Northern Ireland.

Nation-states may find it impossible to censor all pro-terrorist websites

The research presented in this book suggests that it may be impossible for nation-states to permanently remove 'pro-terrorist' websites from the Web. Critics assert that the Internet is 'pretty much a free for all' for terrorists, due to the failure of nation-states to agree uniform rules regarding 'harmful' website content (Penfold, 2004: 285). The failure to achieve an international consensus on terrorist proscription may create communicative spaces in which terrorists can operate online. A 'pro-terrorist' webmaster is able to register their website in a nation-state that does not define its subject as a terrorist actor. There is already some evidence to suggest that terrorist groups, such as Hamas, move the registrations of their websites from one nation-state to another in order to remain online. Moreover, the principles behind the global Internet stipulate that its enabling power should be available to both 'good and bad information and communications behaviour'.[8] This can be illustrated by the culture of anonymity that has developed around the domain registration system. There is no legal requirement for web-masters to provide accurate personal information to the companies such as Nominet (www.nominet.co.uk) who administer the domain name system. A webmaster may request that organisations such as Nominet refrain from publishing their personal details on their web-sites. Alternatively, a webmaster may choose to provide the details of a third-party organisation when submitting registration details to one of these companies. This may make it more difficult for nation-states to remove all 'pro-terrorist' websites from the Web.

This study also suggests that 'pro-terrorist' webmasters may adhere to the norms of acceptable behaviour online. The study found that none of the webmasters used their website to justify contemporary acts of terrorism or solicit resources on behalf of proscribed groups. While some webmasters may have removed references to contempo-rary terrorism for this purpose, the majority did so in order to frame themselves as civil society actors. Political fronts used their websites to differentiate themselves from the violent activities of their respective terrorist organisations. There was little to differentiate between Sinn Fein and the SDLP in terms of their online framing. Thus, the Sinn Fein website made only one reference to the Provisional IRA in its 'History' section. This was also the case for dissident Loyalist and Republican groups such as the 32CSM, who might have been expected to glorify the violent activities of their patrons. While some of these groups did allude to their rationale for armed struggle, their respective webmas-ters appeared to choose their words carefully in order to avoid censure under legislation such as the UK Terrorism Act (2000). These actors tended to use their websites to condemn Sinn Fein for its support of the peace process rather than to justify their current military campaigns.

The analysis of solidarity websites showed that webmasters may show their support for proscribed terrorist organisations without con-travening the norms of acceptable behaviour online. Private individuals may purport to be terrorists online, despite compelling evidence to the contrary on their websites. Despite many of these actors purporting to be members of terrorist organisations, many webmasters issued legal disclaimers stating that they had no links to the paramilitaries. Yet this research perhaps illustrates the distinction that should made between terrorist 'wannabes' and amateur terrorists in terms of their website strategy. The Tsouli case demonstrates how private individuals may use the Internet to further the campaigns of terrorists without becoming absorbed into their organisational structure. This form of web activism is qualitatively different from the activities of Loyalist and Republican solidarity actors that were analysed in this book. 'Unofficial' Loyalist and Republican websites did not constitute a new dimension of terrorist threat in Northern Ireland. None of the webmasters responsible for these websites glorified acts of terrorism nor encouraged others to commit atrocities to further the campaigns of dissidents. The Internet provided a space in which these actors commemorated fallen comrades and provided their own history of the Northern Irish conflict. Yet there was limited evidence to suggest that Loyalist and Republican solidarity actors themselves were engaged in acts of terrorism. However, it is conceivable that these actors are using less public forms of computer-mediated communication, such as email, to plan and perpetrate atrocities.

Do the cyber paradigms have limitations as analytical tools?

In a 2007 article in the *Sunday Times*, Brian Appleyard argued that information technology should not be seen as autonomous as it is 'utterly background dependent'.[9] This resonates with the analysis of Northern Irish political actors presented in this book. This research highlights the need for the continuous development of theoretical and analytical tools for researching the Internet usage of sub-state groups, which will have the capacity to evolve in parallel with technological and contextual developments. For example, the evidence presented in this book suggests that social netwar is merely a description of the extraordinary political mobilisation in favour of the EZLN insurgents in Chiapas, as opposed to a durable conceptual tool for characterising online political activism. Furthermore, the cyber paradigms appear too static to provide a theoretical tool for the analysis of web activism without significant modification. The evidence presented in this book suggests that contextual factors, rather than the traditional focus upon the 'digital divide', determine how ICTs impact upon the reality of 'politics as usual' (Norris, 2001: 13). The digital divide itself describes the differential between those who can benefit from ICTs and those are unable to do so, as opposed to who has access to the Internet. Therefore, analytical tools need to incorporate factors that may explain why ICTs generate different outcomes for similar actors.

There are three components that need to be added to the cyber paradigms, namely the purpose of the web activity, the media environment and the online audience. Firstly, researchers should consider what the actor hopes to achieve through their use of ICTs. If the webmaster lacks influence in the 'offline' world, or wishes to remain anonymous online in order to avoid detection, their website is likely to make little or no immediate impact on 'politics as usual'. Thus, individual and group objectives are critical to understanding how new media technologies influence power relations within nation-states. The Internet is used by some political actors as a means of generating soft power, enabling them to attract support from a potential global audience. These actors will use the Web to publish their ideologies free from the ideological refraction of the conventional mass media. However, the three cyber paradigms presuppose that all political actors will use new media technologies for the same purpose, namely to gain political influence. Conversely, not all political actors will use information technology to alter power relations within their respective polities. For example, the Tullycarnet UPRG does not refer to its political objectives on its website, focusing instead upon community events such as a children's disco.[10] Residents' groups may also use their websites to strengthen relationships within their own communities, as opposed to influencing government policy. In a similar vein to residents' groups, political parties use their websites primarily for intra-group communication. Only a few political parties are likely to be in a position to influence decision making within nation-states. The cyber paradigms must consider the objectives of sub-state actors if they are to capture how politics has evolved in the digital age.

The media environment is also critical to understanding how ICTs affects politics within nation-states. Political parallelism, or the extent to which media systems reflect political context, is also relevant to Internet usage within nation-states. As discussed by Hallin and Mancini (2004), the media should be relatively unrestricted in the United States, due to the freedom of expression enshrined in the First Amendment of the US Constitution. These rights can also be applied to computer-mediated communcation in the same polities. Webmasters and Internet hosting companies often cite 'First Amendment Rights' when justifying the continued presence of websites that project controversial views, such as 'pro-terrorist' websites. In contrast, semi-authoritarian nation-states, such as China, will attempt to limit dissent, whether it be transmitted via traditional media forms or on the Internet. This suggests that the potential of the Internet as a mobilising agent and means of generating soft power may be dependent upon the limits placed on the use of these technologies by nation-states. As discussed in this book, political fronts such as Sinn Fein have received routine media coverage courtesy of their electoral success post 1998, in sharp contrast to the censorship they faced in the wake of the UK Broadcasting Ban in 1988. Sinn Fein uses its website to provide further evidence of its democratic credentials, to reflect the normalisation of its relations with both the conventional mass media and civil society itself. Evidently, Sinn Fein would be unable to project this 'peace frame' if the nation-state in which the website was registered defined it as an 'uncivil' organisation. Yet, nation-states may be unable to limit the soft power of sub-state groups online through restrictions on their ability to use the Internet. Diasporas may generate soft power on behalf of a sub-state actor that has restricted access to their local mass media, as demonstrated by the Zapatista social netwar. Future research should consider the extent to which media environment – both domestic and international – determines where a webmaster registers their website.

The online audience should also be added as a component to the cyber paradigms. After all, ICTs will only influence power relations within nation-states if sub-state groups find an audience for their websites that is unavailable to them in the conventional mass media. The evidence presented in this book suggests that the online audience is highly fragmented, as people use the Internet as a private viewing box. As people use the Internet to pursue private interests, only the politically engaged will use the Web for political research. Yet this illustrates another limitation of research into how sub-state actors use the Internet. It is virtually impossible to estimate the size and composition of an online audience for a particular website. While tools such as Google Zeitgeist provide data about the search queries that are 'gaining the most growth', they do not list the most popular queries. In addition, these tools tend to be heavily filtered to remove harmful content (Sullivan, 2006).[11]

In addition, there is no publicly available information about the number of unique visitors to a particular website. An online survey was rejected in this research, as representative sampling of the audience was impossible to achieve, for similar reasons. Nevertheless, this book demonstrates that the potential audience for a website may be modelled using data already in the public domain, such as Internet surveys conducted by the Oxford Internet Institute. This model will enable researchers to assess whether sub-state groups are likely to reach a large audience online using their websites.

A thematic approach towards content analysis?

The analysis of website function tells us only part of the story when it comes to the website strategy of political actors. In particular, this research illustrates how the coding scheme developed by Gibson and Ward (2000, 2004) has limited utility in the analysis of online frames. It suggests that a thematic approach towards content analysis is more flexible in terms of the requirement to adapt to change. For example, analysis of website function may tell us very little about Web 2.0. Research conducted using qualitative frames is able to chart how online discourse evolves in line with political developments in the 'offline' world. For example, this book provides a snapshot of Loyalist and Republican online discourse during a period of conflict transformation, as terrorist-linked groups move into mainstream politics and the number of violent terrorist incidents decreases. This was reflected in the themes of equality and shared responsibility that permeated the websites of Loyalist and Republican parties. The 'benign apartheid' that has developed across the Province was also highlighted by the thematic approach used in this book. The Gibson and Ward coding scheme, in its current formulation, was also unable to capture the 'competition of victimhoods' that was evident on the websites of rival residents' groups. Overall, the research design provides a model for future research into how the online framing of terrorist-linked groups evolves during a period of conflict transformation.

Notes

1 International Telecommunications Union. www.itu.org (accessed 10 March 2007).
2 Independent Monitoring Commission (2005) *Seventh Report of the Independent Monitoring Commission*, London: The Staionery Office, p. 22.
3 The RUC became the PSNI in 2001 as a result of the policing reforms ushered in by the Good Friday Agreement.
4 Dowling, T. 2007. 'I don't think Bloggers read'. *Guardian* (20 July).
5 'Iran Elections: A Twitter Revolution?' *Washington Post*. www.washington-post.com/wp-dyn/content/discussion/2009/06/17/DI2009061702232.html (accessed 17 June 2009).
6 'Internet Used to Plan City Riot'. *Belfast Telegraph* (6 April).
7 See www.belfasttelegraph.co.uk/news/local-national/ardoyne-violence-videos-posted-on-youtube-14413069.html (accessed 10 August 2009).
8 According to Mueller, Mathiason and McKnight (2004), there are six principles that govern behaviour on the Internet, including the global commons principle, the end to end principle, and the principle of moral neutrality.
9 Appleyard, B. 2007. 'Listen to the Luddites, You Digital Disciples'. *Sunday Times* (11 March).
10 Tullycarnet Ulster Political Research. 2004. Group www.tullycarnetuprg.ionichost.com (accessed 16 May 2004).
11 Google filters navigational terms and sexual terms from the Zeitgeist list. Google has also launched Google Trends to provide data about the 100 fastest-rising Google search queries in the United States.

Appendix 1
Selected chronology of the Northern Irish peace process 1985–97

1985

15 November   Anglo-Irish Agreement signed by British Prime Minister Margaret Thatcher and Irish Taioseach Garret Fitzgerald. The Agreement guarantees that the constitutional status of Northern Ireland will only change through the consent of the majority of people in the Province. Unionists react angrily to the treaty that recognised the role of the Irish government in the management of the Northern Irish conflict.

1988

11 January   First meetings between John Hume (SDLP) and Gerry Adams (Sinn Fein).

19 October   UK Broadcasting Ban placing restrictions on media appearances by members of Sinn Fein, RSF and the UDA.

3 November   Secretary of State for Northern Ireland Peter Brooke makes speech in which he concedes that the Provisional IRA cannot be defeated militarily and does not rule out talks with Sinn Fein, should the Republican movement end its campaign of political violence.

1990

9 November   Peter Brooke makes speech in which he states that Britain will accept unification of Ireland if it is the wish of the people of Northern Ireland.

1992

9 April
UK general election sees Sinn Fein President Gerry Adams lose his West Belfast seat to Dr Joe Hendron of the SDLP.

3 November
Belfast division of Republican organisation the Irish People's Liberation Organisation (IPLO) announces that it is to disband after feud with Provisional IRA.

7 November
IPLO Army Council in Dublin announces an end to its campaign.

1993

11 April
Secret talks between John Hume and Gerry Adams are revealed in *Sunday Tribune* newspaper. Talks are criticised by the main Unionist parties.

24 April
John Hume and Gerry Adams issue first joint statement on hopes for peace process.

4 October
Provisional IRA releases statement welcoming the Hume/Adams initiative.

16 November
UK newspaper reports that there has been a series of secret talks between the UK government and Sinn Fein.

15 December
UK and Irish governments issue a joint declaration detailing basis for a political settlement of the conflict in Northern Ireland. The Downing Street Declaration saw Prime Minister John Major reiterate that the United Kingdom would not stand in the way of the reunification of Ireland should the majority of citizens in Northern Ireland wish it. The Declaration also established a basis for Sinn Fein to be included in all-party talks on the future of the Province.

1994

19 January
Broadcasting restrictions in Republic of Ireland limiting Sinn Fein media appearances are lifted.

19 May
Northern Ireland Office publishes 21-page clarification of Sinn Fein questions that arose from the Downing Street Declaration.

31 August
Provisional IRA announces a complete cessation of military activities in statement to media.

16 September
Broadcasting Ban on proscribed paramilitary organisations lifted in United Kingdom.

13 October	The Combined Loyalist Military Command (CLMC), speaking on behalf of all Loyalist paramilitary organisations, announces a ceasefire.

1995

22 February	UK and Irish governments publish 'Framework for Agreement'.
13 August	Gerry Adams, President of Sinn Fein, addresses a Republican demonstration at Belfast City Hall. During his speech, a member of the crowd calls out to Adams to 'bring back the IRA'. Adams replies: 'They haven't gone away, you know.'
8 September	David Trimble elected leader of the UUP after meeting of Ulster Unionist Council.

1996

24 January	Mitchell Report published by Independent Body on Arms Decommissioning. Report provides the Mitchell Principles that included a number of confidence-building measures that would be required in order for all-party talks to take place including Sinn Fein. Report is rejected by the DUP while the UUP expresses concern over some of its recommendations.
9 February	Provisional IRA ends its ceasefire and detonates large bomb in the docklands of London, killing two people and causing extensive damage.
4 March	Proximity talks begin between the Northern Irish political parties. The UUP and the DUP refuse to participate while Sinn Fein is denied entry to the talks.
30 May	Elections to the proposed Northern Ireland Forum and all-party negotiations are held across Northern Ireland. Sinn Fein attracts a record vote of 15.5%.
10 June	All-party talks begin at Stormont, chaired by US Senator George Mitchell.
8 July	Catholic taxi driver Michael McGoldrick murdered outside Lurgan by Loyalist paramilitaries. Attack is one of the first to be attributed to the LVF, an anti-Agreement Loyalist paramilitary organisation that opposed the ceasefires announced in October 1994.

9 September	The 'General Head Quarters' (GHQ) faction of the INLA announces that the group is disbanding.
12 October	Leaders of the PUP use their annual conference to appeal to the loyalist paramilitary groups to maintain their ceasefire.

1997

1 May	UK general election sees Sinn Fein become the third-largest party in the region and win two seats. The UUP wins 10 seats and receives the most votes. The SDLP retains 3 seats and the DUP wins 2.
3 May	Mo Mowlam appointed Secretary of State for Northern Ireland.
16 May	UK Prime Minister Tony Blair makes speech in Belfast reaffirming the government's commitment to the Framework Document and stating that it would meet Sinn Fein to clarify any issues regarding the proposals.
3 June	Stormont talks resume. LVF and the Continuity IRA both proscribed after being linked to a number of terrorist attacks in the previous months.
20 July	Provisional IRA renews its ceasefire.
26 August	UK and Irish governments set up Independent International Commission on Decommissioning (IICD).
29 August	Northern Ireland Secretary of State Mo Mowlam announces that Sinn Fein will be able to participate in the all-party talks, as the government had accepted the validity of the Provisional IRA ceasefire.
9 September	Sinn Fein signs Mitchell Principles.
15 September	Multi-party talks resume with the three Unionist parties absent in protest at decision to include Sinn Fein.
7 October	After a few weeks of agreeing format and rules for negotiations, substantial talks begin at Stormont.

1998

26 January	UDP expelled from talks after it is revealed that the UFF had been involved in the killing of three Catholic civilians in previous weeks.
20 February	Sinn Fein expelled from multi-party talks after Provisional IRA linked to murder of two men in Belfast.
23 March	Sinn Fein rejoins multi-party talks.

10 April	Chair George Mitchell announces that the parties have reached agreement. The Good Friday Agreement includes plans for an Assembly with 108 members, the creation of North–South administrative bodies and constitutional change in both the UK and the Republic of Ireland to recognise the principle of consent in determining the future of Northern Ireland.
7 May	Northern Irish media reports that the Real IRA has broken away from Provisional IRA and is committed to the use of political violence to achieve a united Ireland.
15 May	LVF announces an unequivocal ceasefire.
22 May	Referendums on Good Friday Agreement held in Northern Ireland and Republic of Ireland. Results show 71.1 % 'Yes' vote in Northern Ireland based on turnout of 81.10%. The Republic of Ireland vote shows 94.39% 'Yes' vote.
25 June	First election for Northern Ireland Assembly held. Results for 108-member Assembly are UUP 28 seats, SDLP 24 seats, DUP 20 seats and Sinn Fein 18 seats.
1 July	Political parties take up seats in Assembly. UUP leader David Trimble elected First Minster Designate, with Seamus Mallon, deputy leader of the SDLP, elected Deputy First Minster Designate.
10 August	LVF issues statement claiming that its military campaign is over.
15 August	Bomb kills 29 people in Omagh, County Tyrone. Dissident Republican organisation the Real IRA linked to attack. Atrocity represents single worst loss of life since beginning of conflict.
17 August	IRSP makes statement calling on INLA to announce a ceasefire.
18 August	Real IRA announces an immediate suspension of military activities.
22 August	INLA announces ceasefire.
7 September	Real IRA announces complete cessation of its military campaign. This leaves the Continuity IRA as the only dissident Republican organisation to remain committed to a campaign of political violence.
11 September	First paramilitary prisoners released on licence under terms of the Good Friday Agreement
13 November	LVF announces it is willing to decommission some of

	its weapons if Provisional IRA agrees to disarm some of its weaponry.
17 November	UK government recognises LVF ceasefire, paving way for its prisoners to be released early in line with terms of Belfast Agreement.
18 December	Agreement reached on creation of North–South administrative bodies. LVF becomes first paramilitary group to hand over some weapons to be destroyed by International Decommissioning Body.

1999

3 March	Northern Ireland Secretary Mo Mowlam proscribes Loyalist paramilitary groups the Red Hand Defenders and the Orange Volunteers after these groups were linked to a number of terrorist attacks in previous months.
1 April	Hillsborough Declaration agreed by the two Prime Ministers, setting out a framework towards establishing an Executive that includes Sinn Fein. Unionists continue to oppose Sinn Fein's inclusion until Provisional IRA decommissioning has been completed.
13 April	Talks to break deadlock over decommissioning resume at Stormont.
14 June	European elections see Jim Nicholson (UUP), Ian Paisley (DUP) and John Hume (SDLP) returned as Northern Ireland's three representatives.
15 July	Attempt to form Executive of Northern Ireland Assembly fails when UUP leader David Trimble and his party colleagues refuse to take their seats.
6 September	Senator George Mitchell, Chair of the multi-party talks, begins review of Good Friday Agreement.
9 September	Patten Commission on Policing in Northern Ireland publishes its recommendations for reform of RUC.
11 October	Peter Mandelson replaces Mo Mowlam as Northern Ireland Secretary of State.
15 November	Senator George Mitchell and General John de Chastelain, head of the International Decommissioning Body, announce that they are close to agreeing a way forward to overcome decommissioning impasse.
16 November	The UUP, Sinn Fein and the SDLP all issue statements endorsing Belfast Agreement.

18 November	Mitchell Review of Good Friday Agreement ends.
2 December	Powers devolved to Northern Ireland Assembly. Executive meets for the first time with all parties except the DUP in attendance.

2000

11 February	Direct rule reintroduced and the Northern Ireland Executive is suspended after International Decommissioning Body reports that the Provisional IRA has not complied with its deadline for disarmament.
27 May	The UUP agrees to participate in the Executive after Provisional IRA agrees to arms dump inspections.
30 May	Devolution restored to the Province by the UK government.

2001

24 January	Peter Mandelson resigns as Northern Ireland Secretary and is replaced by Dr John Reid.
7 June	UK general election and local council elections see an increase in the percentage of votes cast for both the DUP and Sinn Fein. In the Westminster Election, the UUP wins 6 seats, closely followed by the DUP with 5 seats, including a number won from the UUP. Sinn Fein overtakes the SDLP to become the largest Nationalist/Republican party in the region, taking 4 seats compared to the 3 retained by John Hume's SDLP.
1 July	David Trimble resigns as First Minister and calls for suspension of Northern Ireland Assembly.
9 July	Talks at Weston Park between the political parties and the two governments to decide on way forward after resignation of David Trimble. The talks last five days and do not end in agreement.
1 August	UK and Irish governments publish Implementation Plan for Good Friday Agreement.
10 August	Assembly suspended for one day to allow for another period of six weeks in which the parties could elect a First and Deputy First Minister. The Assembly is suspended again for one day on 21 September to allow for an agreement on who should fill these positions.

12 October	Northern Ireland Secretary Dr John Reid specifies the UDA, the UFF, and the LVF as active terrorist organisations.
18 October	Three UUP and two DUP Ministers resign from Northern Ireland Executive in protest at the failure of the Provisional IRA to decommission its weapons.
23 October	The Provisional IRA makes statement confirming that it has begun to decommission its weapons. The Independent Decommissioning Body releases a statement confirming that it has witnessed an act of decommissioning by the Republican movement.
4 November	The PSNI is formed to replace the RUC.
6 November	David Trimble elected as First Minister with Mark Durkan (SDLP) elected to position of Deputy First Minister.

2002

27 January	The UPRG emerges as the political front of the UDA.
8 April	A second act of Provisional IRA decommissioning is verified by John de Chastelain of the IICD.
21 September	UUP leader David Trimble states that his party will withdraw from the power-sharing executive at Stormont on 18 January 2003 if Republicans do not demonstrate that they have left violence behind for good.
8 October	David Trimble announces that he will pull his ministers out of the Executive within seven days if the UK government does not expel Sinn Fein, following allegations of a Republican spy ring at Stormont.
14 October	Northern Ireland Secretary of State Dr John Reid announces suspension of devolution and reintroduction of direct rule.

2003

22 February	The UDA and UFF announce a 12-months ceasefire.
4 September	ICM assumes responsibility for monitoring paramilitary ceasefires.
21 October	Third act of Provisional IRA decommissioning is criticised by Unionists for not being transparent.
26 November	Northern Ireland Assembly election sees the DUP become the largest pro-Union party, with 30 seats in

the Assembly. Sinn Fein consolidates its position as the largest Nationalist party, securing 24 seats. The UUP and the SDLP see their vote increase slightly in comparison to previous elections, achieving 27 and 18 seats respectively.

2004

25 February	The UDA pledges to maintain its ceasefire.
23 March	UK and Irish governments hold talks in Belfast with the main parties to try to resolve the impasse over decommissioning.
20 April	The ICM recommends financial sanctions be applied to both Sinn Fein and the PUP in response to continued Loyalist and Republican violence.
10 June	European election results see Jim Allister (DUP), Bairbre de Brun (Sinn Fein) and Jim Nicholson (UUP) elected to represent Northern Ireland in the European Parliament.
15 June	Review of Good Friday Agreement resumes after a short break for the European election.
18 September	Three days of talks are held at Leeds Castle in an effort to break the deadlock between Sinn Fein and the Unionist parties.
4 October	Dr Ian Paisley meets with Taoiseach Bertie Ahern to discuss some of the issues from the negotiations at Leeds Castle. This is the first time that the DUP leader has met an Irish government delegation.
28 October	The ICM reports that the Provisional IRA has made no progress towards complete disarmament. The Commission also confirms that the UDAremains involved in organised crime.
12 November	The UK government officially recognises the UDA ceasefire.
8 December	DUP leader Dr Ian Paisley confirms that talks to restore devolution have broken down over the issue of whether photographs should be taken showing Provisional IRA decommissioning. The UK and Irish governments publish their proposals to resolve the impasse.
20 December	The Provisional IRA is linked to the £26.5 million Northern Bank robbery in Belfast.

2005

7 January	PSNI Chief Constable Hugh Orde states that the Provisional IRA was responsible for the Northern Bank robbery.
30 January	Members of the Provisional IRA are linked to the murder of Robert McCartney in a Belfast bar.
6 April	Sinn Fein President Gerry Adams makes a statement calling on the Provisional IRA to accept democratic means.
5 May	UK general election and local district council elections see the DUP win 6 seats, mainly at the expense of the UUP, which is left with only 1 seat. Sinn Fein takes an additional seat (Fermanagh/South Tyrone), giving it 5 seats at Westminster. The SDLP retains its 3 seats from the previous election although its percentage share of the vote is less than during the previous general election.
28 July	The Provisional IRA formally ends its campaign of political violence and commits to the use of exclusively peaceful means.
1 August	The UK government outlines its plans to scale down the Army presence in Northern Ireland.
26 September	The ICM announces that it is satisfied that the Provisional IRA has decommissioned its arms.
8 December	Three men at the centre of an alleged Republican spy ring at Stormont are acquitted of all charges in a Belfast court.
15 December	Sinn Fein member Denis Donaldson reveals that he was a paid British agent during the Troubles.

2006

11 January	The UK government drops plans to make paramilitary fugitives appear in front of a tribunal in order to be freed on licence.
4 April	Denis Donaldson is found shot dead in his home in County Donegal. The Provisional IRA denies responsibility for the killing.
6 April	UK Prime Minister Tony Blair and Irish Premier Bertie Ahern arrive in Belfast with their blueprint for restoring devolution to the Province.

11 May	The Northern Ireland Women's Coalition is formally wound down at an event held in Belfast.
15 May	Northern Ireland politicians take their places in the Stormont Assembly for the first time since October 2002.
13 October	After three days of negotiations at St Andrews in Scotland, the two governments publish their roadmap to restore devolution.
24 November	A transitional Assembly is installed at Stormont

2007

28 January	Sinn Fein party members vote to support the PSNI. This had been a sticking point in the negotiations to restore devolution.
7 March	Northern Ireland Assembly elections see the DUP achieve the highest number of seats (36) and percentage share of the vote (30.09%). Sinn Fein also increases its number of seats (28) and its share of the vote (26.16%). Both the UUP and the SDLP lose support, with the former achieving 18 seats and the latter 16.
8 May	Devolution restored in Northern Ireland as the DUP and Sinn Fein agree to participate in the Northern Ireland Executive. Dr Ian Paisley is elected First Minister with Sinn Fein's Martin McGuinness elected Deputy First Minister.

Sources: CAIN; Bew and Gillespie (1993).

Appendix 2

Websites no longer available in November 2009

Political party	Loyalist solidarity website	Republican solidarity website	Loyalist residents' group	Republican residents' group
Northern Ireland Women's Coalition	Fife Loyalist	Australian Aid for Ireland	Greater Glenbryn Community Initiative	Garvaghy Road Residents' Coalition
United Kingdom Unionist Party	Greenock Loyalists	Cairde Sinn Fein	White City Under Attack	Lower Ormeau Concerned Community
	Larne UVF/YCV/ RHC	Coiste na n-larchimi		
	Loyalist View	Give Ireland Back to the Irish		
	Loyalistvoice.co.uk	Hardline IRA		
	Red Hand Land	Ireland for the Irish		
	Scottish Loyalists	Na Gael		
	The Loyalist			
	Ulster Defence Association			
	United Loyalist Movement			
	Ulster Online			
	Ulster Protestant Movement for Justice			
	UVF-The Peoples Army			
	West of Scotland Ratpack			
	Yorkshire Loyal			

Appendix 3

Website registration data for sites used in this book

Table 1 Website registration data provided by Northern Irish political parties

Website	Host	Location of host	Web-master name	Web-master email address	Regis-tered postal address	Tele-phone/ fax number
Alliance Party of Northern Ireland	Firenet	UK	NIA	NIA	IA	IA
Conservative Party of Northern Ireland	Bargain Hosts	UK	NIA	NIA	NIA	NIA
Democratic Unionist Party	Direct IT	UK	NIA	NIA	IA	NIA
Green Party of Northern Ireland	Kontent	Germany	IA	IA	IA	IA
Irish Republican Socialist Party	Network Solutions	USA	NIA	NIA	IA	IA
Northern Ireland Women's Coalition	UTV Internet	UK	NIA	NIA	NIA	NIA
Progressive Unionist Party	Global.Net	UK	IA	NIA	NIA	NIA
Republican Sinn Fein	IEDR	Republic of Ireland	IA	NIA	NIA	NIA

Table 1   (continued)

Website	Host	Location of host	Web-master name	Web-master email address	Regis-tered postal address	Tele-phone/ fax number
Sinn Fein	IEDR	Republic of Ireland	IA	NIA	NIA	NIA
Social and Democratic Labour Party	IEDR	Republic of Ireland	IA	NIA	NIA	NIA
Socialist Environmental Alliance	Supanet	UK	NIA	NIA	IA	NIA
Socialist Workers Party	IEDR	Republic of Ireland	IA	NIA	NIA	NIA
32 County Sovereignty Committee	Netfirms	Canada	IA	IA	IA	IA
Tullycarnet UPRG	Hyperspace	Canada	NIA	NIA	NIA	NIA
Ulster Unionist Party	TIB	UK	NIA	NIA	IA	IA
Workers Party	UTV Internet	UK	IA	IA	IA	IA

Note: IA = information available; NIA = no information available.

Table 2   Website registration data provided by Loyalist solidarity actors

Website	Host	Location of host	Web-master name	Web-master personal email address	Regis-tered postal address	Tele-phone number/ fax number
Birches Guerrilla Movement	Freewebs	USA	NIA	NIA	NIA	NIA
British Ulster Alliance	Schlund	Germany	IA	NIA	NIA	NIA
Fife Loyalists	Pipex	UK	IA	NIA	NIA	NIA
Greenock Loyalists	Yahoo	USA	NIA	NIA	NIA	NIA
Larne UVF/ YCV/RHC	Lycos	UK	NIA	NIA	NIA	NIA

Table 2 (continued)

Website	Host	Location of host	Web-master name	Web-master personal email address	Regis-tered postal address	Tele-phone number/ fax number
Liverpool UDA	Fasthosts	UK	IA	NIA	NIA	NIA
Loyalist Network	Freeserve	UK	NIA	NIA	NIA	NIA
Loyalist View	Bravenet	USA	NIA	NIA	NIA	NIA
Loyalist Voice. co.uk	Network Solutions	USA	NIA	NIA	NIA	NIA
Red Hand Land	Freeserve	UK	NIA	NIA	NIA	NIA
Scottish Loyalists	Calton Hosting	UK	NIA	NIA	NIA	NIA
The Loyalist	Wanadoo	UK	NIA	NIA	NIA	NIA
The Volunteer	Host Master	USA	NIA	NIA	NIA	NIA
Ulster Defence Association	Freewebs	USA	NIA	NIA	NIA	NIA
Ulster Loyalist Movement	Bravenet	USA	NIA	NIA	NIA	NIA
Ulster Online	Wanadoo	UK	NIA	NIA	NIA	NIA
Ulster Protestant Movement for Justice	Pipex	UK	NIA	IA	NIA	NIA
UVF-The People's Army	Schlund	Germany	IA	NIA	NIA	NIA
West of Scotland Ratpack	n/a	n/a	n/a	n/a	n/a	n/a
Yorkshire Loyal	n/a	n/a	n/a	n/a	n/a	n/a

Note: IA = information available; NIA = no information available.

Table 3 Website registration data provided by Republican solidarity actors.

Website	Host	Location	Web-master name	Web-master email address	Regis-tered postal address	Tele-phone number/ fax number
Australian Aid For Ireland	n/a	n/a	n/a	n/a	n/a	n/a
Cairde Sinn Fein	UTV Internet	UK	NIA	NIA	NIA	NIA
Coiste na n-larchimi	IEDR	Republic of Ireland	IA	NIA	NIA	NIA
Eire Saor	Network Solutions	USA	NIA	NIA	NIA	NIA
Fourthwrite	IEDR	Republic of Ireland	IA	NIA	NIA	NIA
Friends of Irish Freedom	Geocities	USA	NIA	NIA	NIA	NIA
Give Ireland Back to the Irish	Wild West	USA	IA	IA	IA	IA
Hardline IRA	Geocities	USA	NIA	NIA	NIA	NIA
Commemorative Web Project (Hunger Strike)	Pairnic	USA	IA	IA	IA	IA
Ireland for the Irish	Bravenet	USA	NIA	NIA	NIA	NIA
Irelands Own	Ipower	NIA	NIA	NIA	NIA	NIA
Irish American Unity Conference	Network Solutions	USA	IA	IA	IA	IA
Irish Anti-Partition League	Wild West	USA	IA	IA	IA	IA
Irish Freedom Committee	Network Solutions	USA	NIA	IA	IA	NIA
Irish Republican Political Prisoners	Pairnic	USA	IA	IA	IA	IA
Mise Eire	Tripod	USA	NIA	NIA	NIA	NIA
Na Gael	Yahoo	USA	IA	IA	IA	IA
National Irish Freedom Committee	Ipower	USA	NIA	NIA	NIA	NIA
New Republican Forum	IEDR	Republic of Ireland	NIA	NIA	NIA	NIA
NORAID	Network Solutions	USA	NIA	IA	IA	IA

Note: IA = information available; NIA = no information available.

Table 4 Website registration data provided by Northern Irish residents' groups

Website	Host	Location of host	Web-master name	Web-master personal email address	Regis-tered postal address	Tele-phone number/ fax number
Cluan Place	Fasthosts	UK	IA	NIA	NIA	NIA
Garvaghy Road Residents' Coalition	Go Daddy	USA	IA	NIA	IA	IA
Greater Glenbryn Community Initiative	Schlund	Germany	NIA	NIA	IA	NIA
Lower Ormeau Concerned Community	n/a	n/a	n/a	n/a	n/a	n/a
Short Strand Under Siege	n/a	n/a	n/a	n/a	n/a	n/a
White City Under Attack	n/a	n/a	n/a	n/a	n/a	n/a

Note: IA = information available; NIA = no information available; n/a = site no longer registered so no information available.

Appendix 4

Northern Irish terrorist groups currently proscribed in the United Kingdom

Table 1

Group	Estimated strength	Pro/anti Good Friday Agreement	Website of politically linked group	Unofficial (solidarity) website
Continuity Army Council[a]	Under 50 active members.	Anti	Yes (as Republican Sinn Fein)	Yes
Cumann na mBan	No data available	No data available	No	No
Fianna na hEireann	Unknown	Anti	Yes	No
Irish National Liberation Army	Under 50 active members	Anti	Yes (as Irish Republican Socialist Movement)	Yes
Irish Peoples Liberation Organisation[b]	No data available	No data available	No	No
Irish Republican Army (aka PIRA)	Several hundred active members.	Pro	Yes (as Sinn Fein)	Yes
Loyalist Volunteer Force	50–150 active members, 300 supporters	Anti	No	Yes
Orange Volunteers	20 active members[c]	Anti	No	Yes
Red Hand Commandos	No data available	Pro	No	Yes

Table 1   (continued)

Group	Estimated strength	Pro/anti Good Friday Agreement	Website of politically linked group	Unofficial (solidarity) website
Red Hand Defenders	Up to 20 active members	Anti	No	No
Saor Eire	No data available	No data available	No	No
Ulster Defence Association/ Ulster Freedom Fighters[d]	Few dozen active members	Pro	Yes (as Ulster Political Research Group)	Yes
Ulster Volunteer Force	Few dozen active members	Pro	Yes (as Progressive Unionist Party)	Yes

Notes:

[a] Linked to RSF, Continuity IRA, and according to some sources, the Real IRA.

[b] The Irish People's Liberation Organisation announced its dissolution in October 1992 following an internal feud.

[c] Security sources believe that Red Hand Defenders and Orange Volunteers are served by same pool of volunteers.

[d] These two organisations are defined as autonomous terrorist organisations on the UK list of proscribed terrorist groups (2005). However, the two groups are considered by many sources to be one and the same organisation.

Bibliography

Adams, G. 1986. *The Politics of Irish Freedom*. Dingle: Brandon Books.

Agre, P. 2002. 'Real-Time Politics: The Internet and the Political Process'. *The Information Society* 18, pp. 311–331.

Alali, A.O and Byrd, G.W. 1994. *Terrorism and the News Media: A Selected Annotated Bibliography*. London: McFarland and Company.

Ariza, L.M. 2005. 'Virtual Jihad: The Internet as the Ideal Terrorism Recruiting Tool'. *Scientific American*. www.sciam.com/print_version. cfm?articleID=000b5155-2077-13A8-9E4D83414B7F0101 (accessed 10 June 2007).

ARK. Northern Ireland Life and Times Survey. 2004. www.ark.ac.uk/nilt.

Arquilla, J. and Ronfeldt, D. 2001. *Networks and Netwars: The Future of Terror, Crime, and Militancy*. Santa Monica, CA: RAND.

Baker, P.A and Ward, A.C. 2002. 'Bridging Temporal and Spatial "Gaps": The Role of Information and Communication Technologies in Defining Communities'. *Information, Communication and Society* 5, 2, pp. 207–224.

Bar-Ilan, J. 1999. 'Search Engine Results Over Time – A Case Study on Search Engine Stability'. *Cybermetric: International Journal of Scientometrics, Informetrics and Bibliometrics* 3, 1 www.cybermetrics.cindoc..csic.es/pruebas/v2i191.html (accessed 23 October 2004).

Barnett, B., Reynolds, A., Roselle, L. and Oates, S. 2007. 'Journalism and Terrorism Across the Atlantic: A Qualitative Content Analysis of CNN and BBC Coverage of 9/11 and 7/7'. Paper prepared for the International Communication Division of the Association for Education in Journalism and Mass Communication Annual Convention, Washington, DC.

Bell, Martin. 2008. 'The Death of News'. *Media, War & Conflict* 1, pp. 221–231.

Bennett, W. 2003. 'Communicating Global Activism'. *Information Communication and Society*. 6, 2, pp. 143–168.

Bew, P. and Gillespie, G. 1993. *Northern Ireland: A Chronology of the Troubles 1968–1993*, Dublin: Gill & Macmillan.

Bimber, B. 1998. 'The Internet and Political Mobilisation'. *Social Science Computer Review* 16, 4, pp. 391–401.

Bodard, K. 2003. 'Free Access to Information Challenged by Filtering

Techniques'. *Information and Communication Technology Law* 12, 3, pp. 263–279.

Bolton, R. 1990. *Death on the Rock and Other Stories*. London: W.H. Allen.

Brandenburg, H. 2006. 'Pathologies of the Virtual Public Sphere', in S. Oates, D. Owen and R. Gibson (eds), *The Internet and Politics: Citizens, Voters and Activists*. London: Routledge, pp. 207–222.

Brinkerhoff, J.M. 2006. 'Digital diasporas and conflict prevention: the case of Somalinet.com'. *Review of International Studies* 32: 25–47.

Bruce, S. 2001. 'Terrorists and Politics: The Case of Northern Ireland's Loyalist Paramilitaries'. *Terrorism and Political Violence* 13, 2, pp. 7–48.

Bruce, S. 2004. 'Turf War and Peace: Loyalist Paramilitaries since 1994'. *Terrorism and Political Violence* 16, 3, pp. 501–521.

Bryan, D. 2000. *Orange Parades, the Politics of Ritual, Tradition and Control*. London: Pluto.

Bucy, E.P. 2003. 'Emotion, Presidential Communication, and Traumatic News: Processing the World Trade Center Attacks'. *The Harvard International Journal of Press/Politics* 8, 4, pp. 76–96.

Budge, I. 1996. *The New Challenges of Direct Democracy*. Cambridge: Polity Press.

Byrne, S. 2001. 'Consociational and Civic Society: Approaches to Peacebuilding in Northern Ireland,' *Journal of Peace Research* 38, 2, pp. 327–353.

Carter, N. and Byrne, S. 2000. 'The Dynamics of Social Cubism: A View from Northern Ireland and Quebec', in Byrne, S. and Nixon, C.L. (eds), *Reconcilable Differences: Turning Points in Ethnopolitical Conflict*. West Harford, CT: Kumanan, pp. 41–65.

Castells, M. 2001. *The Internet Galaxy: Reflections on the Internet, Business and Society*. Oxford: Blackwell.

Centre for Young Men's Studies (2009). *Stuck in the Middle (Some Young Men's Attitudes and Experience of Violence, Conflict and Safety)*. Ulster: Centre for Young Men's Studies, University of Ulster Publications.

Chadwick, A. 2006. *Internet Politics: States, Citizens, and New Communication Technologies*. Oxford: Oxford University Press.

Chase, M. and Mulvenon, J. 2002. *You've Got Dissent! Chinese Dissident Use of the Internet and Beijing's Counter Strategies*. Santa Monica, CA: Rand.

Cho, Hichang and Lee, Jae-Shin. 2008. 'Collaborative Information Seeking in Intercultural Computer-mediated Communication Groups: Testing the Influence of Social Context using Social Network Analysis'. *Communication Research* 35, 4, pp. 548–573.

Chong, D. and Druckman, J. 2007. 'Framing and Opinion Formation in Competitive Elite Environments'. *Journal of Communication* 57, pp. 99–118.

Christensen, C. 2008. 'Uploading dissonance: YouTube and the US Occupation of Iraq'. *Media, War and Conflict* 1, 2, pp. 155–175.

Clawson, P. 1990. 'Why We Need More but Better Coverage of Terrorism', in Kegley, C.W. (ed.), *International Terrorism: Characteristics, Causes, Controls*. London: St Martin's Press, pp. 240–250.

Cleaver, Harry M. Jr. 1998. 'The Zapatista Effect: The Internet and the Rise of an Alternative Political Fabric'. *Journal of International Affairs* 51, 2, 621–640.

Clutterbuck, L. 2004. 'The Progenitors of Terrorism: Russian Revolutionaries or Extreme Irish Republicans?' *Terrorism and Political Violence* 16, 1, pp. 154–181.

Clutterbuck, R. 1983. *The Media and Political Violence*. London: Macmillan.

Cochrane, F. 2007. 'Irish-America, the End of the IRA's Armed Struggle and the Utility of Soft Power, *Journal of Peace Research* 2, pp. 215–231.

Cohen, F. 2002. 'Terrorism and Cyberspace'. *Network Security* 5, pp. 17–19.

Conway, M. 2006a. 'Terrorist Websites: Their Contents, Functioning and Effectiveness', in Seib, P. (ed.), *Media and Conflict in the Twenty-First Century*. London: Palgrave Macmillan, pp. 185–215.

Conway, M. 2006b. 'Cybercortical Warfare: Hizbollah's Strategy', in Oates, S., Owen, D. and Gibson, R. (eds), *The Internet and Politics: Citizens, Voters And Activists*. Routledge: London, pp. 100–117.

Cooke, T. 2003. 'Paramilitaries and the Press in Northern Ireland', in Norris, P., Kern, M. and Just, M. (eds), *Framing Terrorism: The News Media, the Government and the Public*. New York: Routledge, pp. 75–91.

Corrado, A. and Firestone, C.M. (eds). 1996. *Elections in Cyberspace: Toward a New Era in American Politics*. Washington, D.C.: Aspen Institute.

Council of Europe. 1997. *Cultural Rights, Media and Minorities*. Strasbourg: Council of Europe Press.

Crelinsten, R.D. 2002. 'Analysing Terrorism and Counter-Terrorism: A Communication Model'. *Terrorism and Political Violence* 14, 2, pp. 77–122.

Curtis, L. 1988. *Ireland: The Propaganda War: The British Media and the Battle for Hearts and Minds*, second edition. London: Pluto.

Dahlberg, L. 2001. 'The Internet and the Democratic Discourse: Exploring the Prospects of Online Deliberative Forums Extending the Public Sphere'. *Information, Communication and Society* 4, 4, pp. 615–633.

Dahlgren, P. 2005. 'The Internet, Public Spheres and Political Communication'. *Political Communication* 2, 2, pp. 147–162.

Deibert, R. 2001. 'Dark Guests and Great Firewalls: Chinese Internet Security Policy'. *Journal of Social Issues* 58, 1, pp. 143–158.

Drezner, D.W. and Farrell, H. 2004. 'The Power and Politics of Blogs'. Paper presented at the 2004 meeting of the American Political Science Association, Chicago, 1–4 September. www.utsc.utoronto.ca/~farrell/blogpaperfinal.pdf.

Eid, M. 2006. 'Cyber-Terrorism in the Information Age: Actors, Communications, Tactics, Targets and Influences'. Paper presented at The 4th International Conference on Information, Information'06, and the 4th Irish Conference on the Mathematical Foundations of Computer Science and Information Technology'06, MFCSIT'06, Information-MFCSIT'06 (August 1–5 August). University College Cork, Cork, Ireland, pp. 5–9.

Elnur, I. 2003. '11 September and the Widening North-South Gap: Root Causes of Terrorism in the Global Order'. *Arab Studies Quarterly* 25.

English, R. 2003. *Armed Struggle: The History of the IRA*. London: Macmillan.

Entman, R.M. 2003. 'Cascading Activation: Contesting the White House's Frame after 9/11'. *Political Communication* 20, pp. 415–432.

Fallows, D. 2007. *Election Newshounds Speak Up: Newspapers, TV and Internet Fans Tell How and Why they Differ*. Pew Internet and American Life Project. www.pewinternet.org/pdfs/PIP_Election_Newshounds_Feb_2007.pdf (accessed 16 April 2007).

Farry, S. 2004. 'A Return to the Centre'. www.allianceparty.org/news.asp?id=259 (accessed 10 February 2005).

Finlayson, A. and Hughes, E. 2000. 'Advertising for Peace: The State and Political Advertising in Northern Ireland 1988–1988'. *Historical Journal of Film, Radio and Television*, 20, 3, pp. 397–412.

Froomkin, M.A. 2003. 'Habermas@Discourse.net: Toward a Critical Theory of Cyberspace'. *Harvard Law Review* 116, 3, January 2003, pp. 749–873.

Furnell, S. and Warren, M.J. 1999. 'Computer Hacking and Cyber Terrorism: The Real Threats in the New Millennium?' *Computers & Security* 18, 1, pp. 28–34.

Di Gennaro, C. and Dutton, W. 2006. 'The Internet and the Public: Online and Offline Political Participation in the United Kingdom'. *Parliamentary Affairs* 59, 2, pp. 299–313.

Dyson, E. 1998. *Release 2.1: A Design for Living in the Digital Age*. London: Penguin.

Gaines, B.J. and Mondak, J. 2008. 'Typing Together? Characteristics of Ideological Types in Online Social Networks'. Paper presented at *Politics: Web 2.0*, London, United Kingdom, 9 April.

Gerhart, S. 2004. 'Do Web Search Engines Suppress Controversy?' *First Monday* 9, 1. www.firstmonday.org/issues/issue9_1/gerhart/index.html (accessed 10 June 2004).

Gerritts, R.P. 1992. 'Terrorists' Perspectives: Memoirs', in Paletz, D. and Schmid, A.P. (eds), *Terrorism and the Media*. London: Sage, pp. 29–61.

Gibson, R. and Ward, S. 2000. 'A Proposed Methodology for Studying the Function and Effectiveness of Party and Candidate Web Sites'. *Social Science Computer Review* 18, 3, pp. 301–319.

Gibson, R. and Lusoli, S. Ward. 'Italian Elections Online: ten years on.' In *The Italian General Election of 2006*, ed. J. Newell, 177–199. Manchester: Manchester University Press, 2008.

Giddens, A. 1995. 'The New Context of Politics: New Thinking for New Times'. *Democratic Dialogue*. www.democraticdialogue.org/publications.htm (accessed 2 March 2003).

Goffman, E. 1974. *Frame Analysis: An Essay on the Organisation of Experience*. New York: Harper & Row.

Goodman, S.E., Kirk, J.C. and Kirk, M.H. 2006. 'Cyberspace as a Medium for Terrorists'. *Technological Forecasting & Social Change* 74, pp. 193–210.

Gorge, M. 2007. 'Cyberterrrorism: Hype or Reality?' *Computer Fraud and Security*, 2, pp. 9–12.

Graber, D. 1997. *Mass Media and American Politics*, fifth edition. Washington, D.C.: Congressional Quarterly Press.

Graham, B. 2004. 'The Past in the Present: The Shaping of Identity in Loyalist Ulster'. *Terrorism and Political Violence* 16, pp. 483–500.

Greenslade, R. 1998. 'Damien Walsh Memorial Lecture'. http://cain.ulst.ac.uk/othelem/media/greenslade.htm (accessed 20 April 2001).

Griffiths, P. 2004. 'The Policy Applications of Social Capital in the Global Exchange Forum'. *Social Capital: A Policy Tool for North and South?* Conference Report, 29 March. London: The Foreign Policy Centre.

Hall, M. 2001. *Community Relations: An Elusive Concept – an Exploration by Community Activists from North Belfast*. Newtownabbey: Island.

Hallin, D.C. 1986. *The 'Uncensored War': The Media and Vietnam*. New York: Oxford University Press.

Hallin, D.C. and Mancini, P. 2004. *Comparing Media Systems: Three Models of Media and Politics*. London: Cambridge University Press.

Hayes, B. and McAllister, I. (2009) 'Religion, Identity and Community Relations among Adults and Young Adults in Northern Ireland'. *Journal of Youth Studies* 12, 4, pp. 385–403.

Hennessey, T. 1994. 'Ulster Unionism and Loyalty to the Crown of the UK 1912–1974', in English, R. and Walker, G. (eds), *Unionism in Modern Ireland: New Perspectives on Politics and Culture*. London: Macmillan, pp. 115–129.

Herman, E. and Chomsky, N. (2002). *Manufacturing Consent*. New York: Pantheon.

Hill, K. and Hughes, J.E. 1997. 'Computer-mediated Political Communication: The USENET and Political Communities'. *Political Communication*, 14, 1, pp. 3–27.

Hindman, M., Tsioutsiouliklis, K. and Johnson, J.A. 2003. 'Googlearchy: How A Few Heavily Linked Sites Dominate Politics on the Web'. www.princeton.edu/~mhindman/googlearchy--hindman.pdf (accessed 30 October 2004).

Hoffman, B. 1993. *Holy Terror: The Implications of Terrorism Motivated by a Religious Imperative*. Santa Monica, CA: Rand Corporation.

Hoffman, B. 1998. *Inside Terrorism*. London: Victor Gollancz.

Hoffman, B. 2006. 'The Use of the Internet by Islamic Fundamentalists, Testimony to the House Permanent Select Committee on Intelligence, May 4, 2006'. Santa Monica, CA: Rand Corporation.

Horgan, J. and Taylor, M. 1999. 'Playing the "Green Card" – Financing the Provisional IRA'. *Terrorism and Political Violence* 11, 2, pp. 1–38.

Hughes, J. and Donnelly, C. 2001. *Integrate or Segregate? Ten Years of Social Attitudes to Community Relations in Northern Ireland*. Belfast: Northern Ireland Life and Times Survey. www.ark.ac.uk/nilt (accessed 3 February 2005).

Hughes, J. and Donnelly, C. 2004. 'Attitudes to Community Relations in Northern Ireland: Signs of Optimism in Post Ceasefire Period'. *Terrorism and Political Violence* 16, 3, pp. 567–592.

Hutcheson, J., Domke, D., Billeaudeaux, D. and Garland, P. 2004. 'U.S. National Identity, Political Elites, and a Patriotic Press Following September 11'. *Political Communication* 21, pp. 27–50.

Independent Monitoring Commission. 2004. *Independent Monitoring Commission Report*. www.news.bbc.co.uk/hol/shared/bsp/hi/pdfs/20_04_04_imcreport.pdf (accessed 22 April 2004).

Institute for Counter-Terrorism. 2004. *Terrorist Group Profiles*. www.ict.org.il/inter_ter/orgdat (accessed 10 June 2004).

Intelligence and Terrorism Information Center. 2005. 'Marketing Terrorism by Internet: The Hamas Terrorist Movement Continues Using Internet Service Providers in Eastern Europe and South East Asia to Operate Its Leading Sites'. Tel Aviv: Center for Special Studies.

International Telecommunication Union. 2007. 'World Information Society Report 2006'. www.itu.org (accessed 10 April 2007).

Internet World Statistics. 2009. *Internet Usage Statistics – The Big Picture*. www.worldinternetstats.com (accessed 10 November 2009).

Jarman, N. 1997. *Material Conflict: Parades and Visual Displays in Northern Ireland*. Oxford, Berg.

Jarman, N. (2002). *Managing Disorder: Responding to Interface Violence in North Belfast*. Belfast: Office of First Minister and Deputy First Minister Research Branch.

Jarman, N. 2005. 'Managing Conflicts by Phone: The Mobile Phones Network in Northern Ireland'. *People Building Peace*. http://peoplebuildingpeace.microhost.nl/thestories/article.php?typ=theme&id=120&pid=28 (accessed 10 July 2008).

Jarman, N. 2004. *Demography, Development and Disorder: Changing Patterns of Interface Areas*. Belfast: Community Relations Council.

Jensen, J.L. 2006. 'The Minnesota Project: Mobilizing the Mobilized?' in Oates, S., Owen, D. and Gibson, R.K. (eds). *The Internet and Politics: Citizens, Voters and Activists*, London: Routledge, pp. 39–59.

Kahneman, D. and Tversky, A. 1979. 'Prospect Theory: An analysis of Decisions under Risk, *Econometrica* 47, 2, pp. 263–292.

Kaldor, M. 2003. 'The Idea of Global Civil Society'. *International Affairs* 79, 3, pp. 583–593.

Keohane, R.O. and Nye, J.S. 1998. 'Power and Interdependence in the Information Age'. *Foreign Affairs* 77, pp. 81–94.

Laqueur, W. 1978. *The Terrorism Reader: A Historical Anthology*. New York: New American Library.

Laqueur, W. 1999. *The New Terrorism: Fanaticism and the Arms of Mass Destruction*. London: Oxford University Press.

Leonard, M. 2008. 'Social and Sucultural Capital among Teenagers in Northern Ireland'. *Youth and Society* 40, 2, pp. 222–242.

Levin, D. 2005. 'Framing Peace Policies: The Competition for Resonant Themes'. *Political Communication* 22, pp. 84–108.

Lewis, H., Dowds, L., McGivern, Y., Hamber, B. and Robinson, G. 2008.

Communities in Transition: An Exploration of Attitudinal Barriers to the Development of Intercommunity Relationships in a Post-conflict Society. INCORE Report Commissioned by Belfast Conflict Resolution Consortium, Belfast: INCORE.

Locke, T. 1999. 'Participation, Inclusion, Exclusion and Netactivism', in Hague, B.N. and Loader, B.D. (eds), *Digital Democracy: Discourse and Decision Making in the Information Age*. London: Routledge, pp. 211–222.

McAuley, J.W. 2004. 'Just Fighting to Survive: Loyalist Paramilitary Politics and the DUP'. *Terrorism and Political Violence* 16, 3, pp. 522–543.

McCartney, C. 2003. 'The Role of Civil Society'. *Accord* 8. www.c-r.org/accord/ireland/accord8/therole.shtml (accessed 15 January 2005).

McGarry, J. 2002. 'Democracy in Northern Ireland: Experiments in Self-rule from the Protestant Ascendancy to the Good Friday Agreement'. *Nation and Nationalism* 8, 4, pp. 451–474.

McGovern, M. 2004. 'The Old Days are Over: Irish Republicanism, the Peace Process and the Discourse of Equality'. *Terrorism and Political Violence* 16, 3, pp. 622–645.

Madden, M. 2006. *Internet Penetration and Impact*. Pew Internet and American Life Project 202, pp. 419–450. Data memo available at www.pewinternet.org.

Margolis, M., Resnick, D. 2000. *Politics as Usual: The Cyberspace 'Revolution'*. Thousand Oaks, CA: Sage.

Menczer, F., Fortunato, S., Flammini, A., and Vespignani, A. 2006. 'Googlearchy or Googlocracy?' *IEEE Spectrum*, 43, 2. Available: http://spectrum.ieee.org/print/2787.

Miller, D. 1995. 'The Media and Northern Ireland: Censorship, Information Management and the Broadcasting Ban', in Philo, G. (ed.), *The Glasgow Media Group Reader Volume 2: Industry, Economy, War, and Politics*. London: Routledge, pp. 45–60.

Moghadam, A. 2003. 'Palestinian Suicide Terrorism: A Neglected Phenomenon?' *Studies in Conflict and Terrorism* 26, pp. 65–92.

Mueller, M., Mathiason, J. and McKnight, L.W. 2004. 'Making Sense of Internet Governance: Defining Principles and Norms in a Policy Context'. Internet Governance Project, Syracuse University.

Muldoon, O., McNamara, N., Devine, P. and Trew, K. 2008. 'Beyond Gross Divisions: National and Religious Identity Combinations'. www.ark.ac.uk/publications/updates/update58.pdf (accessed 25 August 2009).

Nacos, B.L. 2003. 'The Terrorist Calculus behind 9–11: A Model for Future Terrorism?' *Terrorism and Political Violence* 26, pp. 1–16.

Negrine, R. 1994. *Politics and the Mass Media in Britain*, second edition. London: Routledge.

Nelson, T.E., Clawson, R.A. and Oxley, Z.M. 1997. 'Media Framing of a Civil Liberties Conflict and Its Effect on Tolerance'. *American Political Science Review* 91, 3, pp. 567–584.

Nielsen. 2009. 'Global Faces and Networked Places: A Nielsen report on

Social Networking's New Global Footprint.' *The Nielsen Company*. http://blog.nielsen.com/nielsenwire/wp-content/uploads/2009/03/nielsen_globalfaces_mar09.pdf

Nixon, P., Ward, S. and Gibson, R. 2003. 'Conclusions: The Net Change', in Gibson, R., Nixon, P. and Ward, S. (eds), *Political Parties and the Internet: Net Gain?* London: Routledge, pp. 234–243.

Norris, P. 2000. *A Virtuous Circle: Political Communication in Post Industrial Societies*. London: Cambridge University Press.

Norris, P. 2001. *Digital Divide: Civic Engagement, Information Poverty and the Internet Worldwide*. New York: Cambridge University Press.

Norris, P., Kerns, M. and Just, M. (eds) 2003. *Framing Terrorism: The News Media, the Government, and the Public*. London: Routledge.

North Belfast Community Action Group. 2002. *Report of the Project Team*. www.northbelfastcommunityactionproject.org/report/index.htm (accessed 20 February 2005).

Noveck, B.S. 2000. 'Paradoxical Partners: Electronic Communication and Electronic Democracy', in Ferdinand, P. (ed.), *The Internet, Democracy and Democratization*. London: Frank Cass, pp. 18–36.

Ntoulas, A., Cho, J. and Olson, C. 2004. 'What's New on the Web? The Evolution of the Web from a Search Engine Perspective'. *Proceedings of the Thirteenth WWW Conference*, New York, 17–20 May. http://oak.cs.ucla.edu/~ntoulas/pubs/ntoulas_new.pdf (accessed 04 November 2005).

Nye, J. 2004. *Soft Power*. New York: Public Affairs.

O'Connor, F. 1993. *In Search of a State: Catholics in Northern Ireland*. Belfast: Blackstaff.

O'Dochartaigh, N. 2003. 'Building New Transnational Networks Online: The Case for Ulster Unionism. *Development Gateway*. http://topic.developmentgateway.org/ict/rc/ItemDetail.do~346057 (accessed 17 February 2006).

O'Dochartaigh, N. 2007. 'Conflict, Territory and New Technologies: Online Interaction at a Belfast interface'. *Political Geography* 26, pp. 474–491.

O'Doherty, Malachi. 1998. *The Trouble with Guns: Republican Strategy and the Provisional IRA*. Belfast: Blackstaff Press.

O'Halloran, C., Shirlow, P. and Murtagh, B. 2004. *A Policy Agenda for the Interface*. www.belfastinterfaceproject.org (accessed 10 March 2005).

O'Reilly, T. 2005. 'What is Web 2.0: Design Patterns and Business Models for the Next Generation of Software'. www.oreillynet.com/pub/a/oreilly/tim/news/2005/09/30/what-is-web 20.htm (accessed 10 September 2008).

O'Sullivan See, K. 1986. *First World Nationalisms: Class and Ethnic Politics in Northern Ireland and Quebec*. London: University of Chicago.

Oates, S. 2008. *Introduction to Media and Politics*. London: Sage.

Ofcom. 2009. *Communications Market Report Northern Ireland*. www.ofcom.org.uk/research/cm/cmrnr09/ni/cmrnrni.pdf (accessed 10 August 2009).

Ofcom Media Literacy Audit. 2006. *Report on Media Literacy in the Nations and Regions*. www.ofcom.org.uk/advice/media_literacy/medlitpub/medlitpubrss/nations_regions/nations_regions.pdf.

Owen, S. 2006. 'Internet and Youth Civic Engagement in the US', in Oates, S., Owen, D. and Gibson, R.K. (eds), *The Internet and Politics: Citizens, Voters and Activists*. London: Routledge, pp. 20–39.

Pax, S. 2003. *The Baghdad Blog*. London: Guardian Books.

Penfold, C. 2004. 'Converging Content: Diverging Law'. *Information and Communications Technology Law* 13, 3, pp. 273–292.

Pew Internet and American Life Project. 2001. 'How Americans Used the Internet after the Terror Attacks'. www.pewinternet.org (accessed 10 March 2003).

Pew Internet and American Life Project. 2009. www.pewinternet.org/Media-Mentions/2009/The-Internet-has-not-transformed-civic-engagement--yet.aspx (accessed 10 December 2009).

Pew Research Center for the People and the Press. 2007. 'A Portrait of Generation Next: How Young People View Their Lives, Futures and Politics'. www.people-press.org/reports/pdf/300.pdf (accessed 16 May 2007).

Philo, G. 1994. 'The Media in a Class Society'. in Philo, G. (ed.), *Glasgow Media Group Reader Volume 2: Industry, Economy, War and Politics*. London: Routledge, pp. 176–184.

Postmes, T. and Brunsting, S. 2002. 'Collective Action in the Age of the Internet: Mass Communication and Online Mobilisation'. *Social Science Computer Review* 20, pp. 290–301.

Pridham, G. 1990. *Securing Democracy: Political Parties and Democratic Consolidation in Southern Europe*. London: Routledge.

Purcell, B. 1991. 'The Silence in Irish Broadcasting', in Rolston, B. *The Media and Northern Ireland: Covering the Troubles*. London: Macmillan, pp. 51–68.

Putnam, R.D. 2000. *Bowling Alone: The Collapse and Revival of American Community*. London: Simon and Schuster.

Reilly, P. 2008. 'Googling Terrorists: Are Northern Irish Terrorists Visible on Internet Search Engines', in Spink, A. and Zimmer, M. (eds), *Search Engines: Interdisciplinary Perspectives*. New York: Springer, pp. 151–177.

Rheingold, H.1993. *The Virtual Community: Homesteading on the Electronic Frontier*. Reading, MA: Addison-Wesley Publishing Company.

Richards, A. 2001. 'Terrorist Groups and Political Fronts: The IRA, Sinn Fein, the Peace Process and Democracy'. *Terrorism and Political Violence* 13, 4, pp. 72–89.

Roe, M.D., Pegg, W., Hodges, K. and Trimm, R. 1999. 'Forgiving the Other Side: Social Identity and Ethnic Memories in Northern Ireland', in Harrington, J.P. and Mitchell, E.J. (eds), *Politics and Performance in Contemporary Northern Ireland*. Amherst, MA: University of Massachusetts.

Rogan, H. 2006. *Jihadism Online: A Study of How Al Qaida and Radical Islamist Groups Use the Internet for Terrorist Purposes*. FFI/Rapport-206/00915, Kjeller, Norway: Norway Defence Research Establishment.

Romer, D., Jamieson, K.H. and Pasek, J. (2009) 'Building Social Capital in Young People: The Role of Mass Media and Life Outlook,' *Political Communication* 26, 5, pp. 65–83.

Ronfeldt, David and Arquilla, John. 2001. 'Emergence and Influence of the Zapatista Social Netwar'. In Arquilla, John and Ronfeldt, David *Networks and Netwars: The Future of Terror, Crime, and Militancy*. Santa Monica, CA: RAND, pp. 171–199.

Sandvoss, Cornel. 2005. *Fans: The Mirror of Consumption* , Cambridge: Polity Press.

Scheufele, D.A. 1999. 'Framing as a Theory of Media Effects'. *Journal of Communication* 49, 4, pp. 103–122.

Scheufele, D.A. and Tewksbury, D. 2008. 'Framing, Agenda Setting and Priming: The Evolution of Three Media Effects Models'. *Journal of Communication* 57, 1, pp. 9–20.

Schmid, A.P. 1989. 'Terrorism and the Media: The Ethics of Publicity'. *Terrorism and Political Violence* 1, 4, pp. 539–565.

Schmid, A.P. and Jongman, A. 1988. *Political Terrorism*. London: North-Holland.

Search Engine Yearbook. 2003. *Search Engine Statistics 2003*. www.search-engineyearbook.com/search-engines-statistics.shtml (accessed 17 October 2004).

Selnow, G. 1998. *Electronic Whistle Stops: The Impact of the Internet on American Politics*. Westport, CT: Praeger.

Selwyn, N., Gorard, S. and Furlong, J. 2005. 'Whose Internet Is It Anyway? Exploring Adults' Use of the Internet in Everyday Life'. *European Journal of Communication* 20, 1, pp. 5–26.

Shah, D., Kwak, N. and Holbert, R.L. 2001. 'Connecting and Disconnecting with Civic Life; Patterns of Internet Use and the Production of Social Capital'. *Political Communication*, 18, 2, pp. 141–162.

Shepherd, A. and Bryson, I. 2007. *Household and Individual Use of the Internet: Focus on the Digital Age*. www.statistics.gov.uk/downloads/theme_compendia/foda2007/Chapter2.pdf (accessed 10 June 2007).

Shirlow, P. 2003. 'Who Fears to Speak: Fear, Mobility and Ethno-Sectarianism in the 2 Ardoynes'. *The Global Review of Ethnopolitics* 3, pp. 76–91.

Siebert, F.S., Peterson T. and Schramm, W. 1963. *Four Theories of the Press*. Chicago: University of Illinois Press.

Smith-Shomade, B.E. 2004. 'Narrowcasting in the New World Information Order: A Space for the Audience?' *Television and New Media* 5, 1, pp. 69–81.

Softsteel Solutions. 2003. *Improving Your Search Engine Rating*. www.softsteel.co.uk/tutorials/search/searchIndex.html (accessed 10 June 2004).

Sparre, K. 2001. 'Megaphone Diplomacy in the Northern Irish Peace Process: Squaring the Circle by Talking to Terrorists through Journalists'. *Harvard International Journal of Press/Politics* 6, 1, pp. 88–104.

Spears, R. and Lea, M. 1994. 'Panacea or Panopticon? The Hidden Power in Computer-mediated Communication'. *Communication Research* 21, 4, pp. 427–459.

Stohl, M. 2008. 'Old Myths, New Fantasies, and the Enduring Realities of Terrorism'. *Critical Studies on Terrorism* 1, 1, pp. 1–16.

Submit Corner. 2004. *Search Engine Guide*. www.submitcorner.com/Guide/Se (accessed 14 September 2004).

Sullivan, D. 2006. 'Just How Accurate Is the Google Zeitgeist?' blog.searchenginewatch.com/blog/060403-125957 (accessed 10 June 2007).

Sunstein, C.R. 2007. *Republic.com 2.0*. Princeton, NJ: Princeton University Press.

Templegrove Action Research Ltd. 1996. *Hemmed in and Hacking It: Words and Images from the Fountain and Gobnascale*. Londonderry: Templegrove Action Research Ltd.

Thelwall, M. 2001. 'The Responsiveness of Search Engines'. *Cybermetrics: International Journal of Scientometrics, Informetrics and Bibliometrics* 5, 1. www.cybermetrics.cindoc.csic.es/pruebos/v5i1p1.html (accessed 14 October 2004).

Tonge, J. 2004. 'They Haven't Gone Away, You Know: Irish Republican "Dissidents" and "Armed Struggle"'. *Terrorism and Political Violence* 16, 3, pp. 671–693.

Tucker, D. 2001. 'What's New about the New Terrorism and How Dangerous Is It?' *Terrorism and Political Violence* 13, pp. 1–14.

Walker, J. 2002. *Links and Power: The Political Economy of Linking on the Web*. Baltimore: ACM Press. www.cnc.uib.no/jill/txt/linksandpower.html (accessed 20 October 2004).

Webopedia Computer Dictionary. 2004. 'What is a Meta Tag?' www.webopedia.com/TERM/m/Meta_tag.html (accessed 10 November 2005).

Weimann, G. 2004. *WWW.terror.net: How Modern Terrorists Use the Internet*. Washington, D.C.: United States Institute for Peace.

Weimann, G. 2005. 'Cyberterrorism, the Sum of All Fears?' *Studies in Conflict and Terrorism* 28, pp. 129–149.

Weimann, G. 2006. *Terror on the Internet: The New Arena, the New Challenges*. Washington, D.C: United States Institute of Peace.

Wellman, B. (2001). 'Physical Place and Cyber-place: The Rise of Networked Individualism'. *International Journal for Urban and Regional Research*, 25, 227–252.

Wellman, B., Quan-Haase, A., Boase, J., Chen, W., Hampton, K., de Diaz, I.I., and Miyata, K. 2003. 'The Social Affordances of the Internet for Networked Individualism'. *Journal of Computer-mediated Communication*, 8, 3. www.ascusc.org/jcmc/vol8/issue2/wellman.html (accessed 10 April 2009).

Whine, M. 1999. 'Cyberspace: A New Medium for Communication, Command, and Control by Extremists'. *Studies in Conflict and Terrorism* 22, pp. 231–245.

Wieviorka, M. 1993. *The Making of Terrorism*. Chicago: University of Chicago.

Wilkinson, P. 1997. 'The Media and Terrorism: A Reassessment'. *Terrorism and Political Violence* 9, 2, pp. 51–64.

Williams, K.P., and Jesse, N.G. 2001. 'Resolving Nationalist Conflicts: Promoting Overlapping Identities and Pooling Sovereignty'. *Political Psychology* 22, 3, pp. 571–600.

Wolfsfeld, G. 2001. *The News Media and Peace Processes: The Middle East and Northern Ireland*. Washington, D.C.: United States Institute for Peace.

Wouters, P. and Gerbec, D. 2003. 'Interactive Internet? Studying Mediated Interaction with Publicly Available Search Engines'. *Journal of Computer Mediated Communication* 8, 4. http://jcmc.indiana.edu/vol8/issue4/wouters.html (accessed 16 November 2005).

Wouters, P., Helsten, I. and Leydesdorff, L. 2004. 'Internet Time and the Reliability of Search Engines,' *First Monday* 9, 10. www.firstmonday.org/issues/issue9_10/wouters/index.html (accessed 16 October 2004).

Zanini, M. and Edwards, J.A. 1994. 'The Networking of Terror in the Information Age', in Arquilla, J. and Ronfeldt, D. (eds), *Networks and Netwars: The Future of Terror, Crime and Militancy*. Santa Monica, CA: Rand Corporation, pp. 29–61.

Zittrain, J. and Edelman, B. (2005) 'Localized Google Search Result Exclusions'. http://cyber.law.harvard.edu/filtering/google (accessed 10 November 2005).

Index